Myths of the
Origin of Fire

Sir James George
FRAZER

Myths of the Origin of Fire

HACKER ART BOOKS
NEW YORK 1974

First published 1930. London
Reissued 1974 by Hacker Art Books, Inc.

Library of Congress Catalogue Card Number 76-143348
ISBN 0-87817-068-5

Printed in the United States of America

MYTHS OF
THE ORIGIN OF FIRE

AN ESSAY

BY

SIR JAMES GEORGE FRAZER

O.M., F.R.S., F.B.A.

FELLOW OF TRINITY COLLEGE, CAMBRIDGE
MEMBRE DE L'INSTITUT DE FRANCE

MACMILLAN AND CO., LIMITED
ST. MARTIN'S STREET, LONDON

1930

PREFACE

MYTHOLOGY may perhaps be defined as the philosophy of primitive man. It is his first attempt to answer those general questions concerning the world which have doubtless obtruded themselves on the human mind from the earliest times and will continue to occupy it to the last. Thus the task which it sets the inquirer is identical with that which at a later stage is taken up by philosophy and at a still later stage by science. Surrounded by mysteries on every hand, we are impelled by an invincible instinct to lift the veil that seems to hide them, in the hope that, once uprolled, it may disclose the grand secret which generation after generation of seekers has sought in vain to discover. It is an endless quest, an endless succession of systems, mythical, philosophical, scientific, confidently propounded, strenuously defended like fortresses built for eternity, glistening in rainbow radiance for a time, then bursting and vanishing like gossamer threads in the sunbeams or bubbles on a river. So it has been and so it will be ; it is not for the philosopher or the naturalist to cast stones at the glasshouses of his predecessor the myth-maker. Indeed, one of the greatest of philosophers, Plato himself, was fain to span not a few chasms in his system with bridges built of myth, which, light and airy as they seem, may in the end outlast the structure they were designed to consolidate. To this supreme builder of mythical bridges—this *Pontifex Maximus* —we owe the flights of angel fancy in the *Phaedrus* and the sublime simile of the cave in the *Republic*.

Thus, to be complete, a history of philosophy and even of science should begin with an account of mythology. The

v

importance of myths as documents of human thought in the embryo is now generally recognized, and they are collected and compared, no longer for the sake of idle entertainment, but for the light they throw on the intellectual evolution of our species. In that work of collection and comparison much remains to be done before all the myths of the world can be classified and arranged in a *Corpus Mythorum*, in which, as in a museum, these fossils of the mind can be exhibited to illustrate an early stage in the progress of thought from its lowly beginnings to heights as yet unknown With my other writings I offer this essay as a contribution to that great palaeontology of the human mind which remains to be written.

J. G. FRAZER.

8th December 1929.

CONTENTS

CHAPTER I

INTRODUCTORY

OF all human inventions the discovery of the method of kindling fire has probably been the most momentous and far-reaching. It must date from an extreme antiquity, since there appears to be no well-attested case of a savage tribe ignorant of the use of fire and of the mode of producing it.[1] True, there are many savage tribes and some civilized peoples who tell stories of a time when their ancestors were without fire, and who profess to relate how their forefathers first became acquainted with the use of fire and with the mode of eliciting it from wood or stones. But it is very unlikely that these narratives embody any real recollection of the events which they profess to record ; more probably they are mere guesses invented by men in the infancy of thought to solve a problem which would naturally obtrude itself on their attention as soon as they began to reflect on the origin of human life and society. In short, most if not all such tales are apparently myths. Yet even as myths they deserve to be studied ; for, while myths never explain the facts which they attempt to elucidate, they incidentally throw light on the mental condition of the men who invented or believed them ; and, after all, the mind of man is not less worthy of investigation than the phenomena of nature, from which, indeed, it cannot be ultimately discriminated.

But apart from what we may call the psychological value of myths, a certain number of stories of the origin of fire contain at least possible explanations of the ways in which men first learned the use of that element and the method of

[1] (Sir) E. B. Tylor, *Researches into the Early History of Mankind*[3] (London, 1878), pp. 229 *sqq.*

I

producing it.   It seems, therefore, worth while to collect and
compare the traditions of mankind on this subject, partly as
illustrative of primitive savagery in general, and partly
as perhaps helping us to solve the particular problem in
question.   No comprehensive collection of the traditions, so
far as I am aware, has hitherto been made;[1] what I here offer
is to be regarded merely as a preliminary survey, or as what
Bacon might have called the first vintage,[2] of a wide and
fruitful field.   Others who come after me will doubtless be
able to fill up many of the wide gaps which I have left in the
evidence ; or, to continue the Baconian metaphor, they will
glean many clusters which hung concealed or beyond my
reach in the vineyard

In order to exhibit the diffusion of these stories, and to
determine as far as possible their relations to each other, I
will take them in geographical or what, roughly speaking,
amounts to the same thing, in ethnical order, beginning with
the lowest savages known to us, who are the Tasmanians.

---

[1] Stories of the origin of fire were
treated by Adalbert Kuhn in a famous
essay (*Die Herabkunft des Feuers und
des Göttertranks*, second edition,
Güttersloh, 1886), marked by great
learning and ingenuity ; but he confined himself to Aryan myths, chiefly
Indian and Greek.   Andrew Lang had
the merit of calling attention to the
wide diffusion of stories of fire-stealing
among savages, and he tells us that he
made " a small collection " of such
myths in his work *La Mythologie* (pp.
185-195), which I have not seen.   See
his article " Mythology " in *The
Encyclopædia Britannica*, Ninth
Edition, xix. 807 *sq.*; *Modern*

Mythology (London, 1897), pp. 195
sqq. Compare A. Bastian, " Die Vor-
stellungen von Wasser und Feuer,"
Zeitschrift für Ethnologie, i. (1869)
pp. 379 *sq.*; S. Reinach, *Cultes,
Mythes, et Religions*, iii. (Paris, 1908),
" Aetos Prometheus," pp. 83 *sq.*; E.
E. Sikes, " The Fire-Bringer," pre-
fixed to his edition of Aeschylus,
Prometheus Vinctus (London, 1912),
pp. ix-xv ; Walter Hough, *Fire
as an Agent in Human Culture*
(Washington, 1926), pp. 156-165
(*Smithsonian Institution, United
States National Museum, Bulletin*
139).

[2] *Novum Organum*, ii. 20.

CHAPTER II

THE ORIGIN OF FIRE IN TASMANIA

A NATIVE of the Oyster Bay tribe in Tasmania gave the following account of the introduction of fire among his people :

" My father, my grandfather, all of them lived a long time ago, all over the country : they had no fire. Two black fellows came, they slept at the foot of a hill—a hill in my own country. On the summit of a hill they were seen by my father, my countrymen, on the top of the hill they were seen standing : they threw fire like a star, it fell among the black men, my countrymen. They were frightened—they fled away, all of them; after a while they returned,—they hastened and made a fire,—a fire with wood; no more was fire lost in our land. The two black fellows are in the clouds ; in the clear night you see them like two stars.[1] These are they who brought fire to my fathers.

" The two black men stayed awhile in the land of my fathers. Two women (*Lowanna*) were bathing ; it was near a rocky shore, where mussels were plentiful. The women were sulky, they were sad ; their husbands were faithless, they had gone with two girls. The women were lonely ; they were swimming in the water, they were diving for cray-fish. A sting-ray lay concealed in the hollow of a rock—a large sting-ray ! The sting-ray was large, he had a very long spear ; from his hole he spied the women, he saw them dive ; he pierced them with his spear,—he killed them, he carried them away. Awhile they were gone out of sight. The sting-ray returned, he came close inshore, he lay in still water, near the sandy beach ; with him were the women,

[1] " Castor and Pollux."

3

they were fast on his spear—they were dead! The two black men fought the sting-ray ; they slew him with their spears ; they killed him ;—the women were dead ! The two black men made a fire,—a fire of wood. On either side they laid a woman,—the fire was between : the women were dead !

" The black men sought some ants, some blue ants (*puggany eptietta*) ; they placed them on the bosoms (*parugga poingta*) of the women. Severely, intensely were they bitten. The women revived,—they lived once more. Soon there came a fog (*maynentayana*), a fog as dark as night. The two black men went away, the women disappeared : they passed through the fog, the thick, dark fog ! Their place is in the clouds. Two stars you see in the clear cold night ; the two black men are there, the women are with them : they are stars above ! " [1]

In this story the origin of fire is associated with the two stars, Castor and Pollux, who once appeared as men on earth and threw fire " like a star " among fireless men. But it is not quite clear whether these benefactors were supposed to have brought the fire from heaven in the first instance or only to have transported it thither when they were themselves fixed in the sky for ever. In short, it is doubtful whether the Tasmanians attributed to fire a starry or a terrestrial origin.

---

[1] Joseph Milligan, in *Proceedings of the Royal Society of Tasmania*, vol. iii. p. 274, quoted by James Bonwick, *Daily Life and Origin of the Tasmanians* (London, 1870), pp. 202 *sq.* ; R. Brough Smyth, *The Aborigines of Victoria* (Melbourne and London, 1878), i. 461 *sq.* ; H. Ling Roth, *The Aborigines of Tasmania* (London, 1890), pp. 97 *sq.*

CHAPTER III

THE ORIGIN OF FIRE IN AUSTRALIA

SOME of the aborigines of Victoria " have a tradition that fire, such as could be safely used, belonged exclusively to the crows inhabiting the Grampian Mountains ; and, as these crows considered it of great value, they would not allow any other animal to get a light. However, a little bird called *Yuuloin keear*—' fire-tail wren '—observing the crows amusing themselves by throwing fire-sticks about, picked up one, and flew away with it. A hawk called Tarrakukk took the fire-stick from the wren, and set the whole country on fire. From that time there have always been fires from which lights could be obtained." [1]

The mention of the Grampian Mountains, which are situated in south-western Victoria, seems to show that this story was current among the aborigines of that neighbourhood. But a similar story is reported to have been told by the aborigines of Gippsland in the extreme south-east of Victoria. According to them, there was a time when the aborigines had not fire. The people were in sad distress. They had no means of cooking their food, and there was no camp-fire at which they could warm themselves when the weather was cold. Fire (*tow-er-a*) was in the possession of two women who had no great love for the blacks. They guarded the fire very strictly. A man who was friendly to the blacks determined to get fire from the women, and in order to do so he pretended to be very fond of the women and accompanied them on their journeys. One day, seizing a favourable opportunity, he stole a fire-stick, hid it behind his

---

[1] James Dawson, *Australian Aborigines* (Melbourne, Sydney, and Adelaide, 1881), p. 54.

back, and made off. So he returned to the blacks and gave them the fire which he had stolen. Ever afterwards they regarded him as their benefactor. He is now a little bird with a red mark over its tail, which is the mark of the fire.[1]

In this Gippsland story the little bird with the red mark on its tail is doubtless the same as the " fire-tailed wren " of the preceding tale. But the legend has been rationalized by representing the fire-thief as a man who was afterwards transformed into a bird. A much abridged version of the same story runs that " fire, according to the traditions of the Gippsland people, was originally obtained ages ago by their ancestors from *Bimba-mrit* (the fire-tailed finch) in a very curious way." [2]

Far away from Gippsland, in northern Queensland, the natives in like manner associate the first fire with the same little bird. In the days of long ago, according to the aborigines of Cape Grafton, on the eastern coast of Queensland, there was no such thing as fire on earth ; so Bin-jir Bin-jir, a small wren with a red back (*Malurus* sp.), went up into the skies to get some. He was successful, but lest his friends on earth should have the benefit of it, he hid it away under his tail. Asked on his return how he had fared, he told his friend that his quest had been fruitless, but at the same time he suggested that his friend should try to extract the fire from various kinds of wood. His friend set to work on pieces of wood of different sorts, endeavouring to elicit a flame by twirling one of them on the top of another. But he laboured in vain and at last gave up the task in despair. Then turning round he burst out laughing. Being asked by Bin-jir Bin-jir why he laughed, " Why," said he, " you have got some fire stuck on to the end of your tail," referring to the red spot on the bird's back. Bin-jir Bin-jir was therefore obliged to admit that he did get some fire, and finally he showed his friend from what particular wood to extract it.[3]

Thus in two versions of this story the fire-bringing bird is described as a wren and in one of them as a finch. As there

[1] R. Brough Smyth, *The Aborigines of Victoria* (Melbourne and London, 1878), i. 458.

[2] E. M. Curr, *The Australian Race* (Melbourne and London, 1886–1887), iii. 548.

[3] Walter E. Roth, " Superstition, Magic, and Medicine," *North Queensland Ethnography*, Bulletin No. 5 (Brisbane, 1903), p. 11.

appear to be no wrens in Australia, I conjecture that the bird in question is the scrub-bird *Atrichornis*, a bird about the size of a small thrush, which inhabits the densest parts of the Australian scrub or brushwood forest. Two species of it are known, the *A. clamosa* and the *A. rufescens*. The former, which is the larger, is brown above, each feather being barred with a darker shade ; the throat and belly are reddish white, and there is a large black patch on the breast ; while the flanks are brown and the lower tail-coverts rufous. *A. rufescens* has the white and black of the fore-parts replaced by brown, barred much as is the upper plumage.[1] The ruddy under-tail of this bird would account for the story that it hid the fire under its tail : apparently the narrative is merely a myth devised to explain the colour of the bird's plumage.

In other Australian legends it is not a wren-like bird but a hawk which figures as the first bringer of fire. One such legend runs as follows. A long time ago, a little bandicoot was the sole owner of a firebrand, which he cherished with the greatest jealousy, carrying it about with him wherever he went and never lending it to anybody. So the other animals held a council at which it was resolved that fire must be got from the bandicoot by hook or crook. The hawk and the pigeon were deputed to carry out the resolution. All attempts to persuade the bandicoot to share the boon with his neighbours having proved abortive, the pigeon seized what he thought was an unguarded moment and made a dash to snatch the prize. In despair the bandicoot threw the fire towards the water, intending to quench it for ever. But the sharp-eyed hawk, hovering near, swooped down on the fire before it fell into the water, and with a stroke of his wing he knocked the brand far over the stream into the long dry grass on the opposite bank. The grass blazed up, and the flames spread over the face of the country. The black man then felt the fire, and said that it was good.[2]

Again, among the tribes of New South Wales there is, or rather used to be, a very widespread tradition that the earth

[1] Alfred Newton and H. Gadow, *A Dictionary of Birds* (London, 1893-1896), p. 822.

[2] James Browne, in the *Canadian Journal*, vol. i. p. 509, quoted after Wilson by R. Brough Smyth, *The Aborigines of Victoria*, i. 460. We are not told the name of the particular tribe who relate this story.

was originally peopled by a race much more powerful, especially in magical arts, than that which now inhabits it. That race is known by different names in different tribes. The Wathi-wathi call them Bookoomuri and say that they were finally changed into animals. The story of the origin of fire runs thus. Once upon a time two Bookoomuri were the sole possessors of fire : one of them was Koorambin, that is, a water-rat ; and the other was Pandawinda, that is, a cod-fish. The two jealously guarded the secret of fire in an open space among the reed-beds of the Murray River. Many efforts were made both by the other Bookoomuri and by the present race of men to obtain a spark of the fire, but without success, till one day Karigari, that is, hawk, who of course had originally been a Bookoomuri, discovered the water-rat and the cod-fish in the act of cooking mussels, which they had got from the river. He flew up to such a height that they could not see him, and then caused a whirlwind to blow among the dry reeds, scattering the fire in every direction, so that the whole of the reed-beds were soon in a blaze. The con-flagration spread to the forest and laid waste vast tracts of woodland, where never a tree has grown since. That is why you now see the Murray River flowing among vast bare plains, which were once clothed with forests.[1]

The Ta-ta-thi, another tribe of the same region, tell a similar tale. They say that a water-rat, whom they call Ngwoorangbin, lived in the Murray River and had a large hut, where he kept fire to cook the mussels which he brought out of the water. This fire he jealously guarded. But one day whilst he was down in the river gathering mussels, a spark flew out and was caught by a small hawk (*Kiridka*), who, having some inflammable materials ready, kindled a fire, by means of which he burned down, not only the house of the water-rat, but a large tract of forest beside. That is why the plains thereabout are now so bare. But ever since the black fellows have known how to procure fire by friction.[2]

According to the Kabi, a tribe of south-eastern Queens-land, the deaf adder (*Mundulum*) had formerly the sole

---

[1] A. L. P. Cameron, " Notes on some Tribes of New South Wales," *Journal of the Anthropological In-* *stitute*, xiv. (1885) p. 368.

[2] A. L. P. Cameron, *op. cit.* pp. 368 *sq.*

possession of fire, which he kept securely in his inside.   All
the birds tried in vain to get some of it, until the small hawk
came along and played such ridiculous antics that the adder
could not keep his countenance and began to laugh.   Then
the fire escaped from him and became common property.[1]

In the territory of the Warramunga tribe of Central
Australia, to the south of the Murchison Range, two fine
gum-trees may be seen growing on the banks of a dry creek.
The natives say that the trees mark the spot where two hawk
ancestors first made fire by rubbing sticks together.   The
names of these hawk ancestors were Kirkalanji and Warra-
pulla-pulla.   Though they were birds, they were the first to
make fire in this part of the country.   They always carried
about their fire-sticks with them, and one day Kirkalanji
lit a fire that was bigger than he intended to make, with the
result that he himself was caught in it and burnt to death.
Being very grieved at this mishap, Warra-pulla-pulla went
away somewhere in the direction of what is now Queensland,
and he was never heard of again.   The moon then came up,
for in those days he was a man who walked about on earth.
He met a bandicoot woman near the spot where Kirkalanji
had kindled the fire, and he strolled about with her.   Then
they sat down on a bank with their backs to the fire and
weré so long talking to one another that they did not notice
it till it was close upon them.   The bandicoot woman was
badly singed and swooned away or died outright ; however,
the moon man, being no ordinary mortal, brought her to
life or to consciousness, and together they went up into the
sky.   " It is a curious feature," adds Sir Baldwin Spencer,
" amongst all the tribes that the moon is always represented
as a man and the sun as a woman." [2]

The Mara, a tribe who inhabit the south-western coast of
the Gulf of Carpentaria, have a tradition that in the olden
times there was a great pine-tree which reached right away
into the sky.   Every day a number of men, women, and
children used to climb up into the sky and to come down
again by means of this tree.   One day, while they were up

[1] John Mathew, *Two Representative Tribes of Queensland* (London, 1910), p. 186.
[2] Sir Baldwin Spencer, *Wanderings in Wild Australia* (London, 1928), ii. 470 *sq.*   Compare (Sir) Baldwin Spencer and F. J. Gillen, *Across Australia* (London, 1912), ii. 410.

aloft, an old hawk named Kakan discovered the way to make
fire by means of twirling one stick upon another. But in a
dispute which he had with a white hawk the country was set on
fire, and the pine-tree was unfortunately burnt, so that the
people up above could not get down again to the earth, and so
they have remained in the sky ever since. These people had
crystals implanted in their heads, elbows, knees, and other
joints, and it is the flashing of the crystals at night-time which
makes the lights that we call stars.[1]

In these Australian legends it is not easy to distinguish
between the conception of the first fire-maker as a bird and
the conception of him as a man who merely bore a bird's
name or assimilated himself to a bird in other ways. The
difficulty is due to that confusion between animal and man
which totemism fosters, if it does not create, in the mind of
the savage. Identifying a man with his totemic animal, the
native Australian seems to lose the power of clearly discriminating between them ; and if he were asked whether,
for example, in a story about the adventures of a kangaroo,
he meant a kangaroo animal or a man who had a kangaroo
for his totem, he might not be able to answer or even understand the question.

In the legendary lore of the Booandik, a tribe which
formerly inhabited the extreme south-eastern corner of South
Australia, the first fire-bringer appears as a cockatoo. Thus
in one version of the story fire is said to have originated in the
red crest of a cockatoo, a bird which the Booandik called
mar. A certain cockatoo (*Mar*), we are told, concealed the
fire from his tribe for his own sole benefit, and his fellows were
angry with him for his selfishness. The wise cockatoos called
a meeting to concert a plan for worming the secret from Mar.
It was agreed to kill a kangaroo and invite Mar to come and
share the animal with them. Then when Mar carried off his
share to cook it privately at his fire, the other cockatoos would
watch him and see how he made fire. The plan was carried
into execution. So Mar came and received as his portion of
the kangaroo the head, shoulders, and skin. These Mar
carried home and prepared the meat for roasting. The

[1] Baldwin Spencer and F. J. Gillen, *The Northern Tribes of Central
Australia* (London, 1904), pp. 628 *sq.*

other cockatoos watched him, and saw how he got stringy bark and grass and laid them on the ground ready for lighting, then how he scratched his head with his claws, and how fire came forth from his red crest. So the cockatoos knew how fire was made, but they had still to get it. A little cockatoo offered to go and steal the fire from Mar. He crept cautiously through the grass till he came near the coveted fire. Then he put a grass-tree stick to the fire, and, unnoticed by Mar, lit it and flew away to his fellows. The cockatoos were over-joyed at having at last found out the art of obtaining fire ; but Mar was very angry and set the grass on fire, and burnt the whole country from Mount Schanck to Guichen Bay. The musk-duck (*croom*), enraged at the burning of his country, clapped and shook his wings, and so brought the water that fills the lakes and swamps.[1]

In this version the first fire-maker is clearly conceived as a cockatoo pure and simple, and the story is merely a myth devised to explain the red feathers of his crest. But in another version of the Booandik story the fire-maker is represented as a man who was afterwards turned into a cockatoo. A long time ago, it is said, the black people lived without fire to cook their food, and all they knew about it was that a man called Mar (cockatoo), who lived far away in the east, had it and kept it all to himself, concealed under the tuft of feathers which he wore on his head. He was too powerful a man to be openly attacked and dispossessed of his fire by force, so the people resolved to use guile. They proclaimed a great tribal assembly or corroboree and messengers were sent out to announce the day of meeting. Among the rest came Mar, and when a kangaroo was killed to furnish a feast he was offered a dainty bit but refused it, saying he preferred the skin. He got it and carried it away to his camp, which he had fixed some way off. The rest were curious to know what he would do with the skin, " for," said they, " it will not be good eating unless he prepares it with his fire." An active young fellow named Prite undertook to follow and watch him by sneaking through the grass without being seen. He went and saw how Mar, after yawning, put his hand to his head as if to scratch it and so drew fire from its place of concealment.

[1] Mrs. James Smith, *The Booandik Tribe* (Adelaide, 1880), pp. 21 *sq.*

Having learned the secret, Prite returned and reported to the assembled people. Another person named Tatkanna now volunteered to go and learn more about it. He contrived to get close to the fire and felt its heat. Then he also returned to report, and to show how the fire had singed his breast to a reddish colour. Another then went to the fire, taking with him a grass-tree stick. He saw Mar singeing the hair off the kangaroo skin and managed, without being observed, to thrust his stick into the fire. But on withdrawing it he inadvertently set the grass in a blaze. The fire spread rapidly over the long rank grass and dry underwood. In a great rage, Mar grasped his clubs (waddies) and rushed over to where the others were encamped, for he justly suspected them of tampering with his fire. His suspicion was confirmed by the sight of Tatkanna, whose red breast was proof of his having had a hand, or rather a bosom, in the business. Being a little fellow Tatkanna began to whimper; but Quartang stood up to the big bully Mar and offered to fight him, saying that he was more his match than little Tatkanna. The rest of the blacks did not long remain idle spectators. A free fight followed. In the scrimmage Quartang soon received a blow from a bootjack-like club which finished him off. He leaped up from the ground into a tree and was turned into the bird called the laughing-jackass, which still bears the mark of Mar's bootjack under his wing. Little Tatkanna became a robin-redbreast. The gallant Prite was also converted into a bird which now haunts the underwood along the sea-coast. A big fat fellow of the name of Kounterbull received a deep wound from a spear in the nape of his neck Smarting with pain, he rushed into the sea and was often afterwards seen to spout water from the wound in his neck. His English name is whale. Mar himself, uninjured, flew up into a tree, and, still fuming and scolding, became a cockatoo. A bare spot under the crest on the cockatoo's head is the very place where he used to secrete the fire. Since that eventful day, if the natives chance to let their fire go out, they can readily get a light out of the grass-tree by procuring two pieces of its wood, placing one of them horizontally on the ground, inserting the point of the other in a notch of the first, and twirling the upright stick rapidly between the palms of the hands.

In a short time the sticks will ignite, showing that the wood of the grass-tree can still set the bush in a blaze as it did in the days of Mar.[1]

This version of the story purports to explain how the natives came to make fire by the friction of grass-tree wood. But incidentally it accounts for the characteristic features, not of one, but of several birds and of the whale beside. The original form of the narrative appears to have embraced a considerably larger range of beasts and birds ; for Mrs. James Smith, the lady missionary to whom we owe a valuable account of the Booandik tribe, among whom she lived and laboured for more than thirty-five years, informs us that she had forgotten the names of most of those who distinguished themselves in the fight about fire. She adds : " This is to be regretted, as their names are necessary to the full under-standing of the story."[2] So far as the animals are con-cerned, the story is clearly a zoological myth told to account for certain characteristic features of the Australian fauna. The robin-redbreast, who plays a conspicuous part in it, can hardly be the robin of our islands, since he seems not to be found in Australia. Some native Australian bird with red plumage on his breast has probably been identified by the early settlers with the familiar feathered friend of their old home.

This story of the origin of fire was found by Mrs. Smith to be current only among the natives in the extreme south-eastern corner of South Australia, between Mount Gambier and MacDonnell Bay. It was unknown to the blacks farther north at Rivoli Bay and Guichen Bay, but still farther north the natives of Encounter Bay, at the mouth of the Murray River, were acquainted with a somewhat similar story.[3] This Encounter Bay version of the tale has been recorded by another observer. It runs as follows. Once upon a time their ancestors assembled at Mootabarringar to hold a corro-boree or dancing festival. As they had no fire, they could not dance by night and were obliged to dance by day. The

---

[1] Mrs. James Smith, *The Booandik Tribe*, pp. 19-21.

[2] Mrs. James Smith, *The Booandik Tribe*, p. 20. She tells us (p. 21) that more than ten years had passed since she last heard the story, and that the blacks who could tell it well had long passed away.

[3] Mrs. James Smith, *The Booandik Tribe*, pp. 18 *sq.*

weather being very hot, the sweat dripped from them and formed the large pools which you may see there down to this day ; and the beat of their dancing feet produced those irregularities of surface in the ground which now are hills and valleys. But they knew that a big powerful man, named Kondole, who lived in the east, was in possession of fire, and they sent messengers, Kuratje and Kanmari, to invite him to the feast. He came, but hid his fire. At that the men were displeased and resolved to take the fire from him by force. At first no one ventured to approach him ; but at last a certain Rilballe plucked up courage to smite him with a spear and rob him of his fire. So he threw the spear and wounded him in the neck. This caused a great laughing and shouting, and nearly all the people were transformed into animals of different sorts. Kondole himself ran to the sea and became a whale, and ever after he spouted water out of the wound which he had received in his neck. The two messengers, Kuratje and Kanmari, were turned into small fish. It so happened that at the moment of their transformation Kanmari was wearing a good kangaroo skin, while Kuratje had on nothing but a mat of seaweed ; that is the reason why the fish called *kanmari* has a great deal of oil under its skin, while the fish called *kuratje* is dry and lean. Other people became opossums and went upon trees. The young dandies who were bedecked with tufts of feathers changed into cockatoos, retaining the tufts of feathers as crests. As for Rilballe, he took Kondole's fire and placed it in the grass-tree, where it still remains, and from which it can be drawn out by rubbing The way in which the Encounter Bay tribe extracted fire from the grass-tree was this. They took a split piece of the flower stem and placed it on the ground, with the flat side up. Then they took a thinner piece of the same wood and pressed the lower end of it on the other, while they held the upper end between the palms of their hands and gave it a revolving motion by moving the hands backwards and forwards till the wood caught fire.[1]

This version of the story probably supplements the

---

[1] H. E. A. Meyer, " Manners and Customs of the Aborigines of the Encounter Bay Tribe," in J. D. Woods, *The Native Tribes of South Australia* (Adelaide, 1879), pp 203 *sq.*

Booandik version as recorded by Mrs. Smith, in so far as it furnishes more details as to the transformation of the people into animals after the discovery of fire. But it differs from the Booandik version curiously enough in representing the whale rather than the cockatoo as the original owner of fire.

Other Australian stories associate the discovery of fire-making with the crow. Thus the aborigines who used to inhabit the valley of the river Yarra, which flows into Port Phillip where the city of Melbourne now stands, said that long ago a certain woman called Karakarook was the only person who knew how to make fire. She kept it in the end of her yam-stick, that is in the staff with which she, like other aboriginal Australian women, was wont to dig up edible roots, insects, and lizards to serve as food for her people ; [1] but she refused to impart her fire to any one else. But Waung, whose name means " crow," fell on a plan to get it from her. The woman was very fond of eating ants' eggs ; so Waung made, or took, a great many snakes and put them under an ant-hill. Then he invited Karaka-rook to come and dig up the eggs. When she had dug up a little, she turned up the snakes. Waung told her to kill them with her yam-stick. She struck them accordingly, and as she did so the fire fell out of the yam-stick in which she had hidden it away. Waung thereupon picked up the fire and made off with it. As for the woman, she was set in the sky by Pund-jel, the Maker of Men, and there she still shines as the Pleiades or Seven Stars. But when Waung had got the fire, he proved nearly as selfish as the woman had been before, for he would give fire to nobody. Therefore Pund-jel, the Maker of Men, was very angry with Waung, and he gathered together all the blacks, and caused them to speak harshly to Waung, and Waung was afraid. To save himself and burn the others, he threw the fire among them, and every one picked up some of the fire and departed. Tchert-tchert and Trrar took some of the fire and lighted the dry grass around Waung, and burnt him. Pund-jel said to Waung, " You shall be a crow to

[1] Baldwin Spencer and F. J. Gillen, *Native Tribes of Central Australia* (London, 1899), pp. 26 *sq.*

fly about, and shall be a man no more." Tchert-tchert
and Trrar were lost or burnt in the fire. They are now
two large stones at the foot of the Dandenong mountain.[1]

The Bunurong tribe, who inhabited the district lying to
the south-east of Melbourne, told a similar tale to explain
the origin of fire ; but in it the crow (*waung*) appears to
be a real bird and not a man who was afterwards turned into
a crow. The story, which involves certain repetitions, runs
as follows : Two women were cutting a tree for the purpose
of getting ants' eggs, when they were attacked by several
snakes. The women fought stoutly, but could not kill the
snakes. At last one of the women broke her fighting-stick
(*kan-nan*), and immediately fire came forth from it. The
crow picked up the fire and flew away with it. Two very
good young men, named Toordt and Trrar, ran after the
crow and caught him. In a fright the crow let fall the fire,
and a great conflagration followed. The blacks were sore
afraid when they saw it, and the good Toordt and Trrar
disappeared. Pund-jel himself came down from the sky
and said to the blacks, "Now you have fire, do not lose it."
He let them see Toordt and Trrar for a moment, and then
he took them away with him, and set them in the sky, where
they now shine as stars. By and by the blacks lost the fire.
Winter came on. They were very cold. They had no place
whereat they could cook their food. They had to eat their
food cold and raw like the dogs. Snakes also multiplied
At length Pal-yang, who had brought forth women from
the water, sent down Karakarook from the sky to guard the
women. She was a sister of Pal-yang, and is held in respect
by the black women to this day. This good Karakarook
was a very fine and very big woman, and she had a very,
very long stick, with which she went about the country
killing a multitude of snakes, but leaving a few here and
there. In striking one snake she broke her big stick, and
fire came out of it. The crow again flew away with the
fire, and for a while the blacks were in great distress. However, one night Toordt and Trrar came down from the sky
and mingled with the blacks. They told the blacks that
the crow had hidden the fire on a mountain named Nun-ner-

[1] R. Brough Smyth, *The Aborigines of Victoria*, i. 459.

woon.   Then Toordt and Trrar flew upwards.   Soon Trrar
returned safely with the fire wrapt up in bark, which he had
stripped from the trees, as the aborigines do on a journey
when they carry fire with them and wish to keep it smouldering.   Toordt returned to his home in the sky and never
came back to the blacks.   They say he was burnt to death
on a mountain named Mun-ni o, where he had kindled a
fire to keep alive the small quantity he had procured.   But
some of the sorcerers deny that he was burnt to death on
that mountain ; they maintain that for his good deeds
Pund-jel changed him into the fiery star which white men
call the planet Mars.   Now the good Karakarook had told
the women to examine well the stick which she had broken,
and from which had come forth smoke and fire ; the women
were never to lose the precious gift.   Yet this was not enough.
The amiable Trrar took the men to a mountain where grows
the particular kind of wood called *djel-wuk* out of which
fire-sticks are made ; and he showed them how to fashion
and use these implements, so that they might always have
the means at hand to light a fire.   Then he flew away upwards and was seen no more.[1]

A similar story of the origin of fire was told by the Wurunjerri, a tribe which, at the time when Melbourne was founded,
occupied the country to the north and north-east of the city,
including the Yarra flats and the valley of that river as far
as its source, together with the northern slopes of the Dende-
rong Mountains.[2]   The Karat-goruk, who are clearly the
same as the Karakarook of the two preceding stories, were a
group of young women who dug up ants' eggs with their
yam-sticks, at the ends of which they had coals of fire.   But
the crow (*waang*) stole the fire from them by a stratagem ;
and when the musk-crow (*bellin-bellin*) let the whirlwind
out of his bag at the command of Bunjil, the women were
swept up by it into the sky, where they still remain as the
stars which we call the Pleiades, and still they carry the fire
at the ends of their yam-sticks.[3]

[1] R. Brough Smyth, *The Aborigines of Victoria*, i. 459 *sq.*

[2] A. W. Howitt, *The Native Tribes of South-East Australia* (London, 1904), pp. 71 *sq.*

[3] A. W. Howitt, *op. cit.* p. 430. For this story, which he seems to give in an abridged form, Dr. Howitt refers to the manuscript work of his daughter, Miss Mary E. B. Howitt,

The same story was taken down, in a slightly different form, from the lips of the older aborigines by the Rev. Robert Hamilton of Melbourne. Though he does not say so, we may probably assume that the natives from whom he obtained the legend inhabited the country near the city. His report of the legend is as follows : " *The first obtaining of fire.*—A maiden, whose native name was Mûn-mûn-dik, had somehow or other become the sole owner of fire, which she kept in the end of a yam-stick. (The yam-stick, it may be explained, is a rod about five feet long, the point of which is hardened by fire to fit it for digging up roots out of the earth.) The maiden used the fire for her own convenience and comfort, but no persuasion could make her share the benefits with others, and all attempts at securing the treasure by force or fraud proved unsuccessful. Bûnd-jil, however, sent his son to the assistance of the race. Failing to persuade the fire-maiden to a voluntary surrender, he had recourse to stratagem. Having buried a poisonous snake in a great ant-hill, he asks her to come and dig up the ants' eggs— considered a delicacy. She, of course, digs up the snake. Tarrang calls out, ' Hit it, hit it ! ' As she strikes the creature with her yam-stick the fire is set free. Tarrang seizes it, and bestows it upon men. To prevent the maiden ever resuming her monopoly, he removes her to a place in the sky, where she became the ' Seven Stars.' She is to be seen there now." [1]

In this version no mention is made of the crow, but we may surmise that he lurks in the person of the artful Tarrang, the son of Bundjil, who wheedles the woman out of fire by the same dodge which the crow employs for the same purpose in the first of the versions. The explanation which Mr. Hamilton gives of the yam-stick suggests the reason why the woman's fire was supposed to be concealed in that implement. As the point of the stick had been thrust into the

Legends and Folklore (of some Victorian Tribes). It is much to be regretted that this valuable work has not yet been published. A good many years ago I was privileged to consult it and to make a few extracts from it, but among these extracts the legend of the origin of fire is unfortunately not included.

[1] Rev. Robert Hamilton, Melbourne, " Australian traditions," *The Scottish Geographical Magazine,* i. (Edinburgh, 1885) pp. 284 *sq.*

fire to harden it, what more obvious than that it should in the process absorb some of the fire into its substance, and that consequently any violent impact might suffice to force out of the stick the igneous element with which it might be said to be charged or saturated ?   On the principles of primitive natural philosophy the reasoning seems impeccable.

In this legend, which we may call the Melbourne legend, since it was current among the tribes in the neighbourhood of that city, it is interesting to observe that the origin of fire is associated with the Pleiades, who are supposed still to carry in the sky the same fire which they bore about with them in their yam-sticks on earth.   It may be a simple coincidence that across the water at no very great distance from these tribes in the extreme south of Australia, the rude aborigines of Tasmania similarly associated the terrestrial with the celestial fires, both these savage peoples assuming that the lights of heaven were first kindled here on earth.

Another Victorian version of the same legend has been reported from Western Port, an inlet of the sea some way to the south of Melbourne   The story runs thus : At the creation a number of young men, in an unfinished state, were sitting on the ground in darkness, when Pundyil, an old man, at the request of his good daughter Karakarok, held up his hand to the sun (*gerer*), who thereupon warmed the earth and made it open like a door.   Then the light came.   And Pundyil, seeing the earth to be full of serpents, gave his kind daughter Karakarok a long staff, with which she went everywhere, destroying serpents.   Unfortunately, as it seemed, her staff broke before she had killed them all ; but as the staff snapped in two, fire came out of it, and thus great good was derived from apparent evil.   The people joyfully cooked their food ; but Wang, a mysterious being in the shape of a crow, flew away with the fire, and left them in a pitiable state.   Karakarok, however, restored the fire, which was never again lost.   As for Pundyil, or Bonjil, he is said to have lived at the falls of Lallal, on the Marrabool River, but he is now in the sky.   The planet Jupiter is his fire and is also called Pundyil.[1]

---

[1] Rev. William Ridley, " Report on Australian Languages and Traditions,"   *Journal of the Anthropological Institute*, ii. (1873) p. 278 ; compare *id.*,

In this Western Port version the crow reappears, but the Pleiades disappear. However, they are no doubt implicitly present in Karakarok, the native name for that constellation. According to the preceding account, it would seem that these savages regarded the planet Jupiter as the father of the Pleiades.

Far away from these natives the Boorong tribe, which inhabited the dreary " mallee scrub " country about Lake Tyrrell in north-western Victoria, had a tradition that fire was first given to the natives by the crow, whom they identified with the star Canopus.[1]

Sometimes, though seemingly more rarely, the aborigines of Australia traced the origin of fire on earth to a source which seems to us more obvious than the stars, that is, to the sun. Thus the natives about Lake Condah, in south-western Victoria, related that once upon a time a man threw up a spear towards the clouds, and to the spear a string was attached. Then the man climbed up the string and brought down fire from the sun to the earth.[2] One of the tribes near Maryborough in Queensland told how men originally obtained fire from the sun in a different way. In the beginning, when Birral had placed the black fellows on the primitive earth, which was like a great sandbank, they asked him where they should get warmth in the day and fire in the night. He said that if they went in a certain direction they would find the sun, and by knocking a piece off it they could get fire. Going far in the direction indicated, they found that the sun came out of a hole in the morning and went into another hole in the evening. Then rushing after the sun, they knocked a piece off his disc, and so obtained fire.[3]

A somewhat more probable source of the origin of fire

Kamilaroi, and other Australian Languages (Sydney, 1875), p. 137. This tradition is apparently derived by Mr. Ridley from *Remarks on the Probable Origin and Antiquity of the Aboriginal Natives of New South Wales*, by a Colonial Magistrate, Melbourne, a work which I have not seen. The Magistrate perhaps wrote before the separation of Victoria from New South Wales, which took place in 1851.

[1] W. Stanbridge, "Some Particulars of the General Characteristics, Astronomy, and Mythology of the Tribes in the Central Part of Victoria, Southern Australia," *Transactions of the Ethnological Society of London*, New Series, i. (1861) p. 303.

[2] R. Brough Smyth, *The Aborigines of Victoria*, i. 462.

[3] A. W. Howitt, *The Native Tribes of South-East Australia*, p. 432.

is alleged by some natives of the Kulkadone (Kalkadoon) district in north-western Queensland. They say that a long time ago a certain tribe of blacks assembled on some of the open downs of the country. They had had a good day's hunting, and the carcasses of many slain kangaroos were lying about in the camp. Just then a violent thunderstorm broke, and the lightning set fire to the dry grass of the downs, which blazed fiercely, scorching and partly roasting some of the dead kangaroos. When the people came to eat the half-roasted flesh, they found it much more palatable than the raw flesh on which they had hitherto subsisted. So an old woman was despatched to follow up the fire, still to be seen blazing on the downs, and to bring some back with her. After some time she returned bearing a blazing fire-stick. Thereupon she was appointed permanent caretaker of the fire and solemnly admonished by the elders of the tribe never to lose it or let it go out. For many years the old woman faithfully performed her trust until one night in the wet season, when the camp was swamped with water, her vigilance relaxed and the fire was extinguished. As a punishment for her neglect she was condemned to wander alone through the bush until she should find the lost fire. Long did she stray solitary through the trackless wilderness, searching in vain, till one day, passing through a thick scrub, she could bear it no more, and vented her rage by breaking off two sticks from the trees and rubbing them violently together. To her delight, the friction of the wood produced fire, and she returned to her people in triumph with her precious discovery, which has never since been lost by them [1]

The Arunta of Central Australia have a tradition of the origin of fire. They say that in the far-off days to which they give the name of the Alcheringa a man of the Arunga or euro totem started out in the east to pursue a gigantic euro, which carried fire in its body. The man carried with him two big *churinga*, that is, sacred sticks or stones, with which he tried to make fire, but could not. He followed the euro as it travelled westward, trying all the time to kill it.

[1] F. C. Urquhart, " Legends of the Australian Aborigines," *Journal of* *the Anthropological Institute*, xiv. (1885) pp. 87 *sq.*

The man and the euro always camped a little distance away from each other.   One night the man awoke and saw a fire burning by the euro ; he at once went up to it and took some, and with it he cooked some euro flesh which he carried with him, and upon which he fed.   The euro ran away, turning back along its old tracks to the east.   Still trying to make fire, but in vain, the man followed the animal until they both came back to the place from which they had started.   There at length the man succeeded in killing the euro with his *churinga*.   He examined the body carefully to see how the animal made fire, or where it came from ; and pulling out the male organ of generation, which was of great length, he cut it open and found that it contained very red fire, which he took out and used to cook his euro.   For a long time he lived on the body of the big euro, and when the fire which he had extracted from its body went out, he tried again to make fire and succeeded, always singing a chant in these words :

> *Urpmalara kaiti*
> *Alkna munga*
> *Ilpau wita wita.*[1]

The Wonkonguru tribes of Central Australia, among whom are the Dieri, associate the discovery of fire with a sand-hill to the east of Lake Perigundi.   They say that a long time ago, before the white man came into the country, one of their mythical ancestors, whom they call *mooras* or *moora-mooras*, came up from the south and made a camp behind a big sand-hill.   Just about sundown he went over to see a certain Paralana, who was himself a *moora*.   He found Paralana eating raw fish and asked him why he did so.   Paralana answered, " The fish is all right.   How do you eat it ? "   The other replied, " I like to cook the fish ; they are better cooked."   So he asked Paralana to come over to his camp, saying that he would show him how to do it.   Over there he lit a fire, put some fish on the ashes, and when they were cooked he gave them to Paralana, who ate them and asked the other what he called the thing which he had used to dress the fish.   The other told him that it was

---

[1] Baldwin Spencer and F. J. Gillen, *The Native Tribes of Central Australia,* pp. 446 *sq.*

called fire and showed him how to make it. When Paralana
had learned the secret, he killed his instructor and carried
the fire over to his own sand-hill. There he camped and
there, armed with this novel instrument, he levied tribute
on the other blackfellows, who brought him food and young
women. But by and by he got two young wenches who did
not wish to stay with him. So they waited till he was fast
asleep, and then they hastily departed, taking a fire-stick
with them, and they showed all their people how to keep
fire alight.[1]

The Wonkonguru tell another story of a *moora* woman
who stole fire from an old woman called Nardoochilpanie.
Having killed the old woman she turned herself into a swan
and flew away, carrying the fire-stick in her mouth. That is
why all black swans have a red edging to the inside of their
beaks ; it is to show where the *moora* woman burned her
mouth when she was carrying the fire-stick.[2] In the light
of the foregoing stories we may surmise that in an older
form of this Wonkonguru myth the swan brought the first
fire to mankind and burned the inside of its beak in the
process.

The Kakadu of Northern Australia have a tradition of
two men, half-brothers, both named Nimbiamaiianogo, who
went out hunting with two women, their mothers. The men
caught ducks and spur-winged plovers, while the women got
plenty of lily-roots and seeds in the water-pools. Now at
that time the men had no fire and did not know how to make
it, but the women did. While the men were away hunting
in the bush, the women cooked their food and ate it by
themselves. Just as they were finishing their meal they saw
the men returning, away in the distance. As they did not
wish the men to know about the fire, they hastily gathered
up the ashes, which were still alight, and thrust them up
their vulvas, so that the men should not see them. When
the men came close up, they said, " Where is the fire ? " but
the women replied, " There is no fire " ; and then there was
a great dispute and much noise. At last the women gave the

---

[1] G. Horne and G. Aiston, *Savage
Life in Central Australia* (London,
1924), pp. 139 *sq.*

[2] G. Horne and G. Aiston, *Savage
Life in Central Australia*, pp. 140-
141.

men some of the lily-roots which they had gathered and cooked. When they had eaten a great deal of meat and lily-roots they all went to sleep for a long time. Once more, when they awoke, the men went out hunting and the women cooked their food. The weather was very hot, and all that remained of the birds that the men had brought in was now putrid. The men brought in a fresh supply, and again, while they were still afar off, they saw the fire burning brightly in the women's camp. A spur-winged plover flew up and gave warning to the women that the men were coming back. Once more the women hid the fire and ashes in the same way as before, and again the men asked where the fire was, but the women stoutly maintained that they had none at all. The men said, " We saw it," but the women answered, " No, you are mocking us, we have no fire." The men rejoined, " We saw a big fire ; if you have no fire, how do you cook your food ? has the sun cooked it ? If the sun cooks your lilies, why does it not cook our ducks and prevent them from turning putrid ? " To this there was no reply. They all went to sleep, and when they woke up the men left the women and dug up the root of an iron-wood tree and got resin from it. Then they took two sticks and found that they could make fire by rubbing them one on the other. But to punish the women for the lies they had told about the fire they resolved to turn themselves into crocodiles and in that form to pay the women out for their deceit. So they moulded the resin of the iron-wood tree into the shape of crocodile heads, and putting them on their own heads they dived into a pool ; and when the women came to fish at the pool, the crocodile-men dragged them under water and killed them. When all was over, the crocodile-men drew the dead women out on the bank, and said to them, " Get up, go. Why did you tell us lies about the fire ? " But the dead women made no reply. For a time the men kept their crocodile heads on, while their arms and legs were still human. But afterwards they turned into real crocodiles, and they were the first of the species, for up till then there had been no such creatures.[1]

---

[1] (Sir) Baldwin Spencer, *Native Tribes of the Northern Territory of Australia* (London, 1914), pp. 305-308.

CHAPTER IV

THE ORIGIN OF FIRE IN THE TORRES STRAITS ISLANDS AND NEW GUINEA

In the eastern Islands of Torres Straits, between Australia and New Guinea, the following story of the origin of fire has been recorded:

An old woman named Serkar, who lived at Nagir, had six fingers on each hand. She had a finger between the thumb and the forefinger, as all people had long ago. When she wished to make fire, she placed one piece of firewood on another, then put the finger that had the fire under the wood, which accordingly ignited. Now all the animals at Moa often saw the smoke that Serkar made, and they knew that she had fire, and they wished to get some of it, for they had none of their own. So one day they met in council. There was the snake, and the frog, and lizards of various sorts, to wit, the long-tailed lizard (*zirar*), the very small lizard (*monan*), the house-lizard (*waipem*), and two big lizards, one of them called *si* and the other *karom*. They all agreed that they must swim across to Nagir to get the fire. The snake was the first to try; but the sea ran high, and he had to turn back. The frog tried next, but he too failed to battle with the waves. After him the little lizard, the long-tailed lizard, the house-lizard and one of the two big lizards (*si*) plunged into the water, but were all driven back in like manner. At last the other big lizard (*karom*) essayed the task, and with the help of his long neck, which enabled him to hold his head above the billows, he succeeded in swimming across and landing on the sandy beach of Nagir. Once there, he went straight to Serkar's house. She was seated at work plaiting a basket and was very glad

to see him. She bade him sit down, and then went herself
to the garden to get food for her visitor. The long-necked
lizard availed himself of her absence to search the house
for fire, but he could find none. Thinks he to himself,
" Pretty fools we look at Moa. She has got no fire." By
and by the old woman came back, bringing plenty of food
from the garden and plenty of firewood. Then she put one
piece of wood on another, while the long-necked lizard
watched her closely. He saw her put her finger to the wood,
which took fire at once and blazed up. After that, the old
woman cooked the food, and when she had finished cooking,
she took all the wood away from the fire and hid it in the
sand ; for, being thrifty, she did not like to lose the firewood. The fire was now all out, not a spark of it was left ;
nevertheless the old woman had it all the time in her finger.
But the long-necked lizard wished to get the fire to carry
back with him to Moa. So when he had finished his meal,
he said, " Very good, I am going away ; it is a long swim
to Moa." The old woman went down with him to the
beach to see him start. At the edge of the water the long-
necked lizard held out his hand to the old woman. She
offered him her left hand to shake, but he refused to take it.
" You give me the proper hand," says he, and on that he
insisted, till at last the old woman held out her right hand,
in which was the fire. The lizard caught the finger that
had fire in his mouth, bit it off, and swam with it to Moa.
There all the people, or rather the animals, were waiting
for him on the shore. They were all glad to see the fire
which he brought them. They all took fire to Mer (one of
the Murray Islands). They all went into the wood and
every one got a branch from the tree he liked best ; they
asked each tree to come and get a fire-stick. One of them
asked the bamboo (*marep*), another the *Hibiscus tiliaceus*
(*sem*), another the *Eugenia* (*sobe*), and so on. Thus all
these trees got fire and have kept it ever since ; and men
obtain their fire-sticks from the trees. The fire-sticks (*goi-
goi*) are two in number, an upright one and a horizontal one.
The upright stick is twirled on the horizontal stick till fire is
produced : the operation is called " mother gives fire," for
the horizontal stick is named " mother," and the upright

stick is named " child." As for the old woman Serkar, she lost her sixth finger, and ever since men have had only five fingers, though they had six before : you can still see the big gap between the thumb and the forefinger where the sixth finger used to be. According to one account, the long-necked lizard did not bite off the old woman's finger, but sawed it off with a certain river-shell (*cyrena*), which is common in New Guinea.[1]

A slightly different version of the same story has been reported from the Murray Islands by another observer as follows :

On one of the islands near the mainland of New Guinea (Daudai) lived a woman named Sarkar, who had fire between her finger and thumb on her right hand. One day some men fishing saw smoke rising in the island where Sarkar dwelt, and they decided to go and explore, and, if possible, find out the secret of this mysterious power. After considerable dispute amongst themselves as to the best means of acquiring the desired information, they decided to change themselves into animals. They therefore took the form of the rat, the small lizard (*mona*), the snake, the iguana, the big long-necked lizard (*karom*), and so on. The heavy seas soon caused the rat, the small lizard (*mona*), the snake, the iguana, and the rest to give up the attempt ; only the big long-necked lizard held on, and at last landed near the place where Sarkar lived. Going up to the woman in the form of a man, he asked, " Have you any fire ? " She answered, " No ! " for she was anxious to keep her power a secret. But she brought her visitor food, and when he had eaten, he lay down to sleep. However, he slept with one eye open, and saw how the woman struck fire from her hand and kindled some dry leaves and wood. Next morning he decided to leave, and said to Sarkar, " I am going ; shake hands ! " She offered him her left hand, but he would not take it and asked for the other. So she gave him her right hand, and when she did so he whipped out a bamboo knife, cut off her hand, and plunged into the sea with his prize. On reaching his own place he tried to make fire and

[1] *Reports of the Cambridge An-   Straits*, vi. (Cambridge, 1908) pp.
thropological Expedition to Torres   29 *sq.*

succeeded. Some trees saw him make the fire, and went
to look at it.   Certain of them, to wit the bamboo (*marep*),
the *kizo*, *seni*, *zeb*, and *argergi*, took some of the fire with
them, and ever since that time these trees have possessed the
power of producing fire.   From these trees the natives used
to cut the sticks which made fire by friction.[1]

In this version of the story the actors are men who change
themselves into animals for the purpose of stealing the old
woman's fire, whereas in the former and probably more
primitive version they were animals pure and simple.

An abridged version of the same story is reported from
Mowat (Mawatta), in Daudai, a district to the south of the
Fly River in British New Guinea.   " Eguon, described as a
large bat, is fabled to have introduced fire to Mowat.   A
legend goes, that a tribe once inhabited Double Island [Nalgi]
(near Nagir), one of whose members showed fire to come from
the left hand between the thumb and forefinger, whereupon
dissention arose and the people were all transformed into
animals, birds, reptiles, fish (including dugong and turtle).
Eguon found his way to Mowat, the others to different
places in the Straits and New Guinea."[2]   In this version
a large bat has taken the place of the long-necked lizard as
the fire-bringer ; but otherwise the story is in substantial
agreement with the preceding legend, in so far as it relates
how fire was first elicited from between the forefinger and
thumb of a human being, and how the people who aided
and abetted the theft of fire were transformed into animals.

The people of Mawatta say that fire was brought to them
from the island of Mabuiag in Torres Strait after the following
fashion.   In those days the natives of Torres Strait, like those
of New Guinea, did not know fire.   One day some people
saw a crocodile with fire in his mouth wherewith he cooked

[1] Rev. A. E. Hunt, " Ethno-
graphical Notes on the Murray Islands,
Torres Straits," *Journal of the Anthropological Institute*, xxviii. (1899)
p. 18.   The story is also quoted in
*Reports of the Cambridge Anthropo-
logical Expedition to Torres Straits*, vi.
p. 30.   Following Dr. A. C. Haddon
in the *Reports, llcc.*, I have translated
some of the native names for animals

and trees which Mr. Hunt has left
untranslated.

[2] E. Beardmore, " The Natives of
Mowat, Daudai, New Guinea," *Journal
of the Anthropological Institute*, xix.
(1890) p. 462.   The legend is also
quoted in *Reports of the Cambridge
Anthropological Expedition to Torres
Straits*, v. (Cambridge, 1904) p. 17.

his food. They said, " O crocodile, give us fire," but he
refused. They then went to their chief, who was lying ill in his
house. On his recovery he took some food and swam to
Dauan. While he rested there he saw smoke rising across the
water on the coast of New Guinea. Swimming across, he
met a woman setting fire to the grass, and he stole the fire
from her and carried it back to Mabuiag. From Mabuiag
fire went to Tutu, and the Tutu people gave it to Mawatta.[1]

In the island of Kiwai, which lies off the coast of British
New Guinea, at the mouth of the Fly River, various stories
of the origin of fire are current. The first to report one of
them was the pioneer missionary, the Rev. James Chalmers,
who sacrificed his life in his zeal for the improvement of the
natives of New Guinea. His version runs as follows :

" Fire was first produced on the mainland near to Dibiri
by two men, whose names I could not get. All animals
tried to steal some of the fire and swim across to Kiwai with
it, but failed. Then all the birds tried it, and they too failed,
when up flew the black cockatoo, and he said he would get
it. He dropped down and got a good burning stick and
then flew away with it, letting it fall on the various islands
on his way across the estuary, but always picking it up again.
When he came to Iasa, his mouth was terribly burned, hence
the red spot on both sides of his beak. At Iasa he let it drop,
and the people secured it, and have fire ever since." [2]   The
cockatoo referred to in this story belongs no doubt to the
genus *Microglossa*, " whose wholly black plumage is relieved
by their bare cheeks of bright red." [3]

The same story is reported from Kiwai somewhat more
fully by a more recent inquirer. " There was, of course, a
time when the people had no fire and were compelled to eat
all things uncooked. Fire, however, was known at Dibiri
(the mouth of the Bamu), and, aware of this, the animals
endeavoured to steal it. The crocodile tried and was

[1] W. N. Beaver, *Unexplored New
Guinea* (London, 1920), p. 69.

[2] Rev. James Chalmers, " Note on
the Natives of Kiwai Island, Fly
River, British New Guinea," *Journal
of the Anthropological Institute,*
xxxiii. (1903) p. 118. Compare *Reports of the Cambridge Anthropological Expedition to Torres Straits,* v.
17, where it is said that the black
cockatoo " bears the mark of his
accident to this day in the red scar
round his bill."

[3] Alfred Newton and Hans Gadow,
Dictionary of Birds (London, 1893–
1896), p. 93.

unsuccessful, the cassowary failed, and even the dog could not manage it.   Then the birds made an attempt, and the black cockatoo succeeded in picking up some fire and flew to the west with it in his beak.   When he came to Iasa, however, the fire burned his mouth and he dropped the fire-stick. Thus the Kiwais obtained fire, while the black cockatoo carries the red blaze of the burn above his beak to this day. In some other parts of British New Guinea the majority of fire stories say that the dog was the first to bring fire to man, and in one case the dog stole it from the rat.   In practice among the Kiwais fire is made by holding down the usual billet of dry wood with the foot and drawing a piece of split cane swiftly up and down beneath it.   An alternative is the ' fire plough ' method." [1]   By the " fire plough " the writer means what is also called the " stick-and-groove " method of making fire, which consists in rubbing a blunt-pointed stick along a groove of its own making in a piece of wood laid on the ground. [2]

In recent years a number of stories of the origin of fire have been collected in Kiwai by the Finnish anthropologist, Dr. Gunnar Landtman   Among these tales is the one which relates how fire was brought to Kiwai by the black cockatoo. It runs as follows :

A little boy living at Manavete (on the mainland of New Guinea) was once carried off by a crocodile, and his father, whose name was Dave, launched a canoe and set out to see whether he could find him or his spirit somewhere.   Paddling along, he came to Doropa on Kiwai Island, which at that time was a mere sandbank with no trees.   He spent the night there, and next day he arrived at Sanoba on the same island, where lived a man named Meuri.   Now this Meuri had no garden and no fire, and he spent his time in catching fish which he dried in the sun.   He told Dave that he had no fire, and Dave promised to bring him some.   Now Dave had in his possession an extraordinary bird, which knew many things and could speak like a man.   This wonderful bird was a black cockatoo (*kapia*).   So Dave sent the

---

[1] W. N. Beaver, *Unexplored New Guinea* (London, 1920), p. 175.

[2] (Sir) E. B. Tylor, *Researches into the Early History of Mankind* [3] (London, 1878), pp. 237 *sq.*

cockatoo to fetch fire from Manavete. The bird flew away, and after a time returned with a glowing fire-stick in his beak. That was the way the black cockatoo used to carry fire, and that is why he still has a red streak round the corners of his mouth ; the streak is the effect of the fire. Meuri always kept the fire-stick which the cockatoo brought him.[1]

Another story recorded by Dr. Landtman in Kiwai relates how the islanders of Torres Straits first obtained fire. The story is clearly a variant of the legend told by these islanders themselves.[2] It runs thus :

At one end of Badu Island, in Torres Straits, there lived a man named Hawia with his mother, and they had no fire. But at the other end of the island lived a crocodile, and he had fire. One day Hawia and the crocodile were spearing fish at the same time, and returning home the crocodile kindled a fire to cook his catch. Hawia went and asked him to lend him fire that he too might cook his fish, but the crocodile refused gruffly. So the man returned home, and he and his mother cut up the fish, and dried it in the sun, but they had to eat it raw. Many another time did Hawia ask the crocodile for fire, but always in vain.

One day Hawia prepared to go and seek fire elsewhere. He donned a head-dress of white feathers, painted his face black, and put on many ornaments. Thus adorned, he plunged into the water and swam over to Budji, singing as he swam, " Smoke over there, they are burning the bush. I swim along the water and go to take fire." At last he reached Budji. A woman lived there who was burning the bush in order to make a garden. Between the thumb and forefinger of her right hand a fire was constantly burning. On noticing Hawia, she put out all the flames in the bush, lest the stranger should know that she had fire. She asked him where he came from and what he wanted. He told her, and the woman answered, " Very well. Go to sleep, and

---

[1] Gunnar Landtman, *The Folk-tales of the Kiwai Papuans* (Helsingfors, 1917), pp. 331 *sq.* (*Acta Societatis Scientiarum Fennicae*, vol. xlvii.) ; *id.*, *The Kiwai Papuans of British New Guinea* (London, 1927), p. 36.

Doctor Landtman records (*The Folk-tales of the Kiwai Papuans*, pp. 64, 68 *sq.*, 332) a number of slightly variant versions.

[2] See above, pp. 25 *sqq*

to-morrow I will give you some fire." Next day she began to burn the bush again. Hawia said to her, " Come, let us shake hands. I wish to go away." She offered him her left hand, but he asked for the right, and suddenly tore away the fire from her hand. Having got it, he jumped into the water and swam over to Boigu, singing the same song as before. On reaching Boigu, he lighted a fire, and as the smoke rose into the air, his mother over in Badu said, " Oh, smoke over there ! My son is coming back, he has got fire." Next he came to the island of Mabuiag and lighted a similar signal, and his mother said, " Oh, he is at Mabuiag. The smoke is coming near." Lastly he landed on Badu and told his mother, " I have got fire. We will kill fish and cook them on the fire." The crocodile now saw that Hawia and his mother were in possession of fire, and he officiously came and offered to give them some of his own, pretending to show them a kindness. But Hawia said, " No, I do not want your fire, I have got some from another place." And he added, " Do not stop on shore. You are a crocodile. Stop in the water. You are not a man like me to stop on shore." The crestfallen crocodile went into the water, saying, " My name is alligator. Everywhere I will go and catch men." [1]

In this version the head-dress of white feathers worn by the man, and the black paint smeared on his face when he swam across the sea to fetch the fire, may well be the fruit of a primitive rationalism, which substituted a human being thus disguised for the black cockatoo which figures as the fire-bringer in other Kiwaian stories.[2]

The same curious mode of obtaining fire, by wresting it from a person who kept it burning between his forefinger and thumb, meets us in another story reported by Dr. Landtman :

In Muri, one of the islands of Torres Straits, there lived a man named Iku, who had fire burning between the thumb and forefinger of his right hand. That was the only fire in the islands. All the fire now to be seen in the islands originated from the fire between the thumb and forefinger of

<hr />

[1] G. Landtman, *The Folk-tales of the Kiwai Papuans*, pp. 333 *sq.* This story was told to Dr. Landtman by a Mawata man. Another Mawata man gave Dr. Landtman a shorter and slightly different version of the same story (p. 334).

[2] See above, pp. 29-31.

Iku's right hand. To this day we all have a wide empty space between the thumb and forefinger, because Iku used to have a fire-stick there.

Now in Nagir, another island in Torres Straits, there dwelt a man called Naga, who lived on fish, which he speared and dried in the sun. And in Mabuiag, another island of Torres Straits, there lived a man named Waiati with his wife and daughter. These men had no fire ; they always ate their food cold. But one day Naga came to see Waiati in Mabuiag and said to him, " Let us go and look for fire. There is a man called Iku in the island of Muri, who has fire in his hand, while you and I cook our food in the sun." So a hawk took up the two men and flew with them over the sea to Muri and alighted on a big tree. The two men climbed down to the ground and left the hawk to wait for them in the tree. Now Iku was at work making a canoe out of the trunk of a tree. The two men watched him from the bush and they saw the fire in his hand. Putting down his stone axe, Iku set fire to some pieces of wood. Still the men watched him, saying, " He is putting fire to the wood, he is kindling fire with his hand, oh, yes, yes." Then they came out of the bush, and Iku turned round. " Where do you two fellows come from ? " says he ; " there was no man here. Why have you come ? " They said, " We are come to look for fire. We have no fire. We always dry our fish in the sun." At that, Iku at once withdrew the fire into his hand, so that it could not be seen. He said, " I have no fire. Who told you that I had fire ? " But they stuck to it that they knew he had it. And Naga, who had once before been carried by the hawk to Muri and had seen the fire, told Iku, " I saw you the first time before I spoke to my friend." Then Iku exclaimed scornfully, " You are not men. I think you are devils. You have no fire, you eat your food cold. I am a man, I have fire, I will show it to you." At that he opened his hand and said, " Look, the fire comes out now ! " But Naga ran and wrenched the fire from his hand. In vain Iku tried to stop him, saying, " Take not that fire, it is mine ! " And he ran after Naga. " Oh," he cried, " give back my fire ! " But Naga and Waiati quickly betook themselves to the hawk, and the bird flew away with them. So Iku had to give up the pursuit. He returned to his place, bitterly lamenting his loss, and in order to keep up the fire which he had just lit, now that the source of it was gone, he collected a great deal of wood. The place in his hand where the fire had been now shut up.

Naga and Waiati returned to Nagir, Naga's island, where they lit a big fire. Then Waiati went back to his own island of Mabuiag, taking Iku's fire with him. His people were drying fish in the sun. But Waiati lit a fire, and his wife cried out, " What is that ? " He answered, " That is fire for the food. Come and cook food at it." A big flame shot up, and the people were afraid, saying, " Oh, what is that ? " But Waiati reassured them, saying, " Wait while I cook the fish." When the fish was cooked, he gave them some, and they ate, crying out, " Oh, father, that is a good way ! Till now we have dried the fish, and it took a long time."

Another time Naga and Waiati went to Yam Island, carried by the hawk. Waiati soon returned to Mabuiag, but Naga settled down in Yam, and also brought his family over there. He was the first man to live in that island. Iku went over to Davane and gave fire to Kogea, and also to Mereva in Saibai, an island off the coast of Daudai in New Guinea. It is from Saibai that the knowledge of fire has spread to New Guinea. But Iku returned to his own island of Muri.[1]

Another story tells how the first fire-maker was a small boy named Kuiamo, who had an ever-burning fire at the end of the forefinger of his right hand. He was a native of the island of Mabuiag, in Torres Straits, but one day he went to see some people in the island of Badu. Now these people did not know the use of fire, and they roasted their food in the sun. When they gave Kuiamo raw food to eat, he taught them how to cook it. He put his finger to a piece of wood, and it began to burn. At first the people were very frightened at the sight. Being unused to cooked food, they fainted away when they first tasted it, but soon they got to like it. The same thing happened in the island of Moa and in other places where Kuiamo went to teach the people the use of fire.[2]

[1] G. Landtman, *Folk-tales of the Kiwai Papuans*, pp. 134 *sq.*   [2] G. Landtman, *Folk-tales of the Kiwai Papuans*, p. 157.

The Masingara people, to the south of the Fly River, in British New Guinea, have a story of the origin of fire which closely resembles the story told by the islanders of Torres Straits.[1]   They say that in former times they had no fire, and that their only food consisted of ripe bananas and fish dried in the sun. Growing tired of this diet, they sent some animals to fetch fire. The first whom they chose for this task was the rat. They gave him a drink of kava (*gamoda*) and told him to go and look for fire. The rat drank the kava and ran away into the bush, but stayed there without troubling about the fire. The same thing happened to the iguana and the snake. One after the other they drank the kava, took to the bush, and stayed there. At last the people applied to the *ingua*, which is another kind of iguana, known as *iku* in Mawata. The *ingua* drank the kava, plunged into the sea, and swam across to the island of Tudo. There he found fire and brought it back in his mouth, swimming all the way, and lifting his head at every wave, so that the fire did not go out. Since then the people in the bush have fire. They make it by rubbing or drilling a piece of *warakara* wood or bamboo with another piece of *warakara* wood, which they first smear with a little beeswax.[2]

Another story relates how a man named Turuma, who lived at Gibu in Kiwai, used to catch fish and dry them in the sun, because he had no fire. Now a certain mythical being called Gibunogere lived there underground, and he was sorry for Turuma, seeing him drying his fish in the sun for want of fire. So one day while Turuma was away spearing fish, Gibunogere dug a hole in the ground and lay down there, covering himself with earth, so as to hide himself from Turuma. On his return Turuma found Gibunogere's foot-prints and wondered. " Who has been walking here ? " thinks he to himself. " I am the only man that lives in this place." All of a sudden up got Gibunogere and said, " Who are you ? What are you talking about ? " In great alarm Turuma cried out, " Oh, father, where do you come from ? " It was to curry favour with Gibunogere that he called him father. Gibunogere replied, " I live under-

[1] See above, pp 25 *sqq.*
[2] G. Landtman, *Folk-tales of the Kiwai Papuans*, p. 335.

ground. That is my place, and a very good place it is too. There is fire there. You have got no fire. You had better come to my place." Turuma was still afraid, but Gibunogere promised to give him fire and urged him to come. So they went to Gibunogere's place underground, and when Turuma sat down close to the fire, he fainted. But Gibunogere bled him, made him drink water, and washed his body. At last Turuma came round, married Gibunogere's daughter, and gave his father-in-law many stone axes and necklaces of dogs' teeth in payment for the girl. Unfortunately the bride did not survive the wedding night, and before morning broke, Turuma was a widower.[1]

A more prosaic story, without this tragic ending, tells how in the old days, while the island of Kiwai was as yet only a sandbank with no trees but young mangroves growing on it, two men lived not far from each other at Iasa. The name of the one was Nabeamuro and the name of the other was Keaburo. Now Keaburo had no fire and ate his fish raw, only drying them in the sun. But Nabeamuro knew how to make fire by drilling a hole in one stick with another stick, yet he would not impart his knowledge to Keaburo. However, one day Keaburo came upon him in the act of making fire, stole the fire from him, and ran away with it, and Nabeamuro, who was an old man, could not come up with the thief.[2]

A more instructive story, taken down by Dr. Landtman in Kiwai, narrates the first discovery of fire-making as follows :

Formerly all the people used to eat their food raw. But a Gururu or Glulu man once dreamt that a spirit came to him and said, " Your bow has got fire inside it." When the man woke up, he thought to himself, " Fire, what is that ? " Then he fell asleep again, and the spirit returned and said, " To-morrow, try your bow. Rub it along wood so as to cut the wood." In the morning the man fetched a piece of wood, which he began to saw with his bow, using the bow-string as a blade. He found that the friction made the wood hot, and by hard work he elicited first smoke and afterwards fire. He used some dry coco-nut fibre for tinder, and soon had a bright fire blazing. He was much pleased with the discovery, for

---

[1] G. Landtman, *Folk-tales of the Kiwai Papuans*, p. 333.

[2] G. Landtman, *Folk-tales of the Kiwai Papuans*, p. 147.

he warmed himself at the fire and cooked his food at it.   At first he roasted a taro-root at it, broke it in two, and smelt it cautiously.   He hesitated.   " Suppose," said he, " I were to die in consequence of eating it ? "   But after tasting it, he exclaimed, " It is sweet ! "   He now returned to the people in the house and brought them fire.   Everybody was frightened and wished to run away, but he explained to them the use of fire and showed them how to cook food.   At first they were afraid to eat the cooked food, but after a time they all adopted the new mode of preparing their victuals.[1]

To the same effect another story, recorded by Dr. Landt-man, tells how a certain boy called Javagi, the son of a male kangaroo, was once sawing a piece of wood in two with his bamboo rope, when the wood caught fire.   The boy was at first much frightened, but in the night his mother, or rather foster-mother, the kangaroo came to him and said, " That fire of yours is a good thing   Fear not.   Cook your food at it."   Some bushmen, the story adds, still make fire in that way, namely, by sawing wood with a bamboo rope.[2]

By some natives of British New Guinea on the Gulf of Papua, apparently at Perau, Mr. James Chalmers was informed that fire was first brought from the bowels of the earth, but that after some generations it went out.   In the days when fire was thus extinct on earth, it chanced that a woman, who had just given birth to a child, felt very cold and wished for warmth.   Very opportunely a little fire came down from heaven, and the woman's father fed it with dry leaves. It soon blazed up, and the woman sat and warmed herself at it.   People came with presents for the baby and received in return a burning stick.   Since then fire has never gone out.[3]

At Motumotu, in British New Guinea, they say that fire was first produced in the mountains.   Before that everything was eaten raw, until one day Iriara, a mountaineer, who was

---

[1] G. Landtman, *Folk-tales of the Kiwai Papuans*, pp. 334 *sq.* Compare *id.*, *The Kiwai Papuans of British New Guinea*, p. 37.

[2] G. Landtman, *Folk-tales of the Kiwai Papuans*, pp. 82 *sq.* ; *id.*, *The Kiwai Papuans of British New Guinea*, pp. 37, 109. This Javagi was born, like Erichthonius, from the

ground.   He had a kangaroo father, but no mother.   The female kangaroo, which informed him of the true value of fire, was not really his mother but only his foster-mother.

[3] Rev. James Chalmers, *Pioneering in New Guinea* (London, 1887), pp. 76 *sq.*

sitting with his wife, suddenly rubbed one stick against another, and fire sprang out.[1]

The Motu tribe of British New Guinea tell the following story of the origin of fire among them. They say that their ancestors used to eat their food raw or cooked in the sun. One day they saw smoke at Taulu, which is said to mean " ocean space." The dog, the snake, the bandicoot, a bird, and a kangaroo all looked and exclaimed, " Smoke at Taulu! Smoke at Taulu! The Taulites have fire. Who will go and fetch us some ? " The snake went, but the sea was rough and he soon came back. The bandicoot tried, but he too returned. The bird started, but could not fly against the strong wind, so he also came back. Next the kangaroo went, but he likewise failed. Then the dog said, " I'll go and fetch the fire." He swam to an island, where he landed and saw a fire and women cooking. They said, " Here is a strange dog, kill him." But the dog seized a burning fire-brand and jumped into the sea with it. He swam back, the people watching him from the shore as he drew near to the land, bearing the smoking fire-brand. When he landed, the women rejoiced to have fire, and women came from other villages to buy it of them. But the other animals were jealous of the dog and vilipended him He ran after the snake, which retreated into a hole in the ground. The bandicoot did likewise. As for the kangaroo, he went to the mountains, and ever since there has been enmity between the dog and the other animals.[2]

The Motu story is reported with some small variations by James Chalmers. In his version, the animals which tried in vain to bring back fire are the bush pheasant, the snake, the iguana, the quail, the wallaby, and the pig. As in the former version, it is the dog which finally succeeds in the attempt.[3]

The Orokaiva, who live near the River Mambare in north-eastern Papua (British New Guinea), also look upon the dog as the animal which brought the first fire to their ancestors. They say that some people lived in a village on the shore.

[1] Rev. James Chalmers, *op. cit.* pp. 174 *sq.*

[2] Rev. W. G. Lawes, " Ethnological Notes on the Motu, Koitapu and Koiari Tribes of New Guinea,"

Journal of the Anthropological In-stitute, viii. (1879) p. 369.

[3] Rev. James Chalmers, *Pioneering in New Guinea*, pp. 174 *sq.*

They felt very cold and were tired of their raw, hard food. They looked across the water and saw smoke rising on the other side, and they all wondered what it was, and wanted very much to get the thing that made the smoke. Suddenly one of their dogs said, " I will get it for you." So he swam over the water to the smoking village, and there, sure enough, he got a fire-stick and started to swim back, holding it in his mouth. But although he was a big, strong dog, he could not keep it above the waves. At last the water put out the fire, and he came back with nothing but a dead stick. After him other dogs tried, one after the other, to fetch the fire, but they fared no better than the first. At last a little mangy cur spoke up. He was covered with sores, and had hardly a hair left on his back. " I will get you the fire," quoth he, and all the people laughed in his face. But off he went, swam to the other side, and there got a burning stick ; and instead of trying to carry it in his mouth as the other dogs had done, he tied it to his tail, and so began to swim back to his people. And as he swam he wagged his tail ; and the sparks flew off from the burning brand, which shone like the bunch of flaring coco-nut leaves that the women carry with them when they go fishing on the reef by night. And seeing the light coming towards them and sparkling in the gloom, the people on shore danced about, and slapped their chests, and cried, " Fetch 'em, boy ! " In that way the little dog brought the fire ashore.

But before he gave the fire to the people, he put it down on the ground. And then the bandicoot tried to steal it and to take it down into his burrow. However, the little dog was too clever for him. He snatched the fire back from the bandicoot and gave it to his own " father and mother," that is, to the man and woman who looked after him. And they were very thankful and gave it to all the other people. And they say even now that the fire really belongs to the dog. That is why he likes to lie down very close to it, even on top of the ashes when the fire is dead ; and that is why he snarls and whimpers when you push him away.[1]

Other people in Papua besides the Orokaiva say that fire

[1] " The Fire and the Dog," *The Papuan Villager*, vol. i. No. 1 (Port Moresby, 15th February 1929), p. 2.

was first given to them by a dog. Thus in the story told at
Mukawa, near Baniara, the dog is said to have gone right
across to Goodenough Island and brought back the fire from
there. But as the distance is great, some twenty miles, he
wisely did not attempt to swim, lest he should be drowned ; so
he paddled across the sea all alone in his canoe and brought
back a fire-brand safely And he ran his canoe ashore, and
landed, and walked up a hill near Mukawa. There he set
fire to the grass, or perhaps the grass caught light by accident
from the brand he was carrying ; but at any rate all the
people in the neighbouring villages saw the smoke, and they
came and got fire for themselves. And to this day they call
the hill Dog's Hill, because the dog landed there. And the
white men have put up a lighthouse on it for the ships that
pass in the darkness, so that now every night a light is seen
twinkling on the hill. But whatever the white men may say,
the black men know that it was the dog who first put the
fire there.[1]

The writer who has recorded these two stories of the dog
and the fire tells us further that " long ago the people of
Papua had no fire. They used to shake with cold in the
south-east wind ; and they had to eat their yams and taro
in raw, hard lumps. But now they have fire. In every
village the fires burn brightly by night, and the women cook
the food in pots or bamboos or with hot stones in the ground.
Where did they get the fire ? Who gave it to them ? Some
people say it came down from the sky ; some say that an
old woman had it hidden under her grass *rami* ; some say
that a cockatoo brought it in his beak ; some say that a little
lizard had it tucked away in his armpit." [2]

The natives of the Purari Delta in Papua (British New
Guinea) tell the following story of the origin of fire. They
say that Aua Maku, the Fire-maker, came out of the west.
Some will have it that he came from far away, but others
maintain that he was a Pie River man, born near Kaimari,
the place where he bestowed the first fire on mankind. Be
that as it may, he is said at first to have dwelt under the

---

[1] " The Fire and the Dog," *The Papuan Villager*, vol. i. No. 1, p. 2. The authority cited for this Mukawa story is Mr. Tomlinson, a missionary.

[2] " The Fire and the Dog," *The Papuan Villager*, vol. i. No. 1, p. 2.

waters of the River Pie. But his mother Kea bade him go
up on to dry land, lest he should be caught by a crocodile ;
so up he went. And after performing various exploits he
went up with his brother Biai to live in the sky, and this was
how they did it. They brought a tall *ane* tree and set it up
in the village, where it stood like a great pole. Then they
collected their property and some building materials, and
taking it all with them they climbed up the tree into the sky,
where they built a house with the materials which they had
brought with them. Thenceforward all the Kaimari men
remained down below on earth, and Aua Maku and Biai,
having charged them never to forget their names, remained
up aloft in the sky. But down to that time the people of
Kaimari had no fire ; the only way of cooking their food
which they knew was to let it stand a while in the hot sun,
and often enough they ate it raw.

Now Aua Maku had a daughter named Kauu, who
dwelt with him in the sky, and very sad was she to think
that she must remain a maid to the end of her days, for in
the sky there was never a soul whom she could wed. But
one day, looking down wistfully on the earth, she spied a
handsome young fellow named Maiku sitting quietly with
his fellows before the men's house in the sun, and she made
up her mind to marry him. So down she came in a clap of
thunder and told him that she would be his wife. And, to
cut a long story short, married they were, and her father,
Aua Maku, came down from the sky for the wedding, and
after it he departed to his celestial abode, taking with him
the bride-price that had been paid for his daughter.

Next day the young wife went out with the other women
in the canoes to fish and catch crabs, and she came back
with a bagful of them to her husband and said to him,
" But now for the fire. Where do I get the fire to cook
these crabs ? " But her husband Maiku answered that his
village knew naught of fire ; she must leave her crabs a
while in the hot sun, and then they would eat them together.
So she left them in the sun, but when they were ready she
could not bear the sight of them, and when she tried to eat
of them she vomited. And so it came about that, what with
disgust and want of food, Kauu fell ill, and while all the

people were out fishing on the river, she lay at home in the
hot sun, sick of a fever.

Then her father, Aua Maku, looking down from heaven,
beheld his daughter lying on the platform in front of her
house. So he came down to her, and when he learned the
cause of her sickness, how she would rather starve than eat
raw food, he promised to bring her fire. And, as some tell
the story, he brought down from the sky a piece of smouldering
wood, of the tree called *napera*, with which Kauu kindled a
great fire. And when the people returned from the day's
fishing and saw the rising smoke, they feared to draw near,
for to them the thing was new and strange. Nevertheless,
when Kauu called them, they took courage and came and
saw the fire, and got each man a lighted brand. And Kauu
showed them how to make a fire and to cook, so that thenceforth they had no need to eat their crabs raw.

But others say that Aua Maku sent down the fire in such
a way that it set light to a certain tree called *Kara*, and that
Kauu, seeing the smoke of the burning tree, hastened to it
and so obtained a brand. At any rate, there is no doubt
that it was through Kauu and her father, Aua Maku, that the
Purari people learned the secret of fire, and most people agree
that the place where they first learned it was Kaimari.[1]

Among these people of the Purari delta " fire is made
when necessary by the stick-and-groove method The wood
used is that called *napera*. A length of this is held fast at
one end (with the knee or foot) by the operator, and at the
other end by an assistant. A narrow groove is made along
the wood with a knife or shell-fish, and the operator, taking
a short pointed stick, also of *napera*, proceeds to rub back
and forth. He holds the stick with both hands, the thumbs
of each towards his body, and bears heavily downwards.
Smoke appears very soon, the worker rubs faster and faster,
and finally brings his stick to a standstill, pressing the point
in the groove. A glow should appear, which gradually
spreads through the sawdust ; a little charcoal may be
powdered over it if there is any at hand.

" This method of fire-making is known to all. It is

---

[1] F. E. Williams, *The Natives of the*   pp. 255-259. (*Territory of Papua.*
Purari Delta (Port Moresby, 1924),   *Anthropology, Report* No. 5.)

never practised by the women, because it is too hard work ; it would appear to be too hard work for the men also, for a demonstration seldom reaches the desired consummation. In practice fire is obtained from a neighbour's house when necessary ; a few smouldering brands are carried in the canoe, and a large slow fire is kept going when a party is spending a night in the bush. Formerly a piece of *napera* wood would be carried in the canoe, carefully protected from the damp ; nowadays the occasion for using it would arise very seldom." [1]

Thus we see that, as might have been expected, the same sort of wood which is mentioned in the myth is, or used to be, employed in practice for the kindling of fire.

At Wagawaga, on Milne Bay, near the south-eastern extremity of British New Guinea, the people say that long ago, before men had fire, there lived at Maivara, at the head of Milne Bay, an old woman whom all the boys and youths called Goga. [2] At that time people used to cut their yams and taro into thin slices and dry them in the sun. Now the old woman prepared food in this way for ten of the youths, but when they were away hunting wild pig in the bush, she cooked her own food. She did this with fire taken from her body, but she cleared away the ashes and scraps before the boys came back, so that they should not know how she cooked her taro and yams.

One day a piece of the boiled taro happened to be mixed up with the boys' food, and when all the boys were eating their evening meal, the youngest boy picked up the piece of boiled taro, tasted it, and found it very good. He gave it to his comrades to taste, and they all liked it, for it was soft instead of hard and dry like their taro, and they could not understand how taro came to be so nice. Accordingly, next day when the boys went to the bush to hunt, the youngest boy remained behind and hid in the house. He saw the old woman dry his own and his comrades' food in the sun, but before she cooked her own food she took fire from between her legs. That night, when the boys came back from hunting, and while

---

[1] F. E. Williams, *op. cit.* pp. 25 *sq.*

[2] *Goga* is the ordinary term employed by these people in addressing a man or woman of an older generation, when the person addressed belongs neither to the clan of the speaker nor to the clan of the speaker's father.

they were all eating their evening meal, the youngest told his story. And the boys saw how useful this fire was, and they determined to steal some from the old woman.

So in the morning they all sharpened their adzes and cut down a tree as big as a house ; then they all tried to jump over it, but only the youngest boy succeeded, so he was chosen to steal fire from the old woman. Next morning all the boys went out to hunt in the bush as usual, but when they had gone a little way they all turned back and nine boys hid themselves ; but the youngest went quietly to the old woman's house, and when she was going to cook her taro, he slipped behind and snatched a brand from her. He ran as fast as he could to the felled tree and jumped over it, and the old woman could not follow him over the tree. But as he jumped, the brand burned his hand and he let it fall. It set light to the grass, and then a pandanus tree (*imo*) caught fire.

Now a snake called Garubuiye lived in a hole in this tree, and its tail caught fire and burned like a torch. The old woman caused rain to fall in great torrents so that the fire was put out, but the snake stayed in his hole in the pandanus tree, and the fire in his tail was not extinguished.

When the rain had ceased, the boys went out to look for fire, but found none, till at last they spied the hole in the pandanus tree, and pulled out the snake, and broke off its tail, which was still glowing. Then they made a great pile of wood and set fire to it with branches lighted from the snake's tail, and folk from all the villages came to that fire to take some home with them, and the different folk used different kinds of wood as fire-brands, and the trees from which they took their brands became their totems. As for the snake Garubuiye, he is the totem of the Garuboi clan of Wagawaga.[1]

The people of Dobu, an island belonging to the D'Entre-casteaux Group, which lies off the eastern end of New Guinea, tell a similar story of the origin of fire. Their ancestors, they say, used to hunt pigs and eat the flesh raw. One day when all the people were out hunting, an old woman was left alone

---

[1] C. G. Seligmann, *The Melanesians of British New Guinea* (Cambridge, 1910), pp. 379 *sq*.

in the village. She put the yams for the hunters aside in a dish by itself, and then she took fire out of her body, from between her legs, and boiled her own yams in a pot on the fire. After that she put out the fire, threw the dishes away, and when the hunters came home, she gave them raw food to eat. But by mistake she had let one cooked piece slip in among the hunters' food, and when they tasted it they liked it so much that they determined to watch the old woman. So next day one of them returned to the village and saw the fire, whereupon he gathered leaves to make a torch, and lit it. Then he set fire to the grass, though the woman called out, " My fire ! my fire ! Bring it back ! " And so saying she fell dead. The fire burned much grass and bush, until a great rain fell and put it all out. The people looked for the fire but could find none, until they came across a snake coiled up with fire underneath it ; therefore the underside of that snake is as if it were scorched down to this day. With that fire they cooked food, and they buried the old woman, saying, "Oe! Oe! We are happy now!" So they kept the fire as long as they could, and then found out how to produce it by rubbing the point of a hard piece of wood on a softer piece.[1]

The Marind-Anim, who inhabit the southern coast of Dutch New Guinea, tell of a time when fire was unknown. But one day an initiated man named Uaba or Obē clasped his wife Ualiuamb in so tight an embrace that, struggle as he might, he could not disengage himself from her. At last a spirit or supernatural being (*dema*) came and shook the pair and turned them this way and that in order to part them. As he did so, smoke and flames burst from the friction of the two bodies, and that was the origin of fire and of the fire-drill, which elicits a flame by the friction of two pieces of wood. At the same moment the woman Ualiuamb gave birth to a cassowary and to a giant stork (*Xenorhynchus asiaticus*) ; the black feathers of these two sorts of birds were caused by the smoke and soot of the fire in which their progenitors were born. Moreover, the stork burned its feet

---

[1] Rev. W. E. Bromilow, " Dobuan (Papuan) Beliefs and Folk-lore," *Report of the Thirteenth Meeting of the* *Australasian Association for the Advancement of Science, held at Sydney,* 1911 (Sydney, 1912), pp. 425 *sq.*

and the cassowary its crop ; that is why the feet of the one
and the crop of the other are red to this day.   In the village
nobody could conceive what had happened.   There was a
sudden cry of " Fire ! fire ! "   Everybody rushed to the
spot, but nobody knew where the fire came from till the
hut of Uaba was seen to be in a blaze.   The fire spread
rapidly, for it was the dry season and everything was parched.
The burning stuff fell on the people's heads and singed their
hair, and that is why you see so many bald pates among their
descendants down to the present time.   The east monsoon
drove the flames along the coast ; and that is why a broad
strip of bare treeless land still skirts the shore of the sea.
The creatures that lived on the sea-shore were scorched and
reddened by the flames, and that is why crabs turn red when
you roast them down to this very day.[1]

The myth which the Marind-Anim tell to explain the
origin of fire is clearly based on the analogy which these
people, like many other savages, trace between the process
of kindling fire by the fire-drill on the one hand and the
intercourse of the sexes on the other.   In accordance with
this assumed analogy many savages regard the upright fire-
stick as a male and the flat stick, which is bored by it, as a
female.[2]   Hence, as we should expect, the Marind-Anim
commonly employ the fire-drill (*rapa*) for the kindling of
fire, though they are also acquainted with and commonly
employ for the same purpose the fire-saw, which consists in
rubbing a split bamboo backwards and forwards against
the sharp edge of a bamboo arrow-head fixed obliquely in
the ground.[3]   Indeed, it appears that until lately a Secret
Society among the Marind-Anim logically carried out in
practice their mythical conception of the origin of fire by
accompanying the solemn kindling of fire with sexual orgies
which were deemed essential to the preservation of the
element ; these rites were celebrated annually.[4]

---

[1] P. Wirz, *Die Marind-Anim von
Holländisch-Süd-Neu-Guinea* (Hamburg, 1922–1925), vol. i. Part ii. pp. 80-
83.

[2] For examples of these designations
see *The Golden Bough*, Part i., *The
Magic Art and the Origin of Kings*,
vol. ii. pp. 208 *sqq.*; and my commentary on the *Fasti* of Ovid, vol. iv. pp.
208 *sqq.*

[3] P. Wirz, *op. cit.* vol. i. Part i. p. 85.

[4] P. Wirz, *op. cit.* vol. i. Part ii.
pp. 83 *sqq.*, vol. ii. Part iii. pp. 3, 31-33.

In the island of Nvefoor or Noofoor, off the northern coast of Dutch New Guinea, it is said that the natives were first taught by a sorcerer how to make fire, and that the name of the island, which means " We (have) fire," was derived from that event.[1]

[1] J. B. van Hasselt, " Die Nveforezen," *Zeitschrift für Ethnologie*, viii. (1876) pp. 134 *sq.*

CHAPTER V

THE ORIGIN OF FIRE IN MELANESIA

IN the Admiralty Islands, to the north of New Guinea, the natives say that in the beginning there was no fire on earth. A woman sent the sea-eagle and the starling to fetch fire from heaven. She said, " Go ye two to heaven ! Go ye two to fetch fire hither to me ! " So the two birds flew up to the sky. The fish-eagle took the fire, and the two returned to earth. But midway between earth and heaven they shifted the fire between them ; the starling took the fire and carried it on the back of his neck. The wind blew up the flame, so that it singed the starling. That is why the starling is now so small and the fish-eagle so big. Never would the fire have singed the starling if only the starling had been bigger than the fish-eagle. The two brought the fire hither to us on earth. We eat food cooked on the fire. If it were not for these two birds, we should not eat food cooked on the fire, we should dry our food in the sun.[1]

The natives of the Trobriand Islands, to the east of New Guinea, say that the village of Moligilagi is the place where fire was first found. A woman of the Lukwasisiga gave birth first to the sun, then to the moon, then to the coco-nut. Said the moon, " Throw me up into the sky, so that I may be there before any one else and give light to your place." But the mother was not willing. Said the sun coaxingly, " Well then, I shall go first into the sky, I shall give sun-warmth to your garden-lands ; when you cut the scrub for clearing gardens, I shall dry it with my heat, so that you may burn it and plant the yams." The sun went first into the clouds.

---

[1] Josef Meyer, " Mythen und Sagen der Admiralitätsinsulaner," *Anthropos*, ii. (1907) pp. 659 *sq.*

Soon afterwards the moon was thrown into the sky ; she was angry and interfered with some of the magic used to make the fruits of the gardens grow.

It was this woman, the mother of the sun and moon, who gave birth to fire : she gave birth to fire long before : the fire remained, waiting.   She had a younger sister, and the two lived together.   They subsisted on a kind of wild yam. This woman, the elder sister, remained in the village.   But the younger sister went wandering about in the bush, searching for their food, the wild yams.   When she brought them home, the elder sister cooked them, but the younger sister ate them raw.   At night the younger sister would cough ; but the elder sister would sleep well, for she had roasted her yams and eaten them cooked.

One day when the younger sister had gone away to the bush, she turned back, and stood hiding herself from her elder sister.   She saw how her elder sister drew the fire from her body, taking it from between her legs, and how she roasted her wild yams at the fire.   When the elder sister saw that she was detected, she said to her younger sister, " Hold your peace.   Do not divulge the secret.   May people not hear about it, for if they did, they would not pay us for our fire. Do not shout about it.   Let us take advantage of our valuable possession by eating cooked food."   But the younger sister said, " It is not my opinion that I should be silent.   Indeed, I will take the firewood and give it to others, that it may flare up, so that people may have their share of the fire."   She went and took the fire and put it to wood ; she put it to the *damekui* tree ; she put it to many trees ; they all flared up, till it was all done.   Then the younger sister said to the elder sister, " Now, perhaps, you think you will be able to cook your food and eat it, and keep us, many people, eating raw food ? " [1]

To the south of the Trobriand Islands lies the D'Entrecasteaux Archipelago.   The natives tell how fire was first

[1] For this Trobriand story of the origin of fire I am indebted to the kindness of my friend Professor B. Malinowski, who spent several years in the Trobriand Islands investigating the customs, beliefs, and language of the natives. Compare B. Malinowski, *The Sexual Life of Savages* (New York and London, 1929), ii. 427.   The story agrees substantially with the stories reported from Wagawaga and Dobu. See above, pp. 43 *sqq.*

brought to Wagifa, a small island off Goodenough, which is one of the two largest islands of the group. They say that a number of dogs were fishing on the eastern side of Wagifa. They caught some fish and wished to roast them, but they did not know how to make fire by means of sticks. One of them, by name Galualua, climbed to the top of a rock to sun himself, and across the strait at Kukuya he saw a cloud of smoke ; so he bade his companions stay and fish, while he went over and brought some fire. At Kukuya he found a pot of food cooking over a fire and a woman sweeping the ground beside her hut. She turned and saw him as soon as he shook his head. He said to her, " My friend, give me some fire. My companions are fishing over there, and I want some fire to take back for them." The woman tied a fire-stick to his tail, but as he was swimming back, his tail sank under the water, and the fire was extinguished. He returned to the woman and asked for another brand, and she tied it to his back. But his back dipped under likewise, and he had to return once more. This time she asked him, " Where shall I tie it now ? " and he answered, " On my head." In that way he brought the fire safe to Wagifa. His companions asked him why he had been so long, and Galualua answered, " Oh, twice the fire went out and I had to return for more." They cooked and ate their fish, but afterwards their fire was changed to stone, and the dogs all entered a cave. There they have remained ever since, but in the evenings they sometimes come out and bark. From that time onwards there has always been fire at Wagifa.[1]

The natives of Buin, one of the Solomon Islands, say that formerly there was no fire in the island. So in the olden time the people could not cook nor make a light at night, and they ate all their food raw. But the people in the island of Alu were acquainted with fire. So the people of Buin called out to the people of Alu, " Give us fire." But the people of Alu did not come in answer to this call. So the people of Buin took counsel how they should fetch fire, and who should go to bring it. Then said a small bird (*tegerem tegerika*), " If I please, I can fetch the fire." But the people of Buin did not believe

---

[1] D. Jenness and A. Ballantyne, *The Northern D'Entrecasteaux* (Oxford, 1920), pp. 156 *sq.*

the bird and said, " If you go, you will die in the salt water. You cannot fly so far." Then said the bird, " Very good, I will try." All the people looked after him as he flew away, and soon he was out of sight. The bird reached Alu, hid himself in the wood, and bided his time. Then he saw the people making fire by rubbing two pieces of wood against each other, just as they do in Buin down to this day. So he flew back to Buin and told the people how the people of Alu made fire.[1]

The natives of San Cristoval, one of the Southern Solomon Islands, say that the Creator, whose name was Agunua, and who was incarnate in a serpent, had a twin brother, who was a man. He taught the man to cultivate yams and other fruits. So in time a garden was laid out and yams of all kinds came up, large and small, red and white, smooth and prickly, wild and tame ; and there were likewise banana-trees and coco-nut palms and almond-trees, and fruit-trees of every sort, all bearing fruit after their several kinds. But the man said, " These are all too hard to eat. How am I to make them soft ? " The Creator or the serpent (*figona*) gave him his own staff and said, " Rub on this and see what happens." This was the origin of fire and of the art of cooking.[2]

In Malekula, one of the New Hebrides, the story told to account for the origin of fire is as follows : A woman and her little boy were out in the bush. The boy began to cry and refused to eat the raw food. So to amuse him his mother rubbed a stick on a piece of dry wood. In doing so she was astonished to see the stick smoke and smoulder and at last break into flame. Then she laid the food on the fire, and found that the food tasted much better for that. Thenceforth all the people began to use fire.[3]

The natives of New Britain, a large island to the north-east of New Guinea, tell a story which implies that the mode of kindling fire was formerly a secret which initiated

[1] R. Thurnwald, *Forschungen auf den Salomo-Inseln und dem Bismarck-Archipel* (Berlin, 1912), i. 394.

[2] C. E. Fox, *The Threshold of the Pacific* (London, 1924), pp. 83 *sq.*

[3] T. Watt Leggatt, " Malekula, New Hebrides," *Report of the Fourth Meeting of the Australasian Association for the Advancement of Science, held at Hobart, Tasmania, in January,* 1892, p. 708.

men jealously guarded from women till it was revealed to them by a dog. The story runs thus :

The members of the Secret Society (*iniet*) held an assembly. The dog was hungry. He went away from them into the plantation. He came to the women and to the uninitiated folk. He had painted his hair with the colours of the Secret Society. He went to them ; he laid him down. They said, " Come not near us." The dog said, " Why ? " They said, " Because thou art an initiated." The dog said, " I am hungry. I have eaten nothing. I should like to have some taro." The women said, " If thou wouldst have some taro, where is the fire ? There is no fire here." The dog said, " Wait a bit, I will do a certain thing which I saw done on the ground of the Secret Society." The women said, " Do it not, lest it hurt us." The dog said, " It will not hurt you. I am very hungry." They said, " Nay, do it not." And the dog said, " Yea, do it I will." The women said, " Come not near us." " Wherefore ? " asked the dog. " Because ye are initiated folk," quoth a woman. But the dog said, " Break yonder piece of *kua* wood in two and bring it here." The woman broke it in two and gave it to him. And she asked, " What is it for ? " The dog said, " Thou shalt see." She handed it to the dog. The dog split off a piece of the wood with his teeth and said to the woman, " Sit down on the *kua* wood." The woman said, " I will not, because ye are initiated folk." " Sit down on it," said the dog. She sat down on it. The dog made fire by rubbing the wood : he rubbed very hard. It smoked. Tears fell from the eyes of the woman. She wept, and said that the dog should marry her. The dog felt glad. The uninitiated folk made fire by rubbing wood in presence of the initiated folk. The initiated folk asked them, " Who taught you that ? " "The dog," said the women. "Oho! it was he that blabbed!" said the initiated men. The man to whom the ground of the Secret Society belonged was wroth. He said, " So ye have brought your dogs that they might blab ! They betrayed the secret, our secret." They made magic over the dog that he should speak no more, and he speaks no more.[1]

---

[1] A. Kleintitschen, *Mythen und Erzählungen eines Melanesierstammes* (St. Gabriel, Mödling bei Wien, 1924), pp. 502-504.

Ongtong Java is a large coral atoll situated to the north-east of the Solomon Islands. It is also known as Lord Howe and, incorrectly, as Leuaniua. The people who inhabit the islands of the atoll bear many resemblances to the Polynesians, but there are some marked differences in their culture, although the language is a Polynesian dialect. Thus social classes are not found, and in their legends there is no trace of the great hero Maui, who, as we shall see presently, plays a great part in the Polynesian myth of the origin of fire. The myth of the origin of fire told in Ongtong Java is totally different from the Polynesian, but, on the other hand, it is practically identical with the Micronesian myth told in the Gilbert Islands.[1] So far as it goes, therefore, it suggests an ethnical relation of Ongtong Java with Micronesia rather than with Melanesia. For a knowledge of the myth, as well as for the foregoing notes on Ongtong Java, I am indebted to the kindness of Mr. H. Ian Hogbin, who spent about eleven months on the atoll, studying the natives and learning their language. The myth runs as follows :

Pa'eva is the god of the sea. Long ago he had a son Ke Ahi, who was fire. They lived together at the bottom of the ocean. One day Pa'eva was angry with his son without cause and Ke Ahi decided to run away from home. He came up to the surface of the ocean and made his way to Luaniua, the principal village of Ongtong Java. Here he was very unwelcome because everything he touched burst into flames. So much of a nuisance was he that the people drove him away, and he fled to a small island owned by a woman named Kapa'ea. Here, too, he did a great deal of damage, and in order to save her property Kapa'ea took a stick and killed him.

As time went on, Pa'eva repented of his anger and came to seek his son. By the ashes he traced him to the house of the woman. He called aloud his son's name many times, but at last, receiving no answer, he understood that his son must be dead. To revenge the murder he began to beat the island below the level of the sea. Before he had gone very far, the woman Kapa'ea, who had killed his son, came out to see what all the ado was about, and in order to save what

[1] See below, pp. 88 *sqq*

was left of her property she offered Pa'eva her hand in marriage. As she was a handsome woman, the god closed with the offer and consented to forgo his revenge.

When they were married, Pa'eva asked his wife Kapa'ea to tell him the details of his son's death. So she explained to him how she had beaten him with a stick till he was dead. The father was really fond of his son, and in his grief he embraced the stick that had been the instrument of his death. Immediately the dead Ke Ahi came to life again. His father Pa'eva was overjoyed, and took him up in his arms to bear him back to the depths of the ocean. This did not suit Ke Ahi at all, and as soon as they had plunged under the water he let himself die again. His father returned with the corpse to the shore, and no sooner had they reached it than once again Ke Ahi came to life. Then he explained that he would never more return to the sea, and that all attempts to persuade him to do so would be vain. That is why to this day it is impossible to make fire burn in water

CHAPTER VI

THE Maoris of New Zealand say that long ago the great primordial hero Maui thought he would destroy the fires of his ancestress Mahu-ika. So he got up in the night, and put out the fires left in the cooking-houses of each family in the village ; then, quite early in the morning, he called aloud to the servants, " I hunger, I hunger ; quick, cook some food for me." One of the servants thereupon ran as fast as he could to make up the fire to cook some food, but the fire was out ; and as he ran round from house to house in the village to get a light, he found every fire quite out—he could nowhere get a light.

When Maui's mother heard this, she called out to the servants, and said, " Some of you repair to my great ancestress Mahu-ika ; tell her that fire has been lost upon earth, and ask her to give some to the world again." But the slaves were alarmed and refused to obey her commands. At last Maui said to his mother, " Well ; then I will fetch down fire for the world ; but which is the path by which I must go ? " And his parents said to him, " Follow that broad path that lies just before you there ; and you will at last reach the dwelling of an ancestress of yours ; and if she asks you who you are, you had better call out your name to her, then she will know you are a descendant of hers; but be cautious, and do not play any tricks with her, because we have heard that your deeds are greater than the deeds of men, and that you are fond of deceiving and injuring others, and perhaps you even now intend in many ways to deceive this old ancestress of yours, but pray be cautious not to do so." And Maui answered, " No, I only want to bring fire away for men, that is all, and I'll return again as soon as I can do that."

Then he went and reached the abode of the goddess of fire ; and he was so filled with wonder at what he saw, that for a long time he could say nothing. At last he said, " Oh, lady, would you rise up ? Where is your fire kept ? I have come to beg some from you." Then the aged lady rose right up, and said, " Au-e ! who can this mortal be ? " and he answered, " It is I." " Where do you come from ? " said she, and he answered, " I belong to this country." " You are not from this country," said she; "your appearance is not like that of the inhabitants of this country. Do you come from the north-east ? " He replied, " No." " Do you come from the south-east ? " He replied, " No." " Are you from the south ? " He replied, " No." " Are you from the west-ward ? " He answered, " No." " Come you, then, from the direction of the wind which blows right upon me ? " and he said, " I do." " Oh, then," cried she, " you are my grand-child ; what do you want here ? " He answered, " I am come to beg fire from you." She replied, " Welcome, welcome ; here then is fire for you."

Then the aged woman pulled out her nail, and as she pulled it out fire flowed from it, and she gave it to him. And when Maui saw she had drawn out her nail to produce fire for him, he thought it a most wonderful thing ! Then he went a short distance off and put the fire out, and returning to her said, " The light you gave me has gone out, give me another." Then she caught hold of another nail, and pulled it out as a light for him ; and he left her, and went a little on one side, and put out that light also ; then he went back to her again, and said, " Oh, lady, give me, I pray you, another light, for the last one has also gone out." And thus he went on and on until she had pulled out all the nails of the fingers of one of her hands ; and then she began with the other hand, until she had pulled all the finger-nails out of that hand, too ; and then she commenced upon the nails of her feet, and pulled them also out in the same manner, except the nail of one of her big toes. Then the aged woman said to herself at last, ' This fellow is surely playing tricks with me."

Then out she pulled the one toe-nail that she had left, and

it too became fire, and as she dashed it down on the ground the whole place caught fire. And she cried out to Maui, " There, you have it all now ! " And Maui ran off, and made a rush to escape, but the fire followed hard after him ; so he changed himself into a fleet-winged eagle, and flew with rapid flight, but the fire pursued and almost caught him as he flew. Then the eagle dashed down into a pool of water, but he found the water almost boiling too. The forests also caught fire, so that the bird could not alight anywhere ; and the earth and the sea both caught fire too, and Maui was very near perishing in the flames.

Then he called on his ancestors, Tawhiri-ma-tea and Whatitiri-matakataka, to send down an abundant supply of water, and he cried aloud, " Oh, let water be given to me to quench this fire which pursues after me," and lo,then appeared squalls and gales, and Tawhiri-ma-tea sent heavy lashing rain, and the fire was quenched ; and before Mahu-ika could reach her place of shelter, she almost perished in the rain, and her shrieks and screams became as loud as those of Maui had been, when he was scorched by the pursuing fire : thus Maui ended this proceeding. In this manner was extinguished the fire of Mahu-ika, the goddess of fire ; but before it was all lost, she saved a few sparks which she threw, to protect them, into the *kaiko-mako*, and a few other trees, where they are still cherished ; hence, men yet use portions of the wood of these trees for fire when they require a light.[1]

The myth is obviously told to explain how it is that fire can be elicited from certain kinds of wood : to preserve the fire from being totally extinguished in the heavy rain, the goddess of fire hid it in certain trees, from which it can still be extracted by friction. This is the gist of the whole story, and it is put somewhat more fully in other versions of the myth. Thus we read that when Maui was pursued by the

[1] Sir George Grey, *Polynesian Mythology* (London, 1855), pp. 45-49. For briefer versions of the same Maori myth, see R. Taylor, *Te Ika A Maui, or New Zealand and its Inhabitants* [2] (London, 1870), pp. 130 *sq.* ; John White, *The Ancient History of the Maori*, ii. (London and Wellington, 1889) pp. 108-110. Taylor speaks of Mauika (Mahu-ika) as a male ancestor, not an ancestress, of Maui. On the sex of this personage in Polynesian mythology there is much difference of opinion. See below. Compare E. Tregear, *Maori-Polynesian Comparative Dictionary* (Wellington, N.Z., 1891), p. 194, *s.v.* " Mahuika."

great conflagration, he called for heavy rain, " which came pouring down in torrents, and soon extinguished the flames, and flooded the land. When the waters reached the *tiki tiki*, or top-knot of Mauika's head, the seeds of fire which had taken refuge there fled to the *rata, hinau, kaikatea, rimu, matai*, and *miro*, but these trees would not admit them ; they then went to the *patete, kaikomako, mahohe, totara*, and *puketea*, which received them. These are the trees from which fire is still obtained by friction." [1] And again we read : " Only a little of the fire escaped from the rain. This Mahu-i-ka put into the *totara*-tree, but it would not burn ; then into the *matai*, but it would not burn ; then into the *mahoe*, where it burnt but little ; then into the *kai-komako*, where it burnt well, and the fire was saved." [2]

Thus the myth is told to account for the more or less combustible qualities of different kinds of wood.

The same myth was told by the Moriories, who inhabited the Chatham Islands to the east of New Zealand. The Moriories are, or rather were, a people of the Maori stock, who migrated from New Zealand to the Chatham Islands and preserved a tradition of their migration. Their version of the fire myth is reported as follows :

" After this Maui went to fetch fire from Mauhika ; [3] he asked Mauhika to give him fire, upon which Mauhika plucked off one of his fingers and gave it as fire for Maui, seeing which Maui put it out ; he went again to Mauhika, and another of his fingers was given. He continued this until the small finger only remained ; then Mauhika perceived he was being tricked by Maui, and his anger arose. Then he threw his small finger up into the trees, on to the *inihina* (Maori, *hinahina* or *mahoe*), *karamu, karaka, ake, rautini*, and *kokopere* (Maori, *kawakawa*). All these burnt, but the *mataira* (Maori, *matipou*) would not burn. [4] For this reason all these trees which burnt were used as a *kahunaki* (the piece of wood rubbed into a hollow, holding the abraded wood, which ultimately takes fire by use of the rubber *ure*).

[1] R. Taylor, *op. cit.* p. 131.

[2] John White, *op. cit.* p. 110.

[3] " It does not appear quite certain, according to the Moriories, whether Mauhika was male or female—the weight of evidence appears to indicate his being a male."

[4] " This is explanatory of the trees from which fire can be raised by friction."

He also threw his fire into stone, *i.e.* flint, so that fire rises from flint. Then Maui was chased by Mauhika's fire ; the seas and hills were burnt up, and Maui was burnt by the fire. Maui's wail went up to the roaring thunder, to Hangaia-te-marama, to the great rain, to the long rain, to the drizzling rain. The rain was sent and Maui was saved." [1]

The natives of the Tonga or Friendly Islands, which lie in the Pacific Ocean far to the north of New Zealand, tell a similar tale to explain why fire can be extracted from certain trees. As briefly recorded by the United States Exploring Expedition in the first half of the nineteenth century, the story runs thus : " Maui had two sons, the eldest called Maui Atalonga, and the younger Kijikiji, but by whom is not known. Kijikiji obtained some fire from the earth, and taught them to cook their food, which they found was good, and from that day food has been cooked which before was eaten raw. In order to preserve the fire, Kijikiji commanded it to go into certain trees, whence it is now obtained by friction." [2]

This Tongan myth has since been recorded much more fully by subsequent inquirers. It may be of interest to compare their versions, which are in substantial agreement. As recorded by an English missionary about the middle of the nineteenth century the story runs thus : [3]

" After the peopleing of the earth it was long before fire was known. Of course no food could be cooked. This want was at last supplied in the following way. Maui Atalonga and (his son) Maui Kijikiji lived at Koloa in Hafaa. Every morning Maui Atalonga left his home to visit Bulotu ; [4] every afternoon he returned bringing with him cooked food. He never took Kijikiji with him, nor did he allow his son to know the mode by which he made the journey ; for Kijikiji was young, full of fun, and fond of practical jokes. Kijikiji's

[1] Alexander Shand, *The Moriori People of the Chatham Islands* (Washington and New Plymouth, 1911), p. 20 (*Memoirs of the Polynesian Society*, vol. ii.).

[2] Ch. Wilkes, *Narrative of the United States Exploring Expedition* (New York, 1851), iii. 23.

[3] Sarah S. Farmer, *Tonga and the Friendly Islands* (London, 1855), pp. 134-137. The authority for the story seems to have been the Rev. John Thomas (p. 125).

[4] In Tongan mythology Bulotu was the home of the departed spirits of chiefs and other great personages. It was said to lie in a westerly direction and to be approached either through the earth or by the sea. See Sarah S. Farmer, *op. cit.* pp. 126, 132.

curiosity was awakened, however, and he determined to find
out his father's path and to follow him to Bulotu. He traced
him to the mouth of a cave, over which grew a large reed
bush, so as to hide it from the observation of passers by.
But young Maui made a prying search, found the entrance,
and descended. Arrived in Bulotu, he saw his father at
work with his back towards him ; he was busy with a plot
of ground that he kept under cultivation. Young Maui
plucked a fruit from the *nonu* tree (this fruit is somewhat
larger than an apple), bit a piece off, and in his mischievous
way, threw the remainder at his father. The father picked
it up, saw the marks of his son's teeth, turned and said,
' What brings you here ? Mind what you are doing. This
Bulotu is a dreadful place.' He then proceeded to warn him
against the dangers attending bad conduct. Maui set Kijikiji
to help him in clearing a piece of ground, and above all,
he begged him not to look behind him. Instead of minding
his father's advice, Kijikiji did his work very badly. He
would pull up a few weeds and then look behind him. All
the morning it was weed and look round, weed and look
round, so that very little good was done. The weeds grew
apace, much faster than father and son could pull up.
Afternoon came, and Maui Atalonga wished to cook his
food. ' Go,' said he to his son, ' and get a little fire.' This
was just what Kijikiji wanted. ' Where shall I go ? ' ' To
the Modua.' [1] Off he went, and found (his grandfather) the
oldest Maui lying on a mat by the fire-side for warmth. His
fire was a large iron-wood tree, heated at one end. Young
Maui appeared. The old man was much surprised at the
intrusion, but did not know his grandson. ' What do you
want ? ' ' Some fire.' ' Take some.' Young Maui put a
little into a cocoa-nut shell and carried it a short way. But
his love of mischief springing up, he blew it out, and went
back to the old man with an empty shell. The same questions
and answers followed. Again young Maui obtained the
precious gift, and again he made away with it. A third time
he appeared before his grandfather. The old man was
nettled. ' Take the whole of it,' said he. Young Maui,

---

[1] By " the Modua " is doubtless
meant Maui Motua, Kijikiji's grandfather, the owner of fire in Bulotu or
the Underworld. See below, pp. 62 *sqq.*

without more ado, took up the immense iron-wood tree and walked off with it. Now the old man knew him to be something more than mortal, and shouted after him, ' *Helo, he, he, Ke-ta-fai*,' a challenge to wrestle. Quite ready for this also, the youth turned. They closed and wrestled. Old Maui seized his opponent by the dress that was tightly girded round his waist, swung him round, his feet clearing the ground, and dashed him towards earth. Kijikiji, cat-like, lighted on his feet. It was now his turn ; and seizing his grandfather in the same way, he swung him round, flung him on the ground, and broke every bone in his body. Old Maui has been in a decrepit state ever since. He lies, feeble and sleepy, underneath the earth. When an earthquake threatens, the Tonguese shout the war-whoop in order to awaken old Maui, whom they suppose to be turning round. They fear lest he should get up, and in rising, overturn the world.

" On the return of Kijikiji to his father, he was asked what had detained him so long. The youth was silent ; and as he refused to answer any questions about the old man, Maui Atalonga suspected that something was wrong. He went to see, found old Maui bruised and disabled, and hastened back to punish his son. The son ran off, and the father chased him vigorously, but without success. Evening came on, and the two prepared to return to earth. Maui cautioned his son against taking any fire with him ; but again the sober spirit of the elder was no match for the trickiness of the younger god. He wrapped up a little fire in the end of the long garment that he wore, and trailed it after him. The father went on first. As he was nearing the summit he began to sniff. ' I smell fire,' said he. Young Maui was close behind. He hurried on, hastily drew up his sash, and scattered its contents all around. The neighbouring trees were soon on fire, and for a time the earth seemed to be in great peril. However, the evil was soon checked, while the good remained. A lasting benefit was conferred on the islanders who have, ever since, been able to light a fire, and cook their food. There is something in this legend of the rude Tonguese that reminds one of the Prometheus of the classic Greeks."

A much fuller version of this Tongan myth has since been recorded by a Catholic missionary as follows :

A certain Mauimotua and his son Mauiatalaga dwelt in Lolofonua, which was the nether world. They were the lords of Lolofonua. And Mauiatalaga had a little son called Mauikisikisi, which means Maui the Little One. They all dwelt in the nether world. But Mauiatalaga said to his kinsfolk, the other Mauis, " I will not stay here in Lolofonua ; I will go up to the earth with my son Mauikisikisi ; he is still small, and has not come to the age of reason. But though we shall both go up and dwell on the earth, I will always come back to see you, and to do my work, and to attend to my plantation here in Lolofonua." So the two went up, Mauiatalaga and his little son Mauikisikisi. They went and dwelt in the island of Koloa, which is one of the Vavau Group, which in its turn forms part of the Tonga or Friendly Islands. The part of the island where they dwelt was called Atalaga ; that is why Mauiatalaga had Atalaga for the second part of his name. And there he married a native woman whose name was also Atalaga.

Now the island of Koloa was small, and there was not room in it for all the plantations of Mauiatalaga ; so he used to return to the nether world, to Lolofonua, to plant and work there. Meantime his son Mauikisikisi began to grow big, and his insolence and disobedience to his father Mauiatalaga were terrible. That is why his father always left him at home when he went to work at his plantations in the nether world ; for he knew the insolent character of his son, and feared that his son might play some wanton pranks in the nether world, if he suffered him to go thither with himself. So he said to his wife, " Wife, when I go to tend my plantations and do my work in Lolofonua, be careful not to wake the child Mauikisikisi, lest he should know of my departure, and follow me, and know the way to Lolofonua, and go and play his pranks there. But let him stay on earth and there play his pranks." So when the cock crew and the morning broke, Mauiatalaga used to wake and steal softly away in the twilight, lest Mauikisikisi should hear him and follow him weeping. So he did every night ; he went away always alone, he fled in the darkness ; he departed very early in the morning, while it was still dark, lest Mauikisikisi should see him.

And Mauikisikisi remained alone, and he thought in his heart and said, " Where does my father go to tend his plantations ?   I am weary of seeking him every day.   Where does he go to tend his plantations and to work ? "   And he thought to himself, " Perhaps my father goes to do his work in Lolofonua !   I will watch him going away in the early morning, in the darkness, I will wake, I will rise and follow him."   So Mauikisikisi watched his father, and one night he saw his father Mauiatalaga stealing away.   His father took his belt and his hoe, and went forth.   And when he was gone a little way, his son Mauikisikisi rose and followed him.   He followed him afar off, lest his father should know that he was following him.   When his father came to the foot of a tree, the *kaho* (" reed "), he stopped and looked around to see whether anybody was following him ; but Mauikisikisi had hidden himself so that his father did not see him.   Then Mauiatalaga laid hold of the tree by the branches, uprooted it and put it on one side, thus blocking up the road to Lolo-fonua.   So his son Mauikisikisi said to himself, " Ah, that is perhaps the way that the old man goes to tend his plantations in Lolofonua."   Then he went up to the *kaho* (" reed "), tore it up and threw it far away.   Thus was the road opened to Lolofonua ; it was not blocked up.   Then Mauikisikisi descended, following his father.   And they came to the place where Mauiatalaga had his plantations, and Mauiatalaga began to weed his plantations   And while he weeded, his son Mauikisikisi climbed a tree, a *nonu* tree, plucked one of the fruits of it, and bit it, and threw it at his father.   And his father picked up the fruit and said, " Surely, this is the mark of the teeth of that naughty child."   And he looked about, but could not see his son, because his son was perched among the boughs of the tree.   So he went on with his weeding. But his son picked another fruit and did as before, and again his father said, " Surely, these are the marks of the teeth of the naughty child."

Then Mauikisikisi called out, " Father, here am I ! " And his father said, " Child, by which way have you come ? " And his son answered, " I followed the way by which you came." And his father Mauiatalaga said, " Come, and let us weed together." So his son Mauikisikisi went and weeded. And his father said, " Do not look behind you when you weed." But Mauikisikisi looked behind him as he weeded, and lo ! the weeds grew again apace. So his father Mauiatalaga was angry. " What ? " said he, " I told that insolent child not to look behind when he weeded ; for it is forbidden to do so lest the weeds should grow again and the bushes revive." So his father went and weeded afresh the ground which his son had already weeded, for the weeds had grown on it again. And they went on with their weeding. But again Mauikisikisi looked behind him, and again the weeds and likewise the bushes sprouted afresh in his tracks. Then his father was angry, and said, " Who told this insolent and disobedient child to come hither ? Insolent child, have done with your weeding, but go at once and fetch fire."

And the child said to his father, " What is the thing that is called fire ? " And his father said to him, " Go to yonder house, there is an old man warming himself there. Bring some of the fire hither to cook our food." So Mauikisikisi went to seek fire, he went to the place where the old man was warming himself. And lo, the old man was Mauimotua, the father of Mauiatalaga and grandfather of Mauikisikisi. But Mauikisikisi did not know his grandfather Mauimotua, and his grandfather did not know him, for they had never met before. And Mauikisikisi called to his grandfather, the old man who was warming himself, and he said, " Old man, give me some fire." And the old man took some fire and gave it to him. And the child took the fire and went away with it ; and on the way he put out the fire by wetting it ; the fire was out. And the child went back to the old man and said, " Give me some fire." And the old man said, " Where then is the fire which you took with you ? " And Mauikisikisi said, " It is out." And the old man gave him fire afresh. And again the child carried away the fire and extinguished it on the way by wetting it with water. And again the child went to ask for fire ; it was the third time he asked for it. And when the old man Mauimotua saw the child coming again, he was angry and said, " Why

does this child come again ?   Where are the fires which you
carried away ? "   And Mauikisikisi answered, " I took the
fire with me, and it went out.   That is why I am come again
to get fire from you."

Now there was left in the hearth only one large brand.
And the old man said angrily, " Perhaps you can lift and carry
away this big brand," for he may have thought to himself
that the child could not lift it ; Mauiatalaga alone could lift
that huge brand.   But Mauikisikisi went and seized the
brand with a single hand.   And Mauimotua said, " Put
down the brand at which I warm myself."   So Mauikisikisi
put it down.   Mauimotua was in a great rage, and he said,
" Come, let us wrestle."   " Very good," replied Mauikisikisi
So saying he arose and lifted up Mauimotua in the air, waved
him this way and that, then dashed him violently to the
ground.   This he did twice, and the old man was broken and
fainted.

And Mauikisikisi went away to carry the fire to his father
Mauiatalaga.   And his father said to him, " You have gone
and insulted the old man."   And Mauikisikisi answered,
" The old man was vexed with me because I went often to ask
for fire, and he said to me, ' Child, come let us wrestle.'
And we wrestled, and the old man fell."   And Mauiatalaga
said to him, " Child, and how is he ? "   And Mauikisikisi
answered, " I knocked him down, and he is dead."   And
Mauiatalaga was much moved at the fate of his father
Mauimotua, whom his own son had killed.   And he took the
hoe and struck his son Mauikisikisi on the head, and Mauikisikisi died on the spot ; he was stretched out dead.   And
Mauiatalaga went and brought herbs—the name of the herb
is *mohukuvai*—to cover up Mauikisikisi.

Then he went to Mauimotua, to see whether he had been
really killed in wrestling with the child.   But he found him
revived, for the fainting-fit was over.   And he said to his
father, " Father, the insolent child came to kill you, but he
did not know you."   And his father Mauimotua answered,
" It is true, and I did not know him."   And Mauiatalaga said,
" My son Mauikisikisi is insolent up there on the earth, and
to think that he should come here to kill you !   That is why
I did not wish to bring him here, lest he should be insolent.

And now he has been insolent to you, and I have killed him for that, and he is dead." And his father Mauimotua said, " What, my friend ! you have killed Mauikisikisi for that ! Why not have let him be ?   He acted like a fool, but we had never met.   Go and gather the leaves of the *nonu* ; with that tree they cover the dead, and they live, and the name of that tree is *nonufiafia.*" So Mauiatalaga went and gathered the leaves of the *nonufiafia,* and with the leaves he covered the dead body of his son Mauikisikisi, and his son came to life.

And when they had eaten, Mauiatalaga set out with his son to ascend to the earth.   And he said to his son, " Go in front of me, lest you play some prank here in Lolofonua, for I am weary of your tricks."   But Mauikisikisi said to his father, " Go you in front, and I will follow you."   And his father did so, though he feared his son would carry away something from Lolofonua to the earth.   So Mauiatalaga went in front, and Mauikisikisi followed behind, and he seized some fire to carry it away   And as they were going up, Mauiatalaga stopped and asked, " Child, whence comes that smell of fire ? "   But Mauikisikisi answered, " No ! Perhaps it is the smell of the place where we cooked our victuals that you smell."   And Mauiatalaga said, " Child, perhaps you are carrying fire ? "   But Mauikisikisi answered, " No." So they continued ascending, always ascending.   Again, there was a smell of fire, and again Mauiatalaga stopped and said, " Where does that smell of fire come from ? "   And Mauikisikisi answered, " I do not know."   But Mauiatalaga looked, and behold the fire which his son Mauikisikisi carried was smoking, for Mauikisikisi carried it hidden and stealthily. And his father ran at him in anger and said, " That I should live to see so malicious and disobedient a child !   Where is he carrying the fire to ? "   And with that he put it out.

After that they ascended.   But Mauiatalaga did not know that his son Mauikisikisi had set fire to his girdle, so that the girdle which Mauikisikisi wore was burning.   His father thought that the smell he smelt was only the smell of the fire which he had put out.   So they ascended and reached the earth.   And Mauiatalaga went and hid himself that he might see Mauikisikisi coming up, lest he should bring something from Lolofonua.   And he saw Mauikisikisi coming up and said, " There is that child still playing his pranks ! He is bringing fire on earth ! " And he cried out, " Let a heavy rain fall ! " And there fell a heavy rain. So Mauikisikisi called out to the fire, " Escape to the coco-nut tree ! Escape to the bread-fruit tree ! Escape to the *fau* ! Escape to the *tou* ! Escape to all the trees of the earth ! "

That is the origin of fire, and that is how the earth became acquainted with it. Mauikisikisi brought it from Lolofonua to cook our food, to give us light, to warm our bodies when they are cold and sick. For there was no fire on earth, and people ate the produce of the earth raw. But since the time of Mauikisikisi, since he brought the fire from Lolofonua, we his descendants have beheld it here. That is why you get fire by rubbing two sticks. For Mauikisikisi told the fire to escape into all the trees and stay there.[1]

Still more recently another version of this Tongan myth has been contributed by a Wesleyan missionary, the Rev. E. E. Collcott. It runs thus : [2]

" *How Fire was brought to this World.*—The Maui were four and lived in the Underworld. Their names were Maui Motua (Maui Senior), Maui Loa (Long Maui), Maui Buku (Short Maui), and Maui Atalanga (perhaps Maui Air-propper, or Air-erecter), and there was also a son of the last-named, Maui Kijikiji (Mischievous Maui). For long they lived together in the Underworld, but at last Atalanga was filled with desire to go up and live on the surface of the earth. With his brothers' approval he departed, promising that he would often return to see them and to attend to his garden, and do whatever work might be necessary. Atalanga, accompanied by his son Kijikiji, on emerging into the upper air settled at Koloa, the oldest part of Vavau.[3] To this district the name of Haafuluhao properly belongs, but it is applied indiscriminately to the whole country. The whole country is correctly called Vavau ; Koloa is the original part of the land, and this is correctly Haafuluhao. The two Maui dwelt in Koloa, and Atalanga married a woman of the

---

[1] Le P. Reiter, " Traditions Ton-guiennes," *Anthropos,* xii.-xiii. (1917–1918) pp. 1026-1040. I have shortened the story.

[2] E. E. Collcott, " Legends from Tonga," *Folk-lore,* xxxii. (1921) pp. 45-48.

[3] Vavau is the northernmost of the three groups which compose the Tonga Islands.

place. Their homestead was called Atalanga. Maui did not garden in Koloa, which is said to have been too small for the purpose, but he still cultivated his garden in the Underworld. In his frequent excursions to the nether regions he never took his son with him, but left him at home to keep his wife company. The lad, moreover, was so annoying and mischievous that his father did not desire his companionship. On the days when he went to the Underworld to tend his garden Atalanga used to steal quietly off before daylight, strictly enjoining upon his wife not to wake the urchin lest he should follow and discover the road. Naturally Kijikiji's curiosity was whetted, and for long he sought in vain his father's garden, but coming finally to the conclusion that it must be in the Underworld, he determined to keep a close watch upon his elder's comings and goings.

" For some time he discovered nothing, but one night, happening to wake, he saw his father take his spade (digging stick) and go out, whereupon he got up and followed, taking care to avoid discovery. The entrance to the Underworld was concealed by a clump of reed, and on reaching this Atalanga looked carefully round, but Kijikiji was discreetly hidden at a safe distance, eagerly watching his father's every movement, though unseen himself. Atalanga seized the reeds, pulled them up by the roots, went down through the opening the plant had concealed, and then reached up his hand and replaced it. After an interval sufficient to allow his father to get well on his way Kijikiji went and pulled up the reed and flung it away, then descended and followed Atalanga. The place where Maui went down is called Tuahalakao (apparently Behind the road of the reed). Kijikiji followed his father down into the Underworld, taking care that he was not observed, and at last they came to the garden.

" When the youth reached the place there was his father hard at work, but he himself climbed up a *nonu* tree, plucked one of the fruit, bit it and threw it at his father. Atalanga picked up the *nonu*, and looking at it thought that he recognised the tooth marks as his mischievous son's ; but, looking all around and seeing nobody, he resumed his work, only to be again disturbed by a tooth-marked *nonu*. On examining this second missile all doubts vanished. ' This,' he said, ' is in truth the tooth-mark of that imp of a boy.' Kijikiji then no longer attempted concealment, but called out, ' Here I am, father.' To his father's question as to how he had come there he replied that he had followed him, and further questioned as to whether he had closed the opening he replied less truthfully that he had. Atalanga then called to Kijikiji to come and cut the weeds with him, warning him that he must not look round as he worked. It is almost needless to say that the youth did look round, and thereupon as quickly as he cut down the weeds they sprang up again behind him. His father did the work over again, and reprimanded his son, but in spite of all, the boy, regardless of the tabu, continued to look behind, and at last his father in disgust told him to stop hoeing weeds, and to go and build a fire.

" Kijikiji had never seen fire, and asked his father what it was. Atalanga told him to go to yonder house, where he would see an old man sitting by a fire. He must get some of it, and bring it to prepare food. When Kijikiji entered the house he found there an old man whom he did not know, but who was Maui Motua, Atalanga's father. He asked for fire. He asked for fire and received it, but as soon as he got outside he extinguished it, and returned for more. He again received fire, and again extinguished it outside ; but on his entering the house the third time for fire the old man was angry ; moreover, only one brand was left, a great casuarina log. Maui Motua, however, jestingly told the boy that if he could carry the log he could have it, never dreaming that he would be able to lift it. Kijikiji, however, picked it up and started to carry it off with one hand. Maui Motua at once called to Kijikiji to put down his fire, and when the lad had obeyed he challenged him to wrestle. The challenge showed more spirit than wit on the part of the old man, for Kijikiji dashed him again and again to the ground, and leaving him for dead picked up the casuarina log and bore it off.

" When he reached his father Atalanga inquired what mischief he had been doing to Maui Motua that he was so long in coming, but Kijikiji merely replied that the fire

kept going out, and so he had to return several times. Further
questioning elicited information about the wrestling match
and its fatal termination. On hearing this Atalanga felled
his son to the earth with his spade, and covered his body
with the grass called *mohuku vai* (water grass, literally).
It is said that on account of having covered Kijikiji's body
it does not die when cut out of the ground. Atalanga then
went to see his father, and found that he had revived. The
old man then for the first time learnt that it was his own
grandson with whom he had quarrelled, and told Atalanga
to pluck *nonu* leaves (*Morinda citrifolia*), and place them
on the body to bring it to life again. This was done, and the
lad recovered. This species of *nonu* does not grow in this
world, but only in heaven and the Underworld.

" Then the two of them ate food, and prepared to return
to the upper air. Atalanga, fearful of his son's mischievous
propensities, wished him to go on ahead, but Kijikiji finally
prevailed in his insistence that his father should lead the
way. As they set off Kijikiji seized a burning brand to
take with him, hiding it behind his back. Presently his
father came to a standstill, and said, ' Where's that smell
of burning ? Are you bringing any fire with you ? ' ' No,'
answered the boy, ' it's probably the smell from the place
where we cooked our food.' The father seemed scarcely
convinced, but they resumed their journey. Presently he
turned round again ; ' Boy, where is this smell of fire from ? '
' Don't know,' responded Kijikiji. ' Boy, haven't you brought
some fire with you ? ' again asked Atalanga. Just then the
father saw smoke from the fire which his son was concealing,
and rushing at him he snatched the brand and extinguished
it, bitterly upbraiding Kijikiji for his disobedience and mis-
chievousness. Then they ascended to the upper world, but
all unknown to his father the end of Kijikiji's loincloth was
ignited, trailing behind him out of sight. On reaching the
surface of the earth Atalanga went on ahead and hid to see
if his son had brought anything up from below, and when
Kijikiji emerged he saw the smoke from the burning waist-
cloth. At once Atalanga called on the rain to fall, but,
although a copious downpour ensued, the boy was not to
be outdone, for he cried to the fire to flee to the coconut-tree

and the breadfruit-tree and the hibiscus and *tou* (*cordia*) and all the trees. This is the manner in which fire was introduced amongst men who had previously eaten their food uncooked, and because the fire resides in the trees it is obtained by rubbing one stick on another."

This Tongan myth is substantially identical with the Maori myth. In both of them the fire is first brought to earth through the cunning of a tricky and daring hero, who outwits the owner of fire in the other world ; in both of them the stolen fire is nearly extinguished by heavy rain, and is only saved by being hidden in trees, where it remains until it is extracted by friction. The chief differences between the two myths appear to be, that whereas in the Maori myth the fire is brought down from the upper world, in the Tongan myth it is brought up from the nether world ; that whereas in the Maori myth the original owner of fire is the hero's grandmother, in the Tongan myth he is the hero's grandfather ; and that, whereas in the Maori myth the original owner of fire contains the fire in her body and extracts it from the nails of her fingers and toes, there is no mention of any such marvellous doings in the Tongan myth, which apparently assumes that the original owner of fire possessed and manipulated it in the usual way

The natives of Niué or Savage Island, which lies to the east of the Tongan or Friendly Islands, tell a story of the origin of fire which, though we only possess it in an abridged form, appears to agree substantially with the Tongan version. According to them, a father and a son, both of them called Maui, descended to the nether world through a reed bush. The younger Maui, " like another Prometheus," stole fire in the nether world, ran up the passage with it, and before his father could catch him, had set the bush in flames in all directions. The father tried to put it out, but in vain ; and the people say that ever since the exploit of young Maui they have had fire and cooked their food in Savage Island.[1] The Niuéan myth was obtained in a slightly different form by Sir Basil Thomson. According to his version, in the early days, soon after the island had emerged from the sea, " Maui lived just below the surface of the earth. He prepared his food

[1] George Turner, *Samoa* (London, 1884), pp. 211 *sq.*

secretly, and his son, who had long been tantalized by the delicious smell of his father's food, lay in hiding to watch the process, and saw fire for the first time. When Maui was out of the way he stole a flaming brand and fled up one of the cave mouths into Niué, where he set an *ovava* tree on fire. And thence it comes that the Niuéans produce fire from *ovava* wood by rubbing it with a splinter of the hard *kavika* tree." [1] Here, as so often, the myth is told to explain the process of procuring fire by friction from certain kinds of wood.

The Samoan story of the origin of fire resembles the Tongan version, though the names of the personages in the story differ somewhat. The Samoans say that there was a time when their ancestors ate everything raw, and that they owe the luxury of cooked food to one Ti'iti'i, the son of a person called Talanga. This Talanga was high in favour with the earthquake god Mafuie, who lived in a subterranean region where there was fire continually burning Whenever he went to a certain perpendicular rock, and said, " Rock, divide ! I am Talanga ; I have come to work ! " the rock opened and let him in, and he went below to his plantations in the land of this god Mafuie. One day Ti'iti'i, the son of Talanga, followed his father, and watched where he entered. The youth, after a time, went up to the rock, and feigning his father's voice, said, " Rock, divide ! I am Talanga ; I have come to work ! " and was admitted too. His father, who was at work in his plantation, was surprised to see his son there, and begged him not to talk loud, lest the god Mafuie should hear him and be angry. Seeing smoke rising, the son inquired of his father what it was. His father said it was the fire of Mafuie. " I must go and get some," said the son. " No," said the father, " he will be angry Don't you know he eats people ? " " What do I care for him ? " said the daring youth ; and off he went, humming a song, towards the smoking furnace.

" Who are you ? " said Mafuie to the young man " I am Ti'iti'i, the son of Talanga," he replied ; " I am come for some fire." " Take it," said Mafuie. He went back to his father with some cinders, and the two set to work to bake

[1] (Sir) Basil Thomson, *Savage Island* (London, 1902), pp. 86 *sq*

some taro. They kindled a fire, and were preparing to put the taro on the hot stones, when suddenly the god Mafuie blew up the oven, scattered the stones all about, and put out the fire. " Now," said Talanga, " did not I tell you that Mafuie would be angry?" In a rage his son went off to Mafuie and asked, " Why have you broken up our oven and put out our fire?" Indignant at this bold remonstrance, Mafuie rushed at him, and there they wrestled with each other. Ti'iti'i seized the right arm of Mafuie with both hands and gave it such a wrench that it broke off. He then grasped the other arm and was about to twist it off also, when Mafuie confessed himself beaten and implored his adversary to have mercy and to spare his left arm. " I need the arm," said he, " to hold Samoa straight and level. Give it to me, and I will let you have my hundred wives." " No, not for that," replied Ti'iti'i. " Well, then," rejoined Mafuie, " will you take fire? If you let me keep my left arm, you shall have fire, and you may ever after eat cooked food." " Agreed," said Ti'iti'i ; " keep your arm, and I have fire." " Go," said Mafuie ; "you will find the fire in every wood you cut." Thus ever since the days of Ti'iti'i the Samoans have eaten cooked food, getting fire by rubbing one piece of dry wood against another. And superstitious people, we are told, still have a notion that the earthquake god Mafuie is down below Samoa somewhere, and that the earth has a long handle, like a walking-stick, to which Mafuie gives a shake now and then. It was common for them to say, when they felt the shock of an earthquake, " Thanks to Ti'iti'i that Mafuie has only one arm : if he had two, what a shock he would give ! " [1]

In this Samoan story the names of the father and son may perhaps be only dialectical variations of the names in the

[1] G. Turner, *Samoa*, pp. 209-211. The story is told in substantially the same form by the Rev. J. B. Stair, *Old Samoa* (London, 1897), pp. 238 *sq.*, though he mentions the descent of only one man, whom he calls Ti'iti'-a-Talanga. He concludes the story thus : " On this Talanga left the lower regions, and on coming to the place where he started, he struck various kinds of wood with his burning brand, which caused them to yield fire. This latter statement apparently has a reference to the kinds of wood from which fire is usually obtained by friction." The story is told in a summary form by George Brown, *Melanesians and Polynesians* (London, 1910), pp. 365 *sq.* See also W. T. Pritchard, *Polynesian Reminiscences* (London, 1866), pp. 114-116

Tongan version, the father's name Talanga in the Samoan
story corresponding to Atalanga or Atalaga (Maui-atalaga)
in the Tongan story, and the Samoan Ti'iti'i corresponding to
the Tongan Kijikiji or Kisikisi (Maui-kisikisi). A notable
feature in this Samoan myth is the derivation of fire on earth
from volcanic phenomena ; for we can hardly doubt that
the perpetual fire, which the earthquake god is said to keep
burning underground, is volcanic fire. And the account of
the way in which the earthquake god blew up the oven and
scattered the stones about may well be a mythical description
of a volcanic eruption.

The natives of Fakaofo, or Bowditch Island, to the north
of Samoa, traced the origin of fire to Mafuike, " but, unlike
the Mafuike of the mythology of some other islands, this was
an old blind *lady*. Talanga went down to her in her lower
regions and asked her to give him some of her fire. She
obstinately refused, until he threatened to kill her, and then
she yielded. With the fire he made her say what fish were to
be cooked with it, and what were still to be eaten raw ; and
then began the time of cooking food." [1] Similarly in the
Union Islands, to the south-east of Bowditch Island, " an
adventurous person named Talanga, having descended into
the lower regions, found an old woman named Mafuike busied
with a cooking fire. Compelling her by threats of death to
part with her treasure, he enclosed the fire in a certain wood,
which was consequently used by his descendants for making
fire by friction." [2] These stories accord substantially with
the Samoan version of the myth, even the names of the
personages, Talanga and Mafuike, agreeing exactly or nearly
with the Samoan names Talanga and Mafuie, though in the
Samoan version Mafuie is a god and in the other version
Mafuike is an old woman.

In Mangaia, one of the Hervey Islands, the origin of fire
on earth is attributed to the great Polynesian hero Maui, and
the story of the way in which he procured fire for mankind
resembles in many points both the Maori and the Tongan
myths. It runs as follows :

Originally fire was unknown to the inhabitants of this

[1] G. Turner, *Samoa*, p. 270.
[2] (Sir) Basil Thomson, *Savage Island*, p. 87.

world, who of necessity ate raw food.   In the nether world
(Avaiki) lived four mighty ones : Mauike, god of fire ; the
Sun-god Ra ; Ru, the supporter of the heavens ; and lastly
Ru's wife Buataranga, guardian of the road to the invisible
world.

To Ru and Buataranga was born a famous son Maui.
At an early age Maui was appointed one of the guardians of
this upper world, where mortals live.   Like the rest of the
inhabitants of the world he subsisted on uncooked food.
His mother, Buataranga, occasionally visited her son ; but
always ate her food apart, out of a basket which she brought
with her from nether-land.   One day, when she was asleep,
Maui peeped into her basket and discovered cooked food.
On tasting it he liked it much better than the raw food to
which he was accustomed.   Now this cooked food came from
the nether world ; hence it was clear that the secret of fire
was there.   So to the nether world, the home of his parents,
Maui resolved to descend, in order that ever after he might
enjoy the luxury of cooked food.

Next day when his mother Buataranga prepared to
descend to the nether world, Maui followed her through the
bush without her knowing it.   This was not difficult, as she
always came and went by the same road.   Peering through
the tall reeds, he saw his mother standing opposite a black
rock, which she addressed as follows :

> " Buataranga, descend though bodily through this chasm.
>   The rainbow-like must be obeyed.
>   As two dark clouds parting at dawn,
>   Open, open up my road to nether world, ye fierce ones."

At these words the rock divided, and Buataranga
descended.   Maui carefully treasured up these magic words ;
and without delay started off to see the god Tane, who owned
some wonderful pigeons.   Maui earnestly begged Tane to
lend him one of the birds.   The god offered him two pigeons,
one after the other, but the fastidious Maui rejected them both.
Nothing would content him but a certain red pigeon called
Akaotu, that is, Fearless, which its owner specially prized.
Tane was loath to part from his pet, but gave it to him on
receiving a promise that the pigeon should be restored to him

uninjured.   Maui now set off in high spirits, carrying the red
pigeon, to the place where his mother had descended.   When
he pronounced the magic words which he had heard, the
rock opened, and Maui, entering into the pigeon, descended.
Some say that he transformed himself into a small dragon-fly,
and perching in that form on the back of the pigeon, went
down to the nether world.   The two fierce demons who
guarded the chasm, enraged at the intrusion of a stranger,
made a grab at the pigeon, intending to devour it ; but they
only grasped and tore off the bird's tail, while the pigeon itself
pursued its flight to the shades.   Maui was grieved at the
mishap which had overtaken the pet bird of his friend
Tane.

Arrived in the under world, Maui sought for the home of
his mother.   It was the first house he saw ; he was guided to
it by the sound of her cloth-flail.   The red pigeon alighted on
an oven-house opposite to the open shed where Buataranga
was beating out bark-cloth.   She stopped her work to gaze
at the red pigeon, which she guessed to be a visitor from the
upper world, because none of the pigeons in the lower world
were red.   Buataranga said to the bird, " Are you not come
from ' daylight ' ? "   The pigeon nodded assent.   " Are you
not my son Maui ? " inquired the old woman.   Again the
pigeon nodded.   At this Buataranga entered her dwelling,
and the bird flew to a bread-fruit tree.   Maui resumed his
proper human form, and went to embrace his mother, who
inquired how he had descended into the nether world, and
what was the object of his visit.   Maui avowed that he had
come to learn the secret of fire.   Buataranga said, " This
secret rests with the fire-god Mauike.   When I wish to cook
an oven, I ask your father Ru to beg a lighted stick from
Mauike."   Maui inquired where the fire-god lived.   His
mother pointed out the direction, and said it was called
Areaoa, " House of banyan sticks."   She entreated Maui to
be careful, " For," said she, " the fire-god is a terrible fellow,
of a very irritable temper."

Maui walked boldly to the house of the fire-god, guided
by the curling column of smoke.   He found the god busy
cooking his food in an oven, and being asked by the deity
what he wanted, he replied, " A fire-brand."   He was given

one, but carried it to a stream that ran past the bread-fruit
tree, and there extinguished it.   He now returned to Mauike
and obtained a second fire-brand, which he also extinguished
in the stream.   A third time he demanded a lighted stick
from the god   The god was beside himself with anger, but
he raked the ashes of his oven and gave some of them on a
dry stick to the daring Maui.   But these live coals likewise
Maui threw into the water.   For he thought that a fire-brand
would be of little use unless he learned the secret of how to
make fire.   So he resolved to pick a quarrel with the fire-
god and compel him to disclose the secret, which as yet was
known to none but himself.   Accordingly for the fourth time
he demanded fire from the enraged fire-god.   Mauike ordered
him away, on pain of being tossed into the air ; for Maui
was small of stature.   But the bold youth declared himself
ready for a trial of strength with the fire-god.   Mauike
entered his dwelling to put on his war-girdle ; but on returning he found that Maui had swelled himself to an
enormous size.   Nothing daunted, Mauike seized him and
hurled him as high as a coco-nut tree.   But Maui contrived
to fall lightly without hurting himself.   A second time the
fire-god tossed him aloft, this time far higher than the
highest coco-nut tree that ever grew ; but again Maui
descended unhurt, while the fire-god lay panting for
breath.

It was now Maui's turn.   Twice he threw the fire-god to a
dizzy height and caught him again like a ball with his hands.
Then Mauike, panting and exhausted, entreated Maui to
stop and spare his life, promising that whatever he desired
should be his.   Maui replied, " Only on one condition will I
spare you ; tell me the secret of fire.   Where is it hidden ?
How is it produced ? "   Mauike gladly promised to tell him
all he knew, and led him inside his wonderful dwelling.   In
one corner there was a quantity of fine coco-nut fibre ; in
another, bundles of fire-yielding sticks—the lemon hibiscus
(*au*), the *Urtica argentea* (*oronga*), the *tauinu*, and particularly
the banyan tree (*aoa, Ficus Indicus*).   These sticks were
all dry and ready for use.   In the middle of the room
were two smaller sticks by themselves.   One of these the
fire-god gave to Maui, desiring him to hold it firmly, while

he himself plied the other vigorously. And as he worked,
he sang :

> " Grant, oh grant me thy hidden fire,
>   Thou banyan tree !
>   Perform an incantation ;
>   Utter a prayer to (the spirit of)
>   The banyan tree !
>   Kindle a fire for Mauike
>   Of the dust of the banyan tree ! "

By the time the song was sung, Maui perceived a faint
smoke rising from the fine dust produced by the friction of
one stick upon another. As they persevered in their work,
the smoke increased ; and fanned by the fire-god's breath a
slight flame shot up, which was nursed by an application of
the fine coco-nut fibre as tinder Mauike now inserted the
different bundles of sticks, and soon a good fire was blazing,
to the astonishment of Maui.

Thus the grand secret of making fire was revealed. But
the victorious Maui resolved to be revenged for his trouble
and for being tossed up in the air ; so he set fire to the abode
of his fallen adversary. Soon all the nether world was in
flames, which consumed the fire-god and all he possessed, and
even the rocks cracked and split with the heat.

But before he left the land of ghosts, Maui picked up the
two fire-sticks, once the property of Mauike, and hastened to
the bread-fruit tree, where the red pigeon, Fearless, awaited
his return. His first care was to restore the missing tail of
the bird, so as to avoid the anger of Tane. There was no
time to be lost, for the flames were rapidly spreading. He
re-entered the pigeon, and carrying the fire-sticks one in each
claw the bird flew to the lower entrance of the chasm. Once
more Maui pronounced the words which he had learned from
his mother Buataranga ; once more the rocks parted, and he
returned safely to the upper world. The red pigeon flew to a
lovely secluded valley, where it alighted ; and the place was
thenceforth named Rupe-tau, " the pigeon's resting-place."
Maui now resumed his original human form, and hastened to
carry back the pet bird of Tane.

Passing through the main valley of Keia, he found that the
flames had preceded him and had found an aperture at

Teaoa, which has since closed up. The kings Rangi and Mokoiro trembled for their land ; for it seemed as if everything would be destroyed by the devouring flames. To save the island of Mangaia from destruction, they exerted themselves to the utmost, and at last succeeded in putting out the fire.

The inhabitants of Mangaia availed themselves of the conflagration to get fire and to cook food. But after a time the fire went out, and as they were not in possession of the secret, they did not know how to kindle it afresh. But Maui was never without fire in his dwelling, to the surprise of everybody. At length he took compassion on the inhabitants of the world and told them the wonderful secret, that fire lies hidden in the hibiscus, the *Urtica argentea*, the *tauinu*, and the banyan. He showed them how the hidden fire might be elicited by the use of fire-sticks, which he produced. Finally, he desired them to chant the fire-god's song in order to give efficacy to the use of the fire-sticks. From that day all the dwellers in this upper world have used fire-sticks with success, and have enjoyed the luxuries of light and cooked food.

Down to the present time, we are told, the same primitive mode of making fire is still in vogue in Mangaia, except that cotton is now substituted for coco-nut fibre as tinder. It was formerly thought that only the four kinds of wood found in the fire-god's dwelling would yield fire. The banyan was sacred to the fire-god. The place where the flames are said to have burst through the ground was named Te-aoa, that is, " the banyan tree," and it was sacred until Christianity induced the owner to convert the holy ground into a taro patch. In the island of Rarotonga, another of the Hervey Islands, the name Buataranga becomes Ataranga ; in Samoa, it becomes Talanga. And in the Samoan dialect Mauike becomes Mafuie.[1]

Another version of the myth is told in the Hervey Islands as follows : In the island of Rarotonga, which is one of the Hervey Group, there once lived a man Manuahifare and his wife Tongoifare, who was a daughter of the god Tangaroa. They had three sons, all called Maui, and a daughter named Inaika ; and the youngest of the three sons, Maui the Third,

[1] W. W. Gill, *Myths and Songs from the South Pacific* (London, 1876), 51-58.

was the youngest of the whole family, and a very clever and precocious boy to boot. This promising youth had noticed that his father, Manuahifare, disappeared mysteriously at dawn every day, and returned mysteriously home every night. It seemed all the stranger because, as the favourite son, he slept at his father's side, yet never knew how and when his father came and went. So he resolved to discover the secret. One night when his father laid aside his girdle in order to sleep, Maui took up one end of it and placed it cautiously under himself, without attracting his father's notice. So next morning he was wakened betimes by feeling the girdle drawn from under him. That was just what he wanted ; so he lay still to see what would follow. His unsuspecting parent went, as he was wont, to the main pillar of the house, and said :

> " O pillar ! open, open up,
> That Manuahifare may enter and descend to the nether world (Avaiki)."

The pillar immediately opened and Manuahifare descended.

That same day, when the four children went to play as usual at hide-and-seek, Maui the youngest told his brothers and sister to go outside the house, whilst he would look out for some place to hide in. As soon as they were out of sight, he went up to the post through which his father had disappeared and pronounced the magic words which he had overheard. To his joy, the post opened up, and Maui boldly descended to the nether world. His father Manuahifare was much surprised to see his son down there, but went on quietly with his work. Thus left to himself, Maui explored the subterranean regions. Amongst other things he found a blind old woman cooking her food over a fire. In her hand she held a pair of tongs made of the green midrib of a coco-nut, and with this implement she would carefully lift a live coal and put it on one side, believing it to be food, while the real food was left to burn to cinder in the fire. Maui inquired her name, and discovered to his surprise that she was no other than Inaporari, that is, Ina the Blind, his own grandmother. Her clever grandson pitied the poor old crone, but would not reveal his own name. Close to where Ina the Blind was cooking there grew four *nono* trees (*Morinda citrifolia*).

Taking up a stick, Maui gently struck the nearest of the four trees. At that Ina the Blind angrily said, " Who is that meddling with the *nono* belonging to Maui the Elder ? " The bold lad then walked up to the next tree and tapped it gently. Again the wrath of Ina the Blind was kindled, and she shouted, " Who is that meddling with the *nono* of Maui the Second ? " Then Maui struck a third tree, and found that it belonged to his sister Inaika. He now tapped the fourth and last *nono* tree, and heard his old grandmother ask, " Who is that meddling with the *nono* of Maui the Third ? " " I am Maui the Third," he replied. " Then," said she, " you are my grandson, and this is your own tree."

Now when Maui first looked at his own *nono* tree, it was quite bare of leaves and fruit ; but after Ina the Blind had spoken to him, he looked at it again, and lo ! it was covered with glossy leaves and fine, though unripe, apples. Maui climbed up into the tree and plucked one of the apples ; then biting off a piece of it, he stepped up to his grandmother and threw the piece into one of her blind eyes. The pain was excruciating, but the sight was completely restored. Maui then plucked another apple, bit a piece out of it, and threw the piece at his grandmother's other eye ; and lo ! sight was restored to it also. Ina the Blind was delighted to see again, and in gratitude she said to her grandson, " All above and all below are subject to thee, and to thee alone."

Thus encouraged, Maui asked her, " Who is lord of fire ? " She replied, " Your grandfather Tangaroa-tui-mata, that is, Tangaroa-of-the-tattooed-face. But do not go to him. He is a terribly irritable fellow ; you will surely perish." Nothing daunted, Maui walked straight up to the fire-god, his grandfather Tangaroa-of-the-tattooed-face. See-ing him advancing, the redoubtable deity lifted up his right hand to kill him ; but Maui lifted his right hand too. Thereupon Tangaroa lifted his right foot, intending to kick the luckless intruder to death ; but Maui did the same with his right foot. Amazed at his audacity, Tangaroa demanded his name. The visitor replied, " I am Maui the Younger." The god now knew him to be his own grandson and asked him what he came for. " To get fire," answered Maui. So Tangaroa gave him a lighted stick and sent him away.

Maui walked a little way off, and coming to water he extinguished the lighted stick. Thrice was this process repeated. The fourth time that Maui asked for fire, all the fire-brands were gone, and Tangaroa had to fetch two dry sticks and rub them together in order to produce fire. Maui held the under stick for his grandfather, while the fire-god rubbed it with the other; but just when the fine dust in the groove was about to ignite, Maui blew it all away. Justly incensed, Tangaroa drove his grandson away and sent for a bird, the tern, to hold down the lower stick while he himself operated in the usual way with the upper one. At last, to the great joy of Maui, fire burst forth from the rubbed sticks. The mystery was solved. Maui now snatched the burning upper stick out of his grandfather's hand; but the bird of white plumage, the tern, still clutched the under fire-stick in her claws, till Maui applied the burning upper stick to either side of the bird's eyes and scorched the place. That is why you see the black marks on either side of the tern's eyes down to this day. Smarting with pain, and indignant at this ill-requital of its services, the tern flew away for ever.

Maui next proposed to his grandfather that they should both fly up to daylight through the hole by which the bird had escaped. The god asked how this could be done. " Nothing is easier," replied Maui, and to prove it he himself flew high like a bird. Tangaroa was charmed by the sight, and at his grandson's suggestion he put on his glorious girdle, which mortals call the rainbow, and soared above the loftiest coco-nut tree. But the crafty Maui took care to fly lower down than Tangaroa, and catching hold of his grandfather's shining girdle by one end, he gave it such a tug that he brought the poor old deity with a crash to the ground. The fall killed Tangaroa dead.

Pleased at having learned the secret of fire and murdered his grandfather, the amiable Maui now returned to his parents, who had both descended to the nether world. He told them that he had got the secret of fire, but said not a word about the murder of his grandfather. His parents expressed their joy at his success, and intimated their wish to go and pay their respects to Tangaroa. But Maui objected to their going at once. " Go," said he, " on the third day   I wish to go

myself to-morrow " His parents acquiesced in this arrangement, so next day Maui repaired to the abode of Tangaroa and
found the corpse of his grandfather in an advanced stage of
decomposition. But he collected the bones, put them in a
coco-nut shell, carefully closed the aperture, and gave the
bones a thorough shaking On opening the coco-nut, he
found his grandfather alive again. Liberating the divinity
from his degrading imprisonment in the coco-nut, he washed
him, anointed him with sweet-scented oil, and then left the
deity to recruit his exhausted energies in his own house.

Maui now returned to his parents, Manuahifare and
Tongoifare, and found them very urgent to visit Tangaroa.
But their son persuaded them to defer their visit till the
morrow. The truth is, he feared the displeasure of his
parents when they discovered the crime of which he had been
guilty, and he secretly resolved to make his way back to the
upper world while his parents were paying their respects tc
Tangaroa. On visiting the resuscitated god on the morning
of the third day, Manuahifare and Tongoifare were greatly
shocked to observe the damaged and battered condition of the
deity. When Manuahifare asked his father what was the
matter, " Oh," said the god, " your terrible boy has been
here ill-treating me. He killed me, then collected my bones,
and rattled them about in an empty coco-nut shell ; he then
finally made me live again, scarred and enfeebled, as you
see. Alas ! that fierce son of yours." At this pitiful tale
the parents of Maui burst into tears, and hastened back to
their old dwelling in the under world, expecting to find there
the young scapegrace, their son, and to give him a good
scolding. But he was not at home, having made his escape
to the upper world, where he found his brothers and sisters
plunged in mourning for him whom they never expected to see
again. He told them of his great discovery, how he had
learned to make fire.[1]

As told in the Marquesas Islands the myth runs thus :

Mahuike, or Mauike, goddess of fire, of earthquakes, and
of volcanoes, dwelt in Havaiki, which is the nether world.
Her only child was a married daughter who lived on earth
and was the grandmother of Maui. Now Maui lived with

[1] W. W. Gill, *Myths and Songs from the South Pacific*, pp. 63-69.

his father and mother on the promontory of an island. He pondered over the want of fire, for he was tired of eating his food raw. The frequent absence of his parents during the night perplexed him, and he was convinced that they went to get fire ; for they always had cooked food. On one occasion his mother said to him, " Child, remain here ; I shall return soon." " I wish to go with you," said the child. " You cannot, pet," she answered ; " I am going to seek for fire. Your ancestress will kill you if you follow me."

However, when the mother went, the child followed afar off. Near the entrance to the path which led down to Havaiki, the nether world, the mother was stopped by a bird which was perched on a *kaku* tree.[1] Thinking that the bird was a *patiotio* (a bird which is now taboo in the Marquesas), she called her husband, and they threw stones at it. But they could not hit it, and the woman conceived that perhaps her grandmother was concealed within the bird. However, her husband dissuaded her, and they continued to throw stones till at last they struck the fowl ; whereupon a voice from the bird proclaimed that it was their son Maui who was in the bird. The parents then went on towards Havaiki by a long and winding road. Maui also penetrated through the aperture where commenced the path to the nether world ; but almost at his first step he perceived his grandmother guarding the entrance. He begged her to let him pass, and when she obstinately refused, he killed her. At the same time some drops of blood fell on the breast of Maui's mother, and she said to her husband, " Somebody has killed my mother." Meantime Maui, meeting with no other obstacle, descended into the bowels of the earth. Soon he met his mother coming back. When she saw him, she said, " What have you done ? You have killed my mother." Her son frankly pleaded guilty. " Yes," said he, " she would not let me pass ; I want to get fire and am determined to have it." His father said, " Do not kill or injure the old goddess," and Maui promised that he would not.

Then he went on till he came to the dwelling of Mauike, the fire-goddess. He said to her, " Give me some fire."

[1] This is the only tree in Nukuhiva (the largest of the Marquesas Islands) of which the wood does not ignite by friction.

" Why do you want it ? " she asked   " I want to cook some bread-fruit," he answered. The goddess requested him to get her some husk of coco-nut. He did so, and she then gave him fire drawn from her toes. Now there are several kinds of fire ; there is one kind of fire drawn from the knees, another kind of fire drawn from the navel, and so on ; but the worst kind of fire is the fire taken from the feet or legs, whereas the sacred fire is taken from the head. So when Maui received the fire which the goddess extracted from her toes, he took it and quenched it in water, and asked for more. She now applied the coco-nut husk to her knees and gave him fire from them. That also he took away and extinguished as he had done before ; then he came back and asked for more. " You tiresome child, you wicked boy, what have you done with the fire ? " asked the goddess. " I fell into water and hurt myself," answered Maui. He then received fire from the back of the goddess ; but that also he put out as before. Lastly, the goddess gave him the coco-nut husk ignited with fire from her navel, but that also he extinguished as he had extinguished all the preceding fires. At that the goddess flew into a terrific rage and assumed an awful aspect. But Maui did not blench. " I know all the secrets of witchcraft," said he, " and care nothing for your magical powers." Then he took a sharp stone and with it he cut off her head. Maui then returned to his parents and told them what he had done. They were very angry and lamented the death of their great relative. Maui then took the fire he had obtained. At first he did not understand its properties, but tried to kindle stones, water, and so on. At last he tried trees, and kindled the *fau* (hibiscus), the *vevai* (cotton - wood), the *keikai*, *aukea*, and indeed all trees except the *kaku* tree, on which he had rested when he assumed the form of the bird.[1]

An earlier, but much briefer, version of the Marquesan myth is reported, with certain variations of detail, by the Frenchman, Max Radiguet, who settled for some time in the Marquesas when France took possession of the islands in 1842, and to whom we owe a valuable account of the natives

---

[1] E. Tregear, " Polynesian Folklore : II. The Origin of Fire," *Transactions and Proceedings of the* *New Zealand Institute*, xx. (1887) pp. 385-387.

as they were at a time when European influence had hardly affected their indigenous culture. Speaking of the native traditions, he says: "The origin of fire is curious. Mahoïke (earthquake), being appointed to guard the fire in the nether world, dutifully acquitted himself of the task. Maui, who had heard of the boasted utility of fire, descended into the nether world to steal some of it. Unable to elude the vigilance of the guardian of the fire, he appealed to his generosity, but Mahoïke turned a deaf ear to his prayers. Then Maui challenged him ; a fight took place, and getting the better of his adversary, Maui wrenched off one of his arms and one of his legs. Thus maimed, the wretched Mahoïke, to save the rest of his limbs, appeared to consent at last to give some of his fire and wished to rub the leg of the victor with it, but luckily Maui detected the fraud ; for if such a fire had been carried to the surface of the earth, it could not have been sacred. So he called on Mahoïke to go about it differently, and at last Mahoïke made up his mind to rub Maui's head with the fire, telling him, ' Return to the place from which you came and touch with your forehead all the trees except the *keïka*. all the trees will yield you fire.' I have explained how the natives procure fire by rubbing two pieces of wood one against the other." [1]

In Hawaii, or the Sandwich Islands, the myth of the origin of fire runs as follows : A certain woman named Hina-akeahi was got with child through the agency of the gods Kane and Kanaloa ; for at their direction, as it seems, she bathed, wearing the girdle of the chief of Hilo, whose name was Kalana-mahiki. In consequence she laid an egg, and from the egg came her son Maui, or, to give him his full name, Maui-kiikii-Akalama. When he was grown up, his mother sent him with the girdle for a token to the chief his father, and his father recognized him as his son and educated him with his other sons, who had been borne to him by different women of the country, and all of whom were named Maui, being distinguished from each other as Maui-Mua (Maui the First), Maui (the Last), and Maui-Waina (Maui the Middle

---

[1] Max Radiguet, *Les derniers Sauvages*, Nouvelle Édition (Paris, 1882), pp. 223 *sq*. In this version the guardian of fire (Mahoïke) appears to be a male, whereas in Tregear's version she (Mahuike) is a goddess.

One).   Once going out to sea with his brothers to fish, Maui-kiikii perceived to his astonishment fire burning on the coast. Till then he had known fire only in the house of his mother ; for her skin burned and everything that she touched took fire.   Going in search of the fire which he saw in the distance in the mountains, Maui found a colony of *alae* birds, one of which was carrying fire about and communicating it to its fellows, that they might roast bananas or taro with it.   After vainly attempting to catch the birds, Maui betook himself to his mother for advice, and learned from her that the *alae* bird was her firstborn, and that living in the wooded hills it had learned the use of fire   She advised him to make a puppet and put it, with a paddle in its hand, in the bow of the canoe the next time his brothers went fishing, in order that the birds might think he was with his brothers in the boat.   He did so, and when the canoe had sailed away, he remained on shore and was able again to surprise the *alae* birds in their haunt. They flew away, but one of them, which had overeaten itself, could not follow fast enough and began to roll down hill. There it was caught by Maui, who questioned it about the production of fire.   The bird confessed to making fire by the friction of two sticks, and pointed out various trees from which fire-sticks could be procured.   But on trial the wood of all these trees proved unsuitable for the purpose.   In a rage at his disappointment, Maui would have wrenched off the bird's beak, if the *hau* tree had not last of all been tried and yielded fire.   But to punish the bird for the labour he had expended in vain, Maui applied a burning brand to its head, as you may still see by the red crest on its poll.[1]

This myth of the origin of fire among men is briefly alluded to in a native history of Hawaii, where we read that a certain hero " sought for fire and found it in the *alae*," which is explained to be a bird the upper part of whose beak is covered with a red skin.[2]

Thus the Hawaiian myth of the origin of fire, like many Australian myths of the same sort, serves at the same time to explain the peculiar colouring of a particular sort of bird.

[1] Adolf Bastian, *Inselgruppen in Oceanien* (Berlin, 1883), pp. 278 *sq.* ; *id. Allerlei aus Volks- und Menschenkunde* (Berlin, 1888), i. 120 *sq.*

[2] Jules Remy, *Ka Movolelo Hawaii, Histoire de l'Archipel Havaiien* (Paris and Leipzig, 1862), pp. 85, 87.

A very different story of the origin of fire is told by the natives of Nukufetau or De Peyster's Island, one of the Ellice Group. They say that men discovered fire by seeing smoke rising from the friction of two crossed branches of a tree, which rubbed against each other in the wind.[1]

In the island of Peru, one of the Gilbert Group, they say that " fire was procured from Tangaloa of the heavens by an old lady, and put in a tree. She told the people to bring it out by friction, and ever since they have had cooked food." [2]

But a much more marvellous story of the origin of fire is also told by these islanders. They say that " in the beginning there were two lords. Tabakea was lord of Tarawa, the land ; he lived on the land. And Bakoa was lord of Marawa, the sea ; he lived in the sea.

" Then Bakoa begot a child, whose name was Te-Ika. When Te-Ika grew up he was forever lying on the surface of the sea watching the sunrise. When the sun's first beams shot up over the horizon, it was his daily endeavour to catch a beam in his mouth and bite it off. So for many days he tried to do that thing, and at last he was successful; he caught a sunbeam in his mouth, and swam away with it to his father Bakoa. When he came to his father's house he went in and sat down with the sunbeam beside him ; but, behold, when Bakoa came in he was amazed at the heat of the place, and said to his son, ' Get hence, thou art burning hot and the house smokes where thou sittest.' So Te-Ika left his father's house, and took his sunbeam to another place ; but, behold, wherever he sat it was the same ; the house began to smoke and everything that was near him shrivelled up with the heat.

" At last Bakoa was afraid that everything he had would be dried up and destroyed by his son, so he drove Te-Ika forth from that place, saying, ' Get hence, for thou wilt be the death of us all.' So Te-Ika fled before his father's face and went eastward to Tarawa, where Tabakea dwelt. When he came to Tabakea's land he went ashore with his sunbeam, but behold, wherever he went the trees and the houses were shrivelled up in his presence, for the sunbeam was burning hot and its heat had entered into the body of Te-Ika also.

" Then Tabakea arose against Te-Ika to drive him forth,

[1] G. Turner, *Samoa*, pp. 285 *sq*.   [2] G. Turner, *Samoa*, p. 297.

but he could not. So he took for his weapons every tree
and branch that he could lay his hands upon ; therewith
he belaboured the body of Te-Ika. He beat him with wood
of the *uri*-tree (*Guettarda speciosa*), he beat him with wood
of the *ren*-tree (*Tournefortii argentea*), he beat him with
the bark of the *kanawa*-tree (*Cordia subcordata*), and with
dry rubbish fallen from the coconut-tree. So mightily he
belaboured Te-Ika that at last he battered both him and
his sunbeam into little fragments, that scattered over the
whole land.

"But when Te-Ika had left his father Bakoa and had
been gone awhile, his father began to grieve after him, for
he loved him dearly. At last he arose and began to search
all the seas for his son, but he found him not. So he began
to search the land ; and at last he went eastward to Tabakea's
land. There he said to Tabakea, ' Hast thou seen my son ?
He has a burning body and carries a sunbeam with him.'
Tabakea said, ' I have seen him. He came hither, and I
would have beaten him hence, for I feared him, but I could
not. Then I belaboured him and his sunbeam so mightily
that they were both broken in fragments and scattered over
my land.' When Bakoa heard that he grieved bitterly, for
he loved his son, so Tabakea said, ' Stay, for I will bring thy
son to life again.' So he took a stick of the *uri*-tree, wherewith he had belaboured Te-Ika, and rubbed it upon a stick
of the *ren*-tree. Lo, it was a great magic, for it began to
smoke, and Bakoa said, ' It smokes as the trees smoked
when my son was near them.' Then Tabakea made a heap
of dry bark of the trees wherewith he had belaboured Te-Ika
and, blowing upon his rubbing sticks where they had been
rubbed together, he made a flame, and lighted a fire. Bakoa
was amazed at that great magic. He said, ' Behold it is my
son that thou hast brought to life again.' Then he would
have taken the fire and carried it back with him to westward,
for he said it was indeed his son ; but behold, when he
entered the sea to take it home, it was put out in the water,
and he could never carry his son away with him. So it is
to this day ; the body and the sunbeam of Te-Ika, which
were broken in pieces by Tabakea, remain forever in the
heart of the sticks and rubbish with which they were

belaboured by Tabakea on Tarawa, and they can never again go back to the sea." [1]

The natives of Yap, or Uap, one of the Caroline Islands, say that formerly they had yams and taro, but as yet there was no fire to cook them. So the people baked their yams and taro by means of the sun's heat playing on the sand. But they suffered grievously from internal pains; so they besought the great god Yalafath, who lives in the sky, to help them. Immediately there fell a great red-hot thunderbolt from the sky and smote a pandanus tree. At the contact of the fiery element the pandanus tree broke out into a regular eruption of prickles down the middle and sides of every leaf. Dessra, the thunder-god, thus found himself fixed fast in the tree-trunk, and he called out in a lamentable voice for somebody to deliver him from his irksome prison. A woman named Guaretin, baking taro in the sun hard by, heard the voice and helped the distressed god. He inquired on what work she was engaged, and when she told him, he bade her fetch plenty of moist clay. This he kneaded into a cooking-pot, to the great joy of the woman. He then sent her in search of some sticks from the *arr* tree (called *tupuk* by the natives of Ponape); these he put under his armpits and infused into them the latent sparks of fire. That is how the art of making fire by the friction of wood and the art of moulding pots out of clay were learned by the primitive folk of Yap.[2]

Another version of the same story, with some variations, has since been reported from Yap by another inquirer. It runs thus:

In the olden time there was neither fire nor pottery in Yap. A woman named Deneman in the now extinct slave village of Dinai, near Gitam, had two children. One day she and her children fetched taro from the field, scraped it, cut it up, and laid the pieces in the sun to dry. Then came Thunder in the likeness of a great dog and fell down on a pandanus tree. He said to the woman, " Come and fetch me down," for he was afraid of the prickles of the pandanus tree. The woman answered, " No, I am afraid." " Pray

---

[1] Arthur Grimble, "Myths from the Gilbert Islands," *Folk-lore*, xxxiv. (1923) pp. 372-374.

[2] F. W. Christian, *The Caroline Islands* (London, 1899), pp. 320 *sq.*

do come," quoth Thunder. Then she went and fetched him down. He saw the taro and asked, " What is that ? " " My food," said she. He begged her for two pieces of it, which he put for a time in his armpits ; then he gave them back to the woman, and lo ! they were cooked and good to eat.

Thunder said, " Fetch a branch of the *ăr* tree." She gave it to him. He peeled the bark off, put the stick under his armpit, and drew it slowly through. Then the wood was quite dry. After that he cut the stick through the middle, pointed the one half, and made a socket in the other. Thus the fire-drill was ready. Then he kindled fire by drilling the one stick in the socket of the other, and roasted the taro. After that the woman and her children went home and slept. Next morning they went again to the field to work, and Thunder accompanied them. He said to the woman, " Fetch clay, but let there be no stone in it." So he took the clay and showed the woman how to make a pot out of it. After that he made a great fire and baked the pot. Next he taught the woman a charm (*matsamato*) to make the pot strong and durable, if the buyer paid a good price for it, and another charm to make the pot soon break, if the buyer haggled. Then he took much *lăk* and *măl* and cooked them, and they were very good to eat. Thereupon the woman and her children went home again to sleep. Next morning Thunder had vanished, but the woman kept on cooking by night, that no one should perceive what she was about.

However, there came a man who saw that her food was not like other food, and he inquired the reason of it. Many other people also came to inquire, but the woman kept her counsel. Then the people set a watch and observed her day and night. One night, when they saw a gleam of fire, they broke through the wall of the house and burst in. A man laid hold of the fire, but he burned himself, for he knew not the effect of fire. Then the people brought firewood and carried the fire to other houses ; and thereupon they required of the woman to make pots and promised her a great reward. But they had not paid for the fire.[1]

---

[1] W. Müller, *Yap* (Hamburg, 1917– 1918), pp. 604-607 (*Ergebnisse der Südsee-Expedition*, 1908–1910, heraus- gegeben von Prof. Dr. G. Thilenius, ii. *Ethnographie*, B. *Mikronesien*, Band 2, 2. Halband).

According to another version of the story the lightning which first brought fire to Yap struck a large hibiscus tree at Ugatam, a slave village at the northern end of the island. A woman begged the lightning-god, whose name in this version is Derra, to give her some of the fire ; he did so and showed her how to bake an earthen pot. When the fire died out, he taught her how to obtain more by means of the fire-drill, that is, by rubbing the point of one stick in the hollow of another. He told her, further, that fire in a new house must always be started in this manner, and for it only the wood of the hibiscus tree should be used ; moreover, this wood ought always to be cut with shell knives or shell axes, it should never be touched by iron or steel.[1]

A Spanish missionary in the early part of the eighteenth century reported the same myth in a brief and probably inaccurate form. According to him the natives of the Caroline Islands " include in the rank of the evil spirits a certain Morogrog, who, having been chased from heaven for his gross and uncivil manners, brought to earth the fire, which had been unknown till then." [2]

---

[1] W. H. Furness, *The Island of Stone Money, Uap of the Carolines* (Philadelphia and London, 1910), p. 151.

[2] J. A. Cantova, in *Lettres Édifiantes et Curieuses*, Nouvelle Edition, xv. (Paris, 1781) p. 306.

CHAPTER VII

THE ORIGIN OF FIRE IN INDONESIA

THE Toradyas of Central Celebes say that the Creator made the first man and woman by carving figures in human shape out of stone and causing the wind to blow on them, for thus they acquired breath and life. He also gave them fire, but did not teach them how to make it. So in those early days people were very careful not to let the fire go out on the hearth. However, one day through carelessness the fire was allowed to go out, and the people were at a loss how to boil their rice. But the sky was then close to the earth, and the people resolved to send a messenger to the gods to ask for a little fire. The messenger chosen for the purpose was a certain insect called *tambooya*. When he came to the sky and asked for the fire, the gods said, " We will give you fire ; but you must cover your eyes with your hands, for you may not see how we make fire." The insect did as he was bidden, but the gods did not know that he had an eye under each shoulder. So while he lifted up his arms to hide the eyes in his head, he saw with his eyes under his arms how the gods made fire by striking a flint with a chopping-knife and thus eliciting a spark, which was then used to kindle dry wood. This fire was given by the gods to the insect, who took with it to earth the secret of how to kindle fire   The mode of kindling fire by flint and steel is still the most usual method practised by the Toradyas. Flints are found in some of their streams and mountains.[1]

[1] A. C. Kruijt, " De legenden der Poso-Alfoeren aangaande de eerste menschen," *Mededeelingen van wege het Nederlandsche Zendelinggenootschap*, xxxviii. (1894) pp. 340 *sq.* ; N. Adriani en Alb. C. Kruijt, *De Bare'e-sprekende Toradja's van Midden-Celebes* (Batavia, 1912–1914), ii. 186 *sq*. The native name of the insect, according to Dutch orthography, is

The same story is told, with trifling variations, by the Toradyas of Pana, Mamasa, and Baroopoo in Central Celebes. In their version the insect which revealed to mankind the method of kindling fire is called *dali* ; it appears to be a sort of gad-fly. They say that the creature was sent to Pooang matooa to ask for fire. The Lord of Heaven bade the gad-fly cover its eyes with its feet in order that it should not see how the deity made fire. The insect obeyed, but with the other eyes which, according to the Toradyas, it has in its armpits, it saw how the Lord of Heaven made fire by rubbing two bamboos against each other. The gad-fly returned to earth without fire, but revealed to mankind the secret of kindling fire. The Toradyas of Mengkendek say that the first man, whose name was Pong Moola, sent a bird to heaven to ask for fire. The native name of the bird is *dena* ; the Dutch call it the little rice-thief (*rijstdiefje*), the propriety of which will appear from what follows. As a reward for this hazardous service the first man promised the bird that it should be allowed to eat the young rice in the fields. The bird succeeded in bringing back fire from heaven ; and therefore its descendants come every year to get their reward by eating the young rice in the fields. However, in Pangala the Toradyas say that it was a buffalo-keeper named Maradonde who made the first fire by rubbing bamboos against each other ; this he did in a legendary island of the sea. Moreover, everywhere in the Toradya lands people tell a tale of the war which fire waged on water. They say that fire was beaten and had to take to flight. He hid in a bamboo and a stone. When the first man, Pong Moola, sought for fire, the bamboo and the stone said to him, " Take me away from here." The man asked, " How may I do that ? " Then the bamboo said that he (the bamboo) must be rubbed, and the stone said that he (the stone) must be struck with a piece of steel in order to yield fire.[1]

The Sea-Dyaks of Borneo say that after the great flood, in which all mankind perished save one woman, the solitary survivor found a dog lying at the foot of a jungle creeper, and

tamboeja, which is pronounced like *tambooya* in English. I do not know the scientific name of the insect.

[1] Alb. C. Kruyt, " De Toradja's van de Sa'dan—, Masoepoe—en Mamasa-Rivieren," *Tijdschrift voor Indische Taal-, Land- en Volkenkunde*, lxiii. (1923) pp. 278 *sq.*

feeling the root of the creeper to be warm, she thought that perhaps fire might be extracted from it. So she took two pieces of its wood and rubbed them together and thus succeeded in kindling fire. Such was the origin of the fire-drill, and such the first production of fire after the great flood.[1]

The Muruts, who inhabit the hilly country in the interior of North Borneo, have a legend that after the great flood the sole survivors were a boy and girl, brother and sister, who married and by their union became the parents of a dog. One day the boy took the dog out hunting. They came upon a *kilian* root. The dog took a piece of the root home with him, put it in the sun and dried it. Then he told the boy to make a hole in the middle of the root, insert a stick in the hole, and rub it vigorously between his hands. As he did so, sparks flew out, and this was the origin of fire. Afterwards a boy and girl were born to the pair. They were given a piece of *kilian* root and sent to another country. And so on till the whole world was peopled and knew the use of fire.

Later they grew tired of this primitive mode of making fire. The boy took the dog out hunting again. They lighted on a *polur* tree (resembling the cotton-tree). The dog barked at it. They cut it down, and the dog told the boy to take the cotton-like substance (*lulup*) inside the pod. The dog then barked at a bamboo, and they took a piece of it. Then the dog barked at a rock, and they took a piece of the rock. After that, they dried the *lulup* and rubbed it against the bamboo with the piece of the rock, and thus the Muruts got their more modern method of kindling fire.[2]

The Kiau Dusuns of North Borneo say that, rubbing against each other in the wind, two growing bamboos caught fire. A dog, passing by, seized one of the burning pieces and carried it home to his master's house, which soon blazed up. The fire charred some cobs of maize which were in the house, and it boiled some potatoes which had been left to

---

[1] Rev. J. Perham, "Sea-Dyak Tradition of the Deluge and Consequent Events," *Journal of the Straits Branch of the Royal Asiatic Society*, No. 6 (December 1880), p. 289 ; H. Ling Roth, *The Natives of Sarawak and British North Borneo* (London, 1896), i. 301.

[2] Owen Rutter, *The Pagans of North Borneo* (London, 1929), pp. 248 *sq.*, 252 *sq.*

soak. Thus the Dusuns learned not only how to kindle fire but how to cook their food.[1]

The inhabitants of Nias, an island to the west of Sumatra, say that in the olden time certain evil spirits called Belas, who are supposed to have been formerly men, used to consort with mankind in a friendly way. Nowadays only the priests can see the Belas, but formerly they were visible to everybody. Belas and men visited each other and borrowed fire from each other, just as the people of Nias do from one another at the present day ; but the Belas alone knew how to make fire, and they kept the art a secret from the human race. One day a man went to fetch fire from the wife of a Bela, but it happened that her fire had gone out. Hence in order to prevent him from seeing how she made it, she proposed to cover him up with a garment. But he said, " I can see through a garment ; put a basket over me " ; for he knew that he could see through the interstices of a basket. She complied with his request, and then proceeded to kindle the fire. The man had now attained his object ; for he had seen how the woman made fire, and he laughed in her face at her simplicity. Therefore the indignant Belas said to men, " From henceforth you shall see us no more, and shall come no more to us." [2]

The Tsuwo, a tribe of head-hunters in the mountainous interior of Formosa, tell how their ancestors obtained fire after the great flood. The survivors had taken refuge on the top of a mountain, but when the water subsided they had no fire, for in their hurried retreat before the rising tide they had had no time to carry it with them. For a while they felt the cold severely, but some one espied a sparkle like the twinkling of a star on the top of a neighbouring mountain. So the people said, " Who will go thither and bring fire for us ? " Then a goat came forward and said, " I will go and bring back the fire." So saying, he plunged into the flood and swam straight for the mountain, guided by the star-like twinkling of the fire on its top. The people awaited its return in great anxiety. After a while it reappeared from the darkness,

---

[1] Owen Rutter, *The Pagans of North Borneo*, p. 253.

[2] L. N. H. A. Chatelin, " Godsdienst en Bijgeloof der Niassers," *Tijdschrift voor Indische Taal-, Land-* en *Volkenkunde*, xxvi. (1880) p. 132 ; E. Modigliani, *Un Viaggio à Nias* (Milan, 1890), pp. 629 *sq.* Compare H. Sundermann, *Die Insel Nias* (Barmen, 1905), p. 70.

swimming with a burning cord attached to its horns. But the nearer it drew to the shore, the lower burned the fire on the cord, and more and more feebly swam the goat, till at last it drooped its head, the water closed over it, and the fire was out. After that the people despatched a *taoron* on the same errand, and it succeeded in bringing the fire safe to land. So pleased were the people at its success, that they all gathered round the animal and patted it. That is why the creature has such a shiny skin and so tiny a body to this day.[1]

The Andaman Islanders also tell of the difficulty which their ancestors experienced in recovering the use of fire after the great flood had extinguished all fires on earth, or at least all fires in the Andaman Islands. The only mountain which then rose above the waste of waters was Saddle Peak, where the Creator, Puluga by name, resided in person. The people did not know how to repair the loss of fire till the ghost of one of their friends, who had perished in the inundation, pitied their distress, and, assuming the form of a kingfisher, flew up to the sky, where he discovered the Creator seated beside his fire. The bird seized a burning log in his beak, but the heat, or the weight, or both, proved too much for him, and he dropped the blazing brand on the Creator. Incensed at the indignity and smarting with pain, the Creator hurled the brand at the bird, but the missile missed its mark and fell very opportunely near the very spot where the few forlorn survivors of the great flood were bewailing their sad condition. That is how mankind recovered the use of fire after the great flood.[2]

This Andamanese myth was recorded by Mr. E. H. Man, who resided in the islands from 1869 to 1880 and was intimately acquainted with the natives. The same myth has

[1] For this Tsuwo story I am indebted to the kindness of Mr. Shinji Ishii, a Japanese gentleman who resided for several years in Formosa for the purpose of studying the natives. I have already told the story in *Folk-lore in the Old Testament*, i. 230 *sq.*

[2] E. H. Man, *On the Aboriginal Inhabitants of the Andaman Islands* (London, N.D.), pp. 98 *sq.* The native name of the kingfisher is *luratut*.

Compare *Census of India, 1901*, vol. iii. *The Andaman and Nicobar Islands*, by Sir Richard C. Temple (Calcutta, 1903), p. 63. Brief versions of the Andamanese fire myth in each of the five languages of the South Andaman group of tribes have been published, with translations, by Mr. M. V. Portman. See M. V. Portman, "The Andaman Fire-legend," *The Indian Antiquary*, xxvi. (1897) pp. 14-18.

since been recorded, with minor variations, by Professor A. R. Brown, who resided in the Andaman Islands from 1906 to 1908. His version, which he obtained from the A-Pucikwar tribe, runs thus :

When the ancestors lived at Wota-emi, Bilik (the equivalent of Puluga in Mr. Man's version) lived at Tol-l'oko-tima across the strait. In those days the ancestors had no fire. Bilik took some wood of the tree called *perat* and broke it and made fire for himself. Kingfisher (*luratut*) came to Tol-l'oko-tima while Bilik was sleeping and stole some fire. Bilik awoke and saw Kingfisher. He took up a lighted brand and threw it at Kingfisher. It hit him in the back of the neck and burnt him. Kingfisher gave the fire to the people at Wota-emi. Bilik was very angry about this and went away to live in the sky. " The Kingfisher of this story (*Alcedo beavani* ?) has a patch of bright red feathers on its neck. This is where it was burnt by the brand thrown by Bilik." [1]

In some versions of the Andamanese myth the dove is associated with, or substituted for, the kingfisher as the bird which brought the first fire to men. Thus, in a free translation, " It was Sir Prawn who first produced or obtained fire. Some yam leaves, being shrivelled and dry by reason of the hot weather, caught fire and burnt. The prawn made a fire with some firewood and went to sleep. The kingfisher stole fire and ran away with it. He made a fire and cooked some fish. When he had filled his belly he went to sleep. The dove stole fire from the kingfisher and ran away. It is implied that it was the dove who gave the fire to the ancestors of the Andamanese." [2]

Another version of the Andamanese myth, in which both the kingfisher and the dove play a part, is as follows :

The ancestors had no fire. Bilika (the equivalent of Puluga) had fire. The kingfisher (*lirtit*) went one night and stole her fire while Bilika [3] slept. Bilika awoke and saw him going away with her fire. She threw a pearl shell at him, which cut off his wings and his tail. The kingfisher

[1] A. R. Brown, *The Andaman Islanders* (Cambridge, 1922), pp. 203 *sq.*
[2] A. R. Brown, *The Andaman Islanders*, pp. 189 *sq.*
[3] In the versions of the myths as recorded by Professor A. R. Brown the mythical being Bilika or Biliku is feminine ; in the myths as recorded by Mr. E. H. Man the corresponding figure Puluga is masculine.

dived into the water and swam with the fire to Bet-'ra-kudu
and gave it to Tepe.   Tepe gave fire to the bronze-winged
dove (*mite*), who gave it to the others.[1]

In another version of the myth the fire-bringer is the
dove alone ;   the kingfisher does not appear at all in it.
The story runs thus :

Biliku had a red stone and a pearl shell.   She struck
them together and obtained fire by their percussion.   She
collected firewood and made a fire.   She went to sleep.   The
bronze-winged dove (*mite*) came and stole fire.   He made a
fire for himself.   He gave fire to all the people in the village.
Afterwards fire was given to all the places.   Each village
had its own.[2]

Another version in which the dove alone is the thief of
fire was briefly recorded by Mr. M. V. Portman as follows :

" Mr. Pigeon stole a firebrand at Kúro-t'ón-míka, while
God was sleeping.   He gave the brand to the late Léch, who
then made fires at Karát-tátak-émi." [3]

In another version of the Andamanese myth the kingfisher (*tiritmo*) is said to have kindled the first fire by taking
some rotten wood of the *piri* tree and striking it on a rock.
Having procured fire in this way the kingfisher gave some
of the fire to the heron ;   the heron gave it to another species
of kingfisher called *totemo*, and this latter sort of kingfisher
passed the fire on to all the others.[4]

In yet another version the Andamanese story of the
origin of fire is told to account for the bright colouring of
certain species of fish.   It is said that of old the people had
no fire.   Dim-dori (a fish) went and fetched fire from the
place of departed spirits.   He came back and threw the fire
at the people and burnt them and marked them all.   The
people ran into the sea and became fishes.   Dim-dori went
to shoot them with his bow and arrows, but he also was
turned into the fish that bears his name.[5]

[1] A. R. Brown, *The Andaman
Islanders*, pp. 202 *sq.*
[2] A. R. Brown, *The Andaman
Islanders*, p. 201.
[3] M. V. Portman, " The Andaman
Fire-legend," *The Indian Antiquary*,
xxvi. (1897) p. 14.

[4] A. R. Brown, *The Andaman
Islanders*, pp. 201 *sq.*

[5] A. R. Brown, *The Andaman
Islanders*, p. 204.   This version was
obtained by Professor A. R. Brown
from the Akar-Bale tribe.

CHAPTER VIII

THE ORIGIN OF FIRE IN ASIA

THE primitive Menri, a tribe of the dwarf Semang, who inhabit the dense forests of the Malay Peninsula, say that they got their first fire from the woodpecker. The story runs as follows :

When the Menri came into contact with the Malays, they found among them a red flower (*gantogn* : Malay *gantang*). They gathered in a circle round it and stretched their arms out over it to warm themselves. Afterwards the Malays kindled fire and set the *lalang* grass in a blaze. The Menri fled before the conflagration into the forest, for they had no fire of their own. A stag came up to the great fire and carried a brand back to his home. Fearing that the fire might be stolen, he put the firebrand high up on his hut while he went to work in his plantation. The woodpecker saw the fire, stole it, and brought it to the Menri, telling them that this was fire, but warning them at the same time to be on their guard because the stag was following him ; should the stag come in search of his stolen property, the wood-pecker advised the Menri to take two spears of *tĕras* and stab him with them. So when the stag appeared to fetch his fire, two men seized the spears and stabbed the animal in the head. Till that time the stag had no horns ; but now, wounded in the head, he turned round and hurried off into the forest, and ever since he has had horns but no fire. The woodpecker made the Menri swear that they would not kill him, because he had brought them fire for warmth and cooking. Ever since that the woodpecker may not be killed.[1]

[1] Paul Schebesta, *Among the Forest Dwarfs of Malaya* (London, N.D.), pp. 274 *sq.* ; compare *id.*, " Religiöse Anschauungen der Semang," *Archiv für Religionswissenchaft*, xxv. (1927) p. 16.

In other versions of the myth the Semang ascribe the theft or the discovery of fire, not to the woodpecker, but to the coconut-monkey (*bĕrok*). According to one account, the coconut-monkey stole a firebrand from Karei, the Supreme Being who lives in the sky and causes the thunder. With this stolen fire the monkey ignited the savannah grass. Soon a great conflagration raged, and the people fled before it. Some ran to the river, boarded rafts, and floated down stream ; these people were the Malays of to-day. Others fled to the mountains and the forests, but, being dilatory in their movements, they were overtaken by the fire which singed their hair ; these people were the ancestors of the dwarf tribes of the Malay Peninsula, who are known collectively as Orang-Utan, and whose hair is curly because the fire singed it on their flight.[1]

In another version of this Semang myth the coconut-monkey (*bĕrok*) obtained fire in a less discreditable fashion than by theft. It is said that, when his wife was in the throes of childbirth, the coconut-ape wished to give her a coco-nut ; so he took it and split it open, and when he did so, fire leaped out of the nut. With this fire the coconut-monkey lit the great conflagration to which the Semang owe the curliness of their hair.[2]

According to another Semang story, fire was discovered by a certain hero Chepampes in the process of cutting rattan to use as a saw.[3]

The Thay, or Tai, of Siam have a tradition of a great flood which destroyed all mankind except a boy and girl, who were saved in a gourd. From the offspring of these two, so runs the story, are descended all the present inhabitants of the world. But in these days, after the flood had subsided, the seven boys of the first pair had no fire. Hence they decided to send one of their number to the sky to fetch some. Their messenger was given some fire by the Spirit of the Sky, but at the gate of the heavenly palace his torch went out. He returned to the threshold of the palace and relit his torch, but

[1] P. Schebesta, *Among the Forest Dwarfs of Malaya*, p. 89. As to the thunder-god Karei, the Supreme Being of the Semang, see *id.*, pp. 47, 88, 163 *sq.*, 184 *sqq.*, 198 *sq.*, 276, 280.

[2] P. Schebesta, *Among the Forest Dwarfs of Malaya*, pp. 216 *sq.*

[3] P. Schebesta, *Among the Forest Dwarfs of Malaya*, p. 239.

a second time it was extinguished. A third time his torch was kindled, and he had carried it half-way to earth, when for the third time the fire went out. So the messenger returned to earth and reported his ill success to his brothers. They held a council and resolved to send the serpent and the owl to present their request for fire. But on the way the owl stopped at the first village to catch rats, and the serpent loitered in the marshes chasing tree-frogs ; and neither of them took any more trouble about their mission. The seven brothers now held a second consultation, and this time applied to the gad-fly. The gad-fly willingly accepted the task of fetching fire, but, before addressing himself to it, he laid down his conditions. " For my pains," said he, " I shall quench my thirst on the thighs of buffaloes and on the calves of the legs of gentle and simple." To this proposal the brothers were constrained to agree. When the gad-fly was come to the sky, the Sky asked him, " Where are your eyes ? and where are your ears ? " For the Thay think that the eyes of a gad-fly are not in its head but at the root of its wings, and this anatomical peculiarity was apparently unknown to the Sky. " My eyes," replied the cunning gad-fly, " are just where other people's eyes are, and my ears are just where other people's ears are." " Then," pursued the Sky, " where will you shut yourself up so as to see nothing ? " The artful gad-fly answered, " I see through the sides of a pitcher just as if they did not exist ; but put me in a basket with interstices, and I see absolutely nothing." The confiding Sky accordingly put the gad-fly in a basket with interstices, and set about making fire in the usual way. Ensconced in the basket the gad-fly observed closely the whole process, and though the lighted torch which he received from the Sky went out on his way to earth, the gad-fly recked nothing of that, for he carried with him the divine secret of how to make fire.

On his arrival he was greeted by the brothers with the eager question, " Where is the fire ? Where is the fire ? " " Listen," replied the gad-fly. " Take a splinter of wood as slender as the leg of a roebuck and as thin as the beard of a shrimp ; make a notch in the wood, put a cord in the notch, and pile tow round it, like a nest of little pigs. Then draw the cord rapidly backwards and forwards with both hands, till the smoke rises up in your face." The brothers followed exactly the advice of the gad-fly ; and soon from a puff of smoke the fire spurted out, and they were able to cook their victuals. Men still make fire in that way , and still the gad-fly quenches its thirst on the thighs of buffaloes and on the calves of the legs of gentle and simple.[1]

In this story the gad-fly's trick of peeping through the interstices of a basket resembles the trick played by the man in the corresponding story from Nias.[2]

The Kachins of Burma say that in the beginning men had no fire ; they ate their food raw and were cold and lean. But on the other side of the Irrawaddy there dwelt a spirit (*nat*) named Wun Lawa Makam, and he was in possession of a fire which burned all kinds of wood, whether dry or green. " That is what we need," said men to themselves. So they sent Kumthan Kumthoi Makam to Wun Lawa Makam to borrow some of his fire. The messenger crossed the river on a raft and soon came to Wun Lawa Makam, and said, " Great father, we are cold, we eat our food raw, and we are very lean. Give us then your fire." The spirit answered, " You men cannot possess the Fire-spirit ; he would cause you too many misfortunes." But the messenger pleaded, " Have pity on us, great father ! We suffer so much." Then the Spirit said, " I cannot give you the Spirit of Fire, but I will tell you how to obtain fire. Let a man named Tu and a woman named Thu rub two pieces of bamboo together, and soon you will have fire." The messenger returned joyfully to the men who had sent him On hearing the message the men at once sent for a man named Tu and a woman named Thu, and these two rubbed two bamboos together. Soon fire issued from the bamboos, and thenceforth men were able to warm themselves and to cook their food.[3]

There is a Chinese story that " a great sage went to walk beyond the bounds of the moon and the sun ; he saw a tree, and on this tree a bird, which pecked at it and made fire come forth. The sage was struck with this, took a branch of the tree, and produced fire from it, and thence this great personage

[1] A. Bourlet, " Les Thay," *Anthropos*, ii. (1907) pp. 921-924.

[2] See above, p. 96.

[3] Ch. Gilhodes, " Mythologie et Religion des Katchins (Birmanie)," *Anthropos*, iii. (1908) pp. 689 *sq.*

was called Suy-jin." Now we are told that in Chinese *suy* means an instrument to obtain fire ; that *muh-say* means an utensil to elicit fire from wood by rotatory friction ; and that *Suy-jin-she* is the name of the first person who procured fire for the use of man.[1] Hence apparently the discovery of the means to kindle fire by the friction of wood is popularly attributed by the Chinese to a wise man who observed a bird producing fire by pecking at a tree.

A Tartar tribe of Southern Siberia has a story of the discovery of fire. They say that when Kudai, the Creator, had fashioned man, he observed, " Man will be naked. How can he live in the cold ? Fire must be discovered." Now a certain man named Ulgon had three daughters. They could not make fire nor discover how it was to be done. Then came Kudai. His beard was long, and he trod on it and stumbled. The three daughters of Ulgon mocked at him, and he went away in a huff. But the three daughters of Ulgon waited on the road to hear what God would say. He said, " The three daughters of Ulgon mock at me and laugh, though they cannot find the sharpness of stone and the hardness of iron." When they heard that, the three daughters of Ulgon took the sharpness of stone and the hardness of iron, and with these two they struck fire.[2]

The Yakuts of Northern Siberia say that " the discovery of fire occurred thus : On a hot summer day an old man who was wandering among the mountains sat down to rest and, having nothing to do, struck one stone against another. Sparks issued from the blow and set alight the dry grass and next dry twigs. The fire extended, and people ran from all parts to gaze at the novel wonder. The further it spread the larger it became and the more the fire bred fear and horror ; but fortunately it was extinguished by a downpour of rain. Henceforth the Yakuts learned to kindle fire and to extinguish it." [3]

A very different story of the discovery of fire is told by

[1] (Sir) Edward B. Tylor, *Researches into the Early History of Mankind* (London, 1878), p. 254.

[2] W. Radloff, *Proben der Volkslitteratur der türkischen Stämme Süd-Sibiriens*, i. (St. Petersburg, 1866) pp. 285 *sq*.

[3] C. Fillingham Coxwell, *Siberian and other Folk-tales* (London, N.D.), p. 285, referring to *The Living Past*, 1891, p. 70 (a periodical of the Imperial Russian Geographical Society).

the Buriats of Southern Siberia. They say that formerly
men knew not fire. They could not cook their victuals and
went about hungry and cold. A swallow took pity on them
and stole fire for them from Tengri, who is the Sky. But
Tengri was angry at the bird and shot at it with his bow.
The arrow missed the body of the bird but pierced its tail ;
and that is why the tail of the swallow is still cleft in two.
It was the swallow that brought fire to men, who ever since
have been happy and would not hurt any swallow. For the
same reason people are glad when a swallow builds its nest
in their hut.[1]

The Semas, a Naga tribe of Assam, have a tradition of a
time when fire was not known, and they believe that in those
days men had long hair like apes to keep out the cold. But
Mr. J. H. Hutton, who has given us a very full and valuable
account of the tribe, never met with a Sema who could say
how fire was discovered. However, their neighbours the
Changs know all about it. They say that the discovery was
made by two women who oversaw a tiger making fire by
pulling a thong under his claw, for till then mankind had
depended for what fire they could get on the good will of
the tiger [2] And still the Semas make fire in the very way
which they learned from the tiger, by pulling a sliver of
pliant bamboo sharply to and fro through a forked stick till
the tinder placed under the fork begins to smoulder, when
it is blown into a flame.[3] However, according to another
Naga tribe it was not a tiger but an ape whom a woman
detected in the act of making fire.[4]

This latter version of the myth is accepted by the Aos, a
Naga tribe which borders the Semas on the north. They
say that long, long ago fire and water fought. Fire could not
stand before water, and fled and hid in bamboos and stones,
where it lurks to this day. But some day they will fight again,
and fire will put forth all its strength, and the Great Fire
(*Molomi*), which old men spoke of long before the missionaries
came into the land, will sweep up from the banks of the

---

[1] Garma Sandschejew, " Weltan-
schauung und Schamanismus der
Alaren-Burjaten," *Anthropos*, xxiii.
(1928) p. 970.

[2] J. H. Hutton, *The Sema Nagas*

(London, 1921), p. 43.

[3] J. H. Hutton, *The Sema Nagas*,
p. 42.

[4] J. H. Hutton, *The Sema Nagas*
p. 43 note [1].

Brahmaputra and burn everything on earth. Yet in the end water will be the conqueror, for a great flood will follow the great fire and swamp the world for ever. Now so it was that, when fire fled from water, nobody but the grasshopper saw where it had taken refuge. With his great staring eyes he saw everything, and marked where fire went and hid in stone and bamboo. In those days men and monkeys alike had hair. And the grasshopper told the monkey where the fire was lying hid, and the monkey made fire come out of a bamboo fire-thong. But man was watchful and stole the fire from the monkey. So nowadays monkeys have no fire, and must keep themselves warm as best they can with their fur. Man, on the other hand, has lost his fur because he no longer needs it, having got fire instead. It is because fire hid in bamboo and stones that the Aos to this day make fire both with a bamboo fire-thong and with hard stone and iron. The fire-thong is of the ordinary Naga type. The end of a dry stick is split and a stone inserted in the fork. Tinder, consisting of fine shavings or cotton wool, is put on the ground, and the fork of the stick is held firmly on it with the foot. The operator slips a bamboo thong under the fork, and, holding one end of the thong in either hand, pulls it rapidly backwards and forwards. In less than half a minute the tinder catches fire.[1]

In the foregoing Ao narrative the war between fire and water has its parallel in myths which, as we have seen, are told by the natives of Ongtong Java and the Gilbert Islands, and the Toradyas of Celebes,[2] and we shall meet with another parallel to it in a myth told by the Sakalava and Tsimihety of Madagascar.[3]

The Loris of Baluchistan, who are blacksmiths by hereditary calling, look upon fire with special reverence as God's gift to David, which the deity produced from purgatory when David begged for the wherewithal to melt iron. They make fire by flint and steel.[4]

In Ceylon " the story current about the blue-black swallow-tailed fly-catcher (*Kawudu panikka*) and its mortal

---

[1] J. P. Mills, *The Ao Nagas* (London, 1926), pp. 100-101.
[2] Above, pp. 53 *sq.*, 88 *sqq.*, 94.

[3] See below, pp. 108 *sqq.*
[4] Denys Bray, *Ethnographic Survey of Baluchistan* (Bombay, 1913), i. 139.

enemy, the crow, is that the former, like Prometheus of old, brought down fire from heaven for the benefit of man. The crow, jealous of the honour, dipped its wings in water and shook the drippings over the flame, quenching it. Since that time there has been deadly enmity between the birds." [1]

[1] " The Folklore of Ceylon Birds," *Nature*, xxxvi. (1887) p. 381.

CHAPTER IX

THE ORIGIN OF FIRE IN MADAGASCAR

THE Sakalava and Tsimihety, who inhabit Analalava, a province of north-western Madagascar, give the following lucid account of the circumstances which led to fire being stored up in wood and stone, from which it can be elicited by the friction of the one and the percussion of the other.

They say that formerly flames were naturally to be found everywhere, for the Sun had sent them to protect the earth, and they were, so to say, the soldiers of the Sun. Nothing here below could withstand them, so they were very proud of their power and very cruel.

Above the earth the Thunder reigned supreme. In summer every afternoon he thundered with a loud crash. The flames were all surprised at the prodigious noise which they heard in the sky. "What is that?" said they. "He who makes such a din must be very strong and powerful. Nevertheless we will send ambassadors to declare war on him."

An ambassador was sent, and Thunder, who was very proud, fell into a rage and answered, "Till now I have never provoked anybody and have never done any harm. I made my lightnings flash and my thunder peal for my own entertainment. But since you come to challenge me in the air, which is my domain, I accept your challenge. We will make war on each other, and the war will be terrible."

A day was fixed for the encounter, and so was the place. It was a great bare tableland on the top of a mountain. On the appointed day the flames mustered on the spot and shot up with tremendous violence, rolling torrents of thick black smoke and hissing and screaming withal. Thunder likewise bestirred himself to the utmost. Though it was still broad day, his flashes were dazzling and of every hue—blue, red, green, and violet—all the colours of the rainbow ; and the roar of the thunder was deafening. Thrice Thunder fell down on the flames and scattered them, but without extinguishing their fire. On the contrary, it seemed as if they gained fresh strength from the contact and returned to the assault like giants refreshed. At last the two adversaries, worn out by their exertions, patched up a truce and retired to staunch their wounds and repair their losses.

A few days afterwards the battle began again as fiercely as before. The flames were decimated, and Thunder was reduced to a deplorable state, but still there was neither victor nor vanquished.

Thunder was now very angry indeed. How could he get the better of his enemies ? He bethought him of his old friends the clouds. He assembled them and addressed them in a long harangue, imploring their assistance. They promised their aid. Thunder thereupon in his turn declared war on the flames and appointed as the field of battle the tableland where the two preceding combats had been fought.

On the day appointed great black clouds were seen advancing from the four corners of the sky. Thunder hid behind them and from time to time rumbled a muffled peal. The flames were at first daunted at the strange sight of the clouds lowering thus menacingly overhead. But they were brave, and taking their courage in both hands they marched intrepidly to the attack. They formed a dense and serried mass, the bravest climbing up on the shoulders of their fellows in order to grapple with the aerial foe. But Thunder, esteeming prudence the better part of valour, was content to launch his bolts from behind the screen of the clouds without exposing his person to the fire of the enemy. On the other hand, no sooner had the clouds arrived at a point of the sky directly above the flames than they opened their sluices and let fall on the heads of the foe the whole volume of water with which they were charged.

It was now for the flames a case of devil take the hindmost. Their king was the first to turn tail, and his troops naturally followed the example of their leader. The officers in command sought safety in the bowels of the mountains, and

there they have stayed down to this day, though they sometimes come forth from the crevices which they have opened
up for themselves on the tops of some of the mountains.
That is the origin of volcanoes. As for the common soldiers,
they hid in a great many things such as wood, iron, and hard
stones. That is why you can get fire by rubbing one dry
stick against another ; and that, too, is why sparks leap out
when you knock flint and steel together. Such is the origin
of the fire which man makes for his use, according to the
Sakalava and Tsimihety.[1]

[1] A. Dandouau, *Contes populaires
des Sakalava et des Tsimihety* (Alger,
1922), pp. 110-112. The Sakalava
kindle fire by means of the fire-drill,
which consists of two pieces of *Urena*
Lobata (Linnaeus) : the drill or upper
part is called male, and the lower part
or board is called female. See A.
Dandouau, *op. cit.* p. 136 note [1].

CHAPTER X

THE Bergdama or Bergdamara, as they are more commonly called, of South-west Africa, say that in the days when people had not yet fire it was once on a time very cold on earth. Then a man said to his wife, " To-night I will cross the river, and over there I will fetch me a firebrand from the village of the lion." His wife warned him not to go, but go he did, waded through the flowing river, and entered the lion's hut. The lion sat with the lioness and their children in a circle round a flickering fire, and the lion's children were gnawing at human bones.

The stranger was shown to the place of honour opposite to the door and behind the fire. He would rather have remained sitting at the entrance in order to be able to bolt with a firebrand. So, while the talk went on, he kept edging gradually sideways till he sat close to the door, and as he did so he kept his eye on a good firebrand. Suddenly he jumped up, with one hand threw the lion's children into the fire, snatched the brand with the other, and rushed with it out of the house.

The lion and lioness sprang up to pursue him. But they had first to rescue their children before they could follow up the hue and cry ; so the thief got a good start, and when the pursuers reached the bank he was already on the other side of the stream. They shrank from plunging into the water, and so gave up the pursuit. But the thief brought the firebrand to his hut, collected firewood of all sorts, and while he lit his fire he said, " Thou fire shalt henceforth be in all wood." Ever since that night men also have had their fire. At the present day the Bergdama prefer to kindle fire by matches, but in case of need they still obtain it by the friction of wood, using for the purpose the fire-drill, of which they call the borer of hard wood the male and the flat board of soft wood the female.[1]

The Thonga, a tribe of South-eastern Africa, whose territory lies about Delagoa Bay, give the name of Lilala-humba to the first male ancestor of humanity, and the name signifies " the one who brings a glowing cinder in a shell." [2] The meaning of the name is explained by a story told by the Hlengwe clan. They say that Tshauke, their first king, took as his wife the daughter of another chief belonging to the Sono tribe. Now the Sono knew how to cook their food, but the Hlengwe did not, because they were still ignorant of fire and therefore ate their porridge raw. However, the son of King Tshauke stole a glowing cinder from the Sono and brought it home in a big shell. The Sono were angry and declared war on the Hlengwe ; but the Hlengwe, strengthened by the cooked food which they had eaten, gained the victory. The son of Tshauke was then named Shioki-sha-humba, " he who brings fire in a shell." [3] From this we may perhaps infer that in the opinion of these people the first ancestor of humanity similarly conveyed or stole the first fire in a shell ; but from whom he borrowed or stole it does not appear.

The Ba-ila, a tribe of Northern Rhodesia, tell how the Mason-Wasp fetched fire from God. They say that formerly

---

[1] H. Vedder, *Die Bergdama* (Hamburg, 1923), i. 20-22.

[2] Henri A. Junod, *The Life of a South African Tribe*, Second Edition (London, 1927), i. 21. The Thonga make fire by means of the fire-drill, using apparently for the purpose the wood of the *bulolo*, a kind of hibiscus. The mode of operation is as follows : " A dry branch of the tree is secured, from half an inch to an inch thick, and cut into two pieces, each of about 18 inches in length ; one half is called the wife (*nsati*), the other half, the husband (*nuna*). The first piece, the female, is laid on the ground and a notch is made in it with a knife ; the notch is cut in two movements : first on the upper part of the wood, secondly on the side of it. The male

is then somewhat rounded, inserted perpendicularly in the notch, held firmly between the palms of the hands and made to revolve by a rapid motion of the hands from top to bottom. The operator having reached the bottom of the male at once starts again from the top ; thus the friction continues without an interval. The motion widens the notch in the female to such an extent that the male penetrates and begins to burn it : the ashes find their way out by the lateral notch ; a little dry grass has been placed there and soon begins to smoulder. An expert obtains fire after six or seven consecutive frictions, especially when using *bulolo* " (Henri A. Junod, *op. cit.* ii. 34 *sq.*).

[3] Henri A. Junod, *op. cit.* i. 24.

Vulture, Fish-eagle, and Crow were without fire, for there was no fire on earth   So, needing fire, all the birds assembled together and asked, " Whence shall we get fire ? "   Some of the birds said, " Perhaps from God." Thereupon Mason-Wasp volunteered, saying, " Who will go with me to God ? " Vulture answered and said, "We will go with you, I and Fish-eagle and Crow."

So on the morrow they took leave of all the other birds, saying, " We are going to see whether we can get fire from God." Then they flew off.   After they had spent ten days on the road, there fell to earth some small bones—that was Vulture ; later there also fell to earth some other small bones—that was Fish-eagle ; Mason-Wasp and Crow were left to go on alone.   When the second ten days were ended, there fell other small bones to earth—that was Crow.   Mason-Wasp was left to go on by himself.   When the third ten days were over, he was going along, reposing upon the clouds.   Nevertheless he never reached the summit of the sky.

As soon as God heard of it, He came to where Mason-Wasp was, and answering His question Mason-Wasp said, " No, Chief, I am not going anywhere particular, I have only come to beg some fire.   All my companions have stopped short ; but nevertheless I have persevered in coming, for I had set my heart upon arriving to where the Chief is."   Thereupon God answered him, saying, " Mason-Wasp, since you have reached Me, you shall be chief over all the birds and reptiles on earth.   You, now, I give a blessing.   You shall not have to beget children.   When you desire a child, go and look into a grain-stalk and you will find an insect whose name is *Ngongwa*.   When you have found him, take and carry him into a house.   When you arrive in the house, look out for the fireplace where men cook, and build there a dwelling for your child *Ngongwa*.   When you have finished building, put him in and let him remain there.   When many days have elapsed, just go and have a look at him ; and one day you will find he has changed and become just as you are yourself." So it is to-day ; Mason-Wasp builds a house, looking for the fireplace, just as he was commanded by God.[1]

[1] Edwin W. Smith and Andrew Murray Dale, *The Ila-speaking Peoples*   *of Northern Rhodesia* (London, 1920), ii. 345 *sq.*

In explanation of this story the authors who have recorded it write as follows : " The Mason-Wasp, the Prometheus of the Ba-ila, with its indigo-blue wings, yellow abdomen, and black and orange legs, is a common object in Central Africa. It builds its cell of mud not only in the fireplace, as the tale narrates, but also (and this is a great nuisance) on walls, books, and pictures in one's dwelling.   In the cell it lays its eggs, together with a caterpillar or grub, and seals them up ; then it builds other cells, until quite a large unsightly lump of clay is left on the wall.   As the young grubs hatch out they eat the insects which have been benumbed, but not killed, by the sting of their parent.   We have here an interesting example of how the observation of natives is correct up to a certain point; but not taking into consideration, because they have not noticed, all the facts, the conclusion they draw is wrong.   They suppose *Ngongwa* to metamorphose into a Mason-Wasp ; and this tale is to explain why it is so, as well as to account for the domestic fire." [1]

The Baluba are a tribe or nation who occupy a large territory in the southern basin of the Congo.   They make fire by means of the fire-drill ; and they say that when the Great Spirit, Kabezya Mpungu, created the first man, whom they call Kyomba, he stuck the seeds of all edible plants in his hair, and placing in his hånds wood and tinder, taught him how to extract fire from them and to cook his food. [2]

The Bakuba or Bushongo, a tribe, or rather nation, who occupy a territory between the rivers Sankuru and Kasai in the southern part of the Congo valley, have a tradition that in the olden times their ancestors obtained their fire from conflagrations kindled by lightning, but did not know how to make it for themselves.   However, in the reign of one of their kings, by name Muchu Mushanga, there lived a certain man called Kerikeri, who acquired the art of producing fire. For Bumba, by whom the Bushongo mean God, appeared one night in a dream to Kerikeri and told him to go along a certain road, to break the branches of a certain tree, and to keep them carefully.   The man did so, and when the branches

[1] E. W. Smith and A. M Dale, *op. cit.* ii. 346 *sq.*

[2] Colle, *Les Baluba*, i. (Brussels, 1913) p. 102.

were quite dry, Bumba appeared to him again in a dream, congratulated him on his obedience, and taught him how to make fire by friction.   Kerikeri kept the secret to himself, and when all the fires of the village chanced to have gone out, he sold his fire at a very high price to his neighbours.   All the men, both wise and foolish, tried to worm the secret out of him, but in vain.   Now the king, Muchu Mushanga, had a very beautiful daughter, named Katenge, and he said to her, " If you can discover this man's secret, you shall be honoured and shall sit among the elders, like a man."   So the fair princess made advances to Kerikeri, and he fell madly in love with her.   When she perceived that, she ordered all the fires in the village to be put out, and sent word by a slave to Kerikeri, that he was to expect her that night in his hut.   When all the world was asleep, the princess glided softly to Kerikeri's hut and knocked at the door.   The night was very dark, Kerikeri opened the door to her, and entering she sat down and remained silent.   " Why so silent ? " asked her lover, " do not you love me?"   " How can I think of loving," she answered, " when I am shivering in your house ?   Go and fetch fire that I may see you, and my heart will warm again." Kerikeri ran to borrow fire from his neighbours, but, obedient to the orders of the princess, they had all put out their fires, and Kerikeri had to return without any.   In vain he entreated her to gratify his passion ;   she insisted that he must first kindle a fire.   At last he gave way, fetched his fire-sticks, and lit the fire by means of them in her presence, while she watched him attentively.   Then she laughed and said, " Did you think that I, the daughter of a king, loved you for your own sake ?   It was your secret that I wished to discover, and now that the fire is lit you may get a female slave to put it out." Then she rose, fled from the house, revealed her discovery to the whole of the village, and remarked to her father, " Where a powerful king would fail, an artful woman will succeed ! " Such was the origin of fire-making, and such is the origin of the office of Katenge among the Bushongo ; for to this day there is amongst the highest councillors a woman who is great among the great and bears the title of Katenge.   In time of peace she wears a bow-string as an ornament round her neck ;   but if the country is in peril she removes it and hands it to the commander of the army, who then sallies forth and destroys the enemy.[1]

A very different story of the origin of fire is told by the Basongo Meno, a group of tribes whose territory lies to the north of the Sankuru and Kasai rivers, and who have been in relations with the Bushongo for many years. They say that from the earliest times they have made their fishing-traps out of the ribs of the raphia palm. One day a man, constructing such a trap, wished to bore a hole in the end of one of the ribs, and he used a small pointed stick for the purpose. In the process of boring the rib fire was elicited, and this method of procuring fire has been employed ever since, whenever it is needed. Hence large plantations of the raphia palm are maintained by the people to supply them with fire-sticks and also with the materials which they use for weaving.[2]

The Boloki or Bangala, a tribe of the Upper Congo, tell of an unsuccessful attempt to procure fire in the early days of the world. They say that there was a time when all the birds and animals lived in the sky   One day it was very rainy and so cold that all the birds and beasts were shivering. So the birds said to the dog, " Go down and fetch us some fire to warm ourselves." The dog descended, but seeing plenty of bones and bits of fish lying about on the ground he forgot to take. the fire to the shivering birds. The birds and beasts waited a while, but when no dog appeared they sent the fowl to hasten him with the fire. However, when the fowl reached the earth, and beheld plenty of palm-nuts, pea-nuts, maize, and other good things, he did not trouble either to hurry the laggard dog or to take any fire himself to his comrades up aloft. That is why of an evening you can hear a bird singing notes which sound like *Nsusu akende bombo ! nsusu akende bombo !* which means, " The fowl has become a slave ! the fowl has become a slave ! " And the heron sometimes sits on a tree near a village and cries, *Mbwa owa ! mbwa owa !* which means, " Dog, you die ! dog, you die ! " The reason why these birds jeer at and abuse the dog and the fowl is

[1] E. Torday et T. A. Joyce, *Les Bushongo* (Brussels, 1910), pp. 236 *sq.* ; E. Torday, *Camp and Tramp in African Wilds* (London, 1913), pp. 292-297.

[2] E. Torday et T. A. Joyce, *Les Bushongo*, pp. 275 *sq.*

because these creatures left their friends to shiver in the cold, while they enjoyed themselves in warmth and plenty.[1]

The Bakongo, a tribe of the Lower Congo, say that fire came first from above by means of lightning, which struck a tree and set it on fire. As for the artificial production of fire, they affirm that fire was first elicited by the friction of wood and afterwards by the concussion of flint and steel. They also tell a legend how that formerly there was no fire on earth, and a man sent a jackal, which then was tame and lived in the villages, to where the sun sets to bring some fire from it ; but the jackal found so many good things there that he never returned again to the abode of man. The people say among themselves that far away to the north there are whole tribes who know nothing about fire and eat their food uncooked and their meat raw ; but they themselves have never seen such folk, they have only heard about them in their talks around the evening fire.[2]

In Loango they say that once on a time the spider span a long, long thread, and that the wind caught one end of the thread and carried it up to the sky. Then the woodpecker climbed up the thread and pecking at the celestial vault made those holes in it which we call stars. After the woodpecker, man climbed up the thread to the sky and fetched down fire. But some say that man found fire at the place where fiery tears had fallen from the sky.[3]

The Ekoi of Southern Nigeria, on the border of the Cameroons, say that in the beginning of the world the Sky God, Obassi Osaw, made everything, but he did not give fire to the people who were on earth   Etim 'Ne said to the Lame Boy, " What is the use of Obassi Osaw sending us here without any fire ? Go therefore and ask him to give us some." So the Lame Boy set out.

Obassi Osaw was very angry when he got the message, and sent the boy back quickly to earth to reprove Etim 'Ne for what he had asked. In those days the Lame Boy had not become lame, but could walk like other people. When

---

[1] John H. Weeks, *Among Congo Cannibals* (London, 1913), p. 209.
[2] John H. Weeks, " Notes on Some Customs of the Lower Congo People," *Folk-lore*, xx. (1909) pp. 475, 476;

id., Among the Primitive Bakongo (London, 1914), pp. 292 *sq.*
[3] *Die Loango-Expedition*, iii. 2, von E. Pechuël-Loesche (Stuttgart, 1907), p. 135.

Etim 'Ne heard that he had angered Obassi Osaw, he set out himself for Obassi Osaw's town and said, " Please forgive me for what I did yesterday. It was by accident." But Obassi would not pardon him, though he stayed for three days begging forgiveness. Then he went home.

When Etim reached his town, the boy laughed at him. " Are you a chief," said he, " yet could get no fire ? I myself will go and bring it to you. If they will give me none, I will steal it." That very day the lad set out. He reached the house of Obassi at evening time and found the people preparing food. He helped with the work, and when Obassi began to eat, the boy knelt down humbly till the meal was ended.

The master saw that the boy was useful and did not drive him out of the house. After he had served for some days, Obassi called to him and said, " Go to the house of my wives, and ask them to send me a lamp." The boy gladly did as he was bidden, for it was in the house of the wives that fire was kept. He touched nothing, but waited until the lamp was given him, then brought it back with all speed. Once, after he had stayed for many days among the servants, Obassi sent him again, and this time one of the wives said, " You can light the lamp at the fire." So saying, she went into her house and left him alone. The boy took a brand and lighted the lamp, then he wrapped the brand in plantain leaves and tied it up in his cloth, carried the lamp to his master and said, " I wish to go out for a certain purpose." Obassi answered, " You can go." The boy went to the bush outside the town where some dry wood was lying. He laid the brand amongst it, and blew till it caught fire. Then he covered it with plantain stems and leaves to hide the smoke, and went back to the house. Obassi asked, " Why have you been so long ? " and the lad answered, " I did not feel well."

That night when all the people were asleep, the thief tied his cloth together and crept to the end of the town where the fire was hidden. He found it burning, and taking with him a glowing brand and some firewood, he set out homeward. When he reached the earth once more, he went to Etim and said, "Here is the fire which I promised to bring you. Send for some wood, and I will show you what we must do."

So the first fire was made on earth. Obassi Osaw looked
down from his house in the sky and saw the smoke rising.
He said to his eldest son Akpan Obassi, " Go, ask the boy if
it is he who has stolen the fire." Akpan came down to earth,
and asked as his father had bidden him. The lad confessed,
" I was the one who stole the fire. The reason why I hid it
was because I feared." Akpan replied, " I bring you a
message. Up till now you have been able to walk. From
to-day you will not be able to do so any more." That is the
reason why the Lame Boy cannot walk. He it was who
first brought fire to earth from Obassi's home in the sky.[1]

The Lendu, a tribe of Central Africa, to the north-west of
Lake Albert, have a tradition that their ancestors migrated
into their present territory from the plains in the north, and
on their arrival they found dwarfs in occupation of the country,
who retreated before the invaders. The Lendu brought
with them fire from their old home, but the dwarfs were
unacquainted with the use of it, and looked with envy on the
newcomers, who warmed themselves at the cheerful blaze and
ate their food cooked instead of raw. One night the dwarfs
stole some of the fire and kindled it for their own benefit
in the forest. They also imparted it to the Wassongora
(Ndjali), who had immigrated into the country from the south,
and who were likewise ignorant of fire.[2]

The Kikuyu of British East Africa tell the following story
of the origin of fire. They say that a long time ago a man
borrowed a spear from a neighbour to kill a porcupine which
was destroying his crops. He lay in wait in the field, and at
last speared a porcupine, but the animal was only wounded,
and running away with the spear in its body disappeared
down a burrow The man then went to the owner of the
spear and told him that the spear was lost, but the owner
insisted on having it back again. The borrower bought a
new spear and offered it to the owner as a substitute ; but the
other refused the offer and persisted in his demand for the
original spear. So in order to recover it the borrower crawled
down the porcupine's burrow until he found himself, to his

---

[1] P. Amaury Talbot, *In the Shadow
of the Bush* (London, 1912), pp.
370 *sq.*

[2] Franz Stuhlmann, *Mit Emin
Pascha ins Herz von Afrika* (Berlin,
1894), pp. 464 *sq.*

surprise, in a place where many people were seated cooking food by a fire. They asked him what he wanted and he told them of his errand. Thereupon they invited him to stay and eat with them ; but he was afraid, and said that he must go back with the spear, which he saw lying there. They made no effort to keep him, but told him to climb up the roots of a *mugumu* tree, which penetrated down into the cavern, and they said that he would soon come out into the upper world. Moreover, they gave him some fire to take back with him. So he took the spear and the fire, and climbed out as he was told. That is the way in which fire is said to have been brought to men ; before that time people ate their food raw. When the man reached his friends, he returned the spear to its owner, saying, " You have given me a great deal of trouble to recover your spear ; and if you want to get some of this fire, which you see is going away into smoke, you will have to climb up the smoke and get it back for me." The owner of the spear tried and tried to climb up the smoke, but he could not do it. Then the elders came and intervened and said, " We will make the following arrangement : fire shall be for the use of all, and because you have brought it, you shall be our chief." The under-world referred to in this tale is called *Miri ya mikeongoi*.[1]

The Wachagga, who inhabit the great mountain of Kilimanjaro in East Africa, say that in the olden time men knew not fire. So they had to eat their food raw, even bananas, just like the baboons. But one day the lads drove the kine as usual out to grass and took their food with them. There they cut arrows and played with them. And one of them set his arrow upright on a log of wood and twirled it between his hands. The shaft of the arrow grew hot and he called to the others, " Who will let me give him a dab ? " The others came and he dabbed at them with the hot end of the shaft ; then they shrieked and ran away. After that he twirled the shaft harder than ever to make it hotter and dab at them again. But now the others helped him, saying, " We will make it right hot." So they twirled away like anything, and lo ! smoke rose from the end of the shaft, and some dry grass, that lay under it, began to smoulder.

[1] C. W. Hobley, *Bantu Beliefs and Magic* (London, 1922), pp. 264 *sq*.

The lads brought more grass to increase the smoke, and while they gazed at it a flame shot up. Soon there was a blazing fire which burned the grass and consumed the bushes, making a noise like *wo-wo-wo-wo-wo*, just as if a whirlwind were sweeping by.

The people of the neighbourhood ran together, gazed, and cried, " Who are they who have brought us this magic ? " They found the lads and shouted at them, " Whence did you get this magic ? " They were very angry, and the lads were afraid. But they took the sticks and showed the men how they had twirled the shaft, and then the flame burst out again. The elders cried, " What are you about ? You have brought us a thing that is eating up all our grass and trees ! "

However, they learned that fire was good when the lads sought their food among the ashes. At first the lads said, " See, all our food is destroyed by Wowo ! " for they called the fire *wowo* because that was the sound it made. But when in their hunger they bit the roasted bananas, they perceived that the fruit tasted much sweeter than before. So they lit the fire again and toasted bananas at it, and again the fruit was sweeter than of old. So all the folk round about carried Wowo (fire) to their homes and roasted their food at it.

And whenever a stranger came and ate of their sweet food, he would ask, " How do you make it like that ? " Then they showed him the fire, and the stranger would go home and fetch wherewithal he might buy the fire. And if anybody met him and asked him, " Whither away with that goat of yours ? " he would say, " I am going to the magician Wowo to get *wowo* from him." Thus many people came and bought fire and spread the use of it in all lands. And the piece of soft wood they called *kipongoro*, and the stick that they twirled they called *ovito*. These two sticks they used to keep ready on the floor of their huts ; for they said, " When the long night comes that shuts people in, nobody can fetch fire from his neighbour." [1]

The Shilluk, a tribe of the White Nile, say that fire comes from the land of the Great Spirit (*pan jwok*). There was a time when nobody knew of fire. People used to warm their food in the sun ; and the upper part of the victuals,

[1] Bruno Gutmann, *Volksbuch der Wadschagga* (Leipzig, 1914), pp. 159 *sq.*

which was thus cooked, was eaten by the men ; and the under part, which remained uncooked, was eaten by the women. But one day a dog stole a piece of flesh that had been roasted by fire in the land of the Great Spirit, and he brought it to the people. The Shilluk tasted it and found it much better than raw flesh. So in order to procure the fire they swathed the tail of the dog in dry straw and drove him back to the land of the Great Spirit. On arriving there the dog rolled, after his wont, on the ash-heap, and the straw on his tail caught fire in the still glowing ashes. Howling with pain, the dog tore back to the land of the Shilluk and rolled in the dry grass to ease his agony. But the grass in its turn caught fire, and from the conflagration which ensued the Shilluk derived the fire which ever since they have kept glowing or smouldering on their ash-heaps.[1]

[1] W. Hofmayr, *Die Schilluk* (St. Gabriel, Mödling bei Wien, 1925), p. 366.

CHAPTER XI

THE ORIGIN OF FIRE IN SOUTH AMERICA

THE Lengua Indians of the Paraguayan Chaco tell the following story of the origin of fire among men. They say that in early times, being unable to produce fire, men were compelled to eat their food raw. One day an Indian had been out hunting, but had been unsuccessful all the morning ; so towards mid-day, in order to stay the pangs of hunger, he repaired to the vicinity of a swamp to gather some snails. While he was eating them, his attention was attracted to a bird coming out from the swamp with a snail in its bill. This it seemed to deposit near a large tree some little way off. It then returned to the swamp and brought up another snail, and repeated the process several times. The Indian also noticed that from the spot where the bird placed the snails there arose, as it were, a thin column of smoke. His curiosity was aroused, and the next time the bird flew away he proceeded cautiously towards the place where the smoke had risen. There he observed a number of sticks, set point to point, the ends quite red and giving forth heat. Drawing still nearer, he saw some snails placed close to the sticks. Being hungry, he tasted the cooked snails, and finding them delicious he made up his mind that he would never eat raw snails again.

So he seized some of the sticks and ran off with them to his village, where he told his friends of his discovery. They at once got a supply of dry wood from the forest in order to keep alive this invaluable acquisition, which they henceforth called *tathla*, or fire. That night they cooked their meat and vegetables for the first time, and gradually found new uses for their discovery.

But when the bird returned to the place where it had left the snails, and discovered the loss of its fire, it was filled with rage and determined to be revenged on the thief, and it was all the angrier because it could not produce more fire. Soaring up into the sky, it circled about in search of the thief, and to its amazement saw the people of the village sitting around the stolen treasure, enjoying its warmth and cooking their food by it. Filled with thoughts of vengeance, it retired to the forest, where it created a thunderstorm, accompanied by terrible lightning, which did much damage and terrified the people. Hence, whenever it thunders, it is a sign that the thunder-bird is angry and is seeking to punish the Indians by fire from the sky ; for ever since the bird lost its fire, it has had to eat its food raw. The missionary who records this story adds : " It is curious that the Indians should believe such a fable as this, since they themselves produce fire by friction ; nor are they particularly careful to keep a fire alight when not required. Neither are they afraid of either thunder or lightning." [1]

This Lengua story records, in mythical form, a belief that men first learned the use of fire from a conflagration kindled by lightning ; for it is a common notion with the American Indians that thunder and lightning are caused by the flapping of the wings and the flashing of the eyes of a gigantic bird.[2]

The Choroti Indians of the Gran Chaco say that long ago all the world known to them was laid waste by a great conflagration, which destroyed all the Chorotis except one man and one woman, who saved themselves by taking refuge in a hole in the earth. When it was all over and the fire had gone out, the man and woman dug their way out of the earth, but they had no fire. However, the black vulture had carried a firebrand to his nest; the firebrand had kindled the nest, and the nest had kindled the tree, so that the fire smouldered in the trunk. The black vulture presented some of the fire to the Choroti man, and since that time the Chorotis have

[1] W. B. Grubb, *An Unknown People in an Unknown Land* (London, 1911), pp. 97-99. Compare G. Kurze, " Sitten und Gebräuche der Lengua-Indianer," *Mitteilungen der Geographischen Gesellschaft zu Jena*, xxiii.

(1905) p. 17.

[2] J. G. Müller, *Geschichte der Amerikanischen Urreligionen*[2] (Bâle, 1867), pp. 120 *sq.* The evidence could easily be multiplied.

possessed fire. All the Chorotis are descended from that
man and woman.[1]

The Tapiete Indians, another tribe of the Gran Chaco,
say that the black vulture obtained fire by means of lightning
from heaven In those days the Tapietes had no fire.
However, a small bird (the *cáca*) stole fire for them (from the
black vulture ?), but the fire went out, so the Tapietes had no
fire wherewith to roast the flesh of the game which they killed.
They were very cold. Then the frog took pity on them and
went to the fire of the black vulture and sat down there.
While the black vulture was warming himself at the fire, the
frog took two sparks and hid them in his mouth. Thereupon
he hopped away and conveyed the fire to the Tapietes.
Since then the Tapietes have had fire. But the fire of the
black vulture was out, for the frog had stolen it all. So the
black vulture sat down with his hands over his head and
wept, and all the birds assembled to prevent anybody from
giving fire to the black vulture.[2]

The Matacos Indians of the Gran Chaco say that the
jaguar was in possession of fire and guarded it before man had
procured it for himself. One day when all the Matacos were
out fishing, a guinea-pig paid a visit to the jaguars, bringing
them a fish ; but when he tried to go up to the fire and get
somé of it, the jaguar in charge of the fire would not let him.
Nevertheless the guinea-pig contrived to steal some of the
fire and to hide it. The jaguar asked him what he was taking
away with him, but the guinea-pig said that he was taking
nothing. However, the guinea-pig carried away some of the
fire and with it he kindled a great fire, at which he roasted
the fish in a twinkling. And when the fishermen went away,
the fire caught the grass and it began to burn. The jaguars
saw it burning, and they came running and brought water
with them to put out the fire. When the fishermen returned
home, they kindled a fire by means of the firebrands that they
had taken with them, and since then the fire has never gone
out ; no Mataco Indian is without fire.[3]

The Toba Indians of the Bolivian Gran Chaco say that

---

[1] E. Nordenskiöld, *Indianerleben.
El Gran Chaco* (Leipsic, 1912), pp.
21 *sq.*

[2] E. Nordenskiöld, *op. cit.* pp. 313
sq.

[3] E. Nordenskiöld, *op. cit.* pp. 110 *sq.*

long ago a great fire devastated the whole earth, so that nothing was left. At that time there did not yet exist any Tobas. The first Tobas emerged from the earth, seized a brand from the great fire and carried it away. Thereafter other Toba men likewise rose from the earth. The men thus had fire, and they maintained life by a root which the Tobas call *tannara*. They moreover caught fish in the river   But there did not yet exist any Toba woman.[1]

The Chiriguanos, a once powerful tribe of south-eastern Bolivia, tell of a great flood in which the whole of their tribe, except a little boy and girl, were drowned and all fires on earth were extinguished. How then without fire could the children cook the fish which they caught ?. In this emergency a large toad came to the help of the children. Before the flood had submerged the whole earth, that prudent creature had taken the precaution of hiding in a hole, taking with him in his mouth some live coals, which he contrived to keep alight all the time of the deluge by blowing on them with his breath. When he saw that the surface of the ground was dry again, he hopped out of the hole with the live coals in his mouth, and making straight for the children he bestowed on them the gift of fire. Thus they were able to roast the fish which they caught and to warm their chilled bodies. In time they grew up, and from their union the whole tribe of the Chiriguanos is descended.[2]

In the sixteenth century the Tupinamba Indians about Cape Frio in Brazil used to relate how the sky, the earth, the birds, and the animals were made by a great being whom they called Monan, and to whom, so we are told, they ascribed the same perfections that we attribute to God. He lived familiarly with men until, disgusted by their wickedness and ingratitude, he withdrew from them and caused the fire of heaven, which they called *tatta*, to descend and burn up everything on the face of the earth. Only one man, named Irin-magé, was saved, having been transported by Monan to heaven or some other place, where he escaped the fury

[1] R. Karsten, *The Toba Indians of the Bolivian Gran Chaco* (Abo, 1923), p. 104 (*Acta Academiae Aboensis, Humaniora* iv.).

[2] Bernardino de Nino, *Etnografia*

Chiriguana (La Paz, Bolivia, 1912), pp. 131-133. I have cited this story in *Folk-lore in the Old Testament*, i. 272 *sq.*

of the flames.   At his entreaties Monan caused it to rain
so heavily that the conflagration was extinguished, and the
water, which had fallen in the form of rain, became the sea,
the saltness of which is due to the cinders that remained
after the great fire.   According to another version of the
story, two brothers with their wives were saved from the
great flood.   With regard to the origin, or rather the recovery, of fire after the great flood, the Indians said that
during the catastrophe Monan saved the fire by placing it
between the shoulders of a large and heavy beast (the sloth),
from which the two brothers extracted it when the waters of
the deluge had subsided.   To this day, said the Indians, the
beast bears the marks of the fire on its shoulders.   In con-
firmation of which the early French writer who reports the
story observes that, " to tell the truth, if you look at this beast
from a distance, as I have sometimes done out of curiosity
when they pointed it out to me, you would suppose that it is
all on fire, so bright is the colour towards the shoulders ; and
near at hand you would suppose that it was burned in the said
place.   And this mark appears only on the males.   Down to
the present time the savages call this impression of fire on the
said beast *tatta-ou pap*, that is to say, ' fire and hearth.' " [1]

Thus the Indians of Cape Frio, like many other savages,
told their story of the origin of fire in part at least in order to
explain the peculiar colouring of an animal which appeared to
them to have been produced by the action of fire.

The Apapocuva Indians, a branch of the Guarani stock,
to which the Tupinamba Indians also belong, relate how the
great hero Nanderyquey stole fire from the vultures with the
help of a toad.   They say that, having secured the assistance
of the toad, the fire-eater, he laid himself down as if he were
dead.   So the vultures, who were then the Lords of Fire,
flocked about him and prepared to make a meal of the
supposed carrion, and for this purpose they lit a fire at which
to cook the corpse.   But a falcon, sitting on a tree-stump

---

[1] André Thevet, *La Cosmographie Universelle* (Paris, 1575), ii. 913 [947] *sq.*, 915 [949].   The pages are wrongly numbered in this part of the book.   I have added the correct numbers in square brackets.   The passage is re-printed by A. Métraux in his book, *La Religion des Tupinamba* (Paris, 1928), p. 230, from which (p. 48) I gather that the beast referred to by Thevet is the sloth.

hard by, was on the watch and marked how the pretended dead man blinked with his eyes ; so he warned the vultures to beware. But the warning was lost on them, and without more ado they lifted up Nanderyquey and heaved him into the fire. At once the brawny hero struck out right and left and sent the glowing embers flying in all directions. The vultures fled in terror, but their chief bade them gather up the scattered and still smouldering embers. Nanderyquey now asked the toad whether he had swallowed the fire. The toad at first prevaricated, but Nanderyquey was peremptory and administered a dose to the creature which compelled him to spew up the embers, and from them the hero relit the fire.[1]

The Sipaia Indians, a tribe of central Brazil, in the basin of the Xingu river, similarly relate how a great tribal hero, whom they call Kumaphari the Younger, contrived to steal fire from a vulture by simulating death. They say that once a vulture (*Gavião de Anta*) came flying with a firebrand in his talons and mocked at Kumaphari because he had no fire. Then the hero pondered how he could get possession of the fire. He observed that the vulture, after perching on a tree, flew down and gorged on carrion. The sight suggested a plan to Kumaphari. He laid himself down on the ground, died and rotted   The vulture came with other birds of prey (*urubus*) to devour the putrid flesh, but he left his fire on a tree-stump so far away that Kumaphari could not reach it. The birds ate up the flesh and left nothing over but the bones. Then Kumaphari turned himself into a stag and died again. The other birds of prey (*urubus*) came to devour the dead stag, but the vulture was suspicious. " Do come," said the other birds, " he is dead."   " Dead indeed ! " answered the vulture, " he is still alive. Catch me going to him ! " At last Kumaphari opened his eyes a little. The vulture perceived it and cried, " See ! Didn't I tell you that he was still alive ? " So saying he took his firebrand and flew away with it. At last Kumaphari lay down on a great slab of stone and died yet again. He spread out his arms, and they penetrated like roots into the ground and then came forth

[1] C. Nimuendajú, " Die Sagen von der Erschaffung und Vernichtung der Welt als Grundlage der Religion der Apapocúva-Guarani," *Zeitschrift für Ethnologie*, xlvi. (1914) pp. 326 *sq.*

again in the shape of two bushes, each of them with five branches springing from a single point of the stem. When the vulture came to devour the carrion, says he to himself, " In these forked branches is a nice place for my fire." So saying he put the firebrand in Kumaphari's hand. The hero clutched it and jumped up : the fire was in his possession. But the vulture shrieked out, " You claim to be the son of your father, Kumaphari the Elder, and yet you do not know how to make fire ! The way is to lay sticks of *urukus* in the sun and then to twirl them one in the other." " Very good," quoth Kumaphari, " now I know that also ; but I prefer to keep the firebrand, you shall not have it again." [1]

The Bakairi, an Indian tribe of central Brazil, relate how in the early days of the world the two great twin brothers, Keri and Kami, procured fire at the bidding of their aunt Ewaki. At that time the Lord of Fire was the animal which naturalists call *Canis vetulus*. This animal had set a trap to catch fish. Keri and Kami went to the trap and found in it a *jejum* fish and a *caramujo* snail. So they concealed themselves by entering into these creatures, Keri assuming the form of the fish, and Kami turning into the snail. By and by the Lord of Fire (*Canis vetulus*) came along singing and kindled fire. Then he looked into the fish-trap, and finding the fish and the snail, he pulled them out and put them on the fire, intending to roast them. But the two brothers, in their guise of fish and snail, poured water on the fire. In a rage, the animal (*Canis vetulus*) tried to seize the snail, but it hopped into the river, fetched more water, and pouring it on the fire almost extinguished it. The animal again grabbed at the snail and would have smashed it on a log, but the snail slipped from his clutches and fell on the other side. That was more than *Canis vetulus* could stand, and he ran away in a very bad temper. But Keri and Kami blew up the dying fire and carried it to their aunt Ewaki.[2]

---

[1] Curt Nimuendajú, " Bruchstücke aus Religion und Überlieferung der Šipáia-Indianer," *Anthropos*, xiv.-xv. (1919–1920) p. 1015. Compare A. Métraux, *La Religion des Tupinamba*, pp. 48 *sq.*, from which I gather that a *Gaviao de Anta* is a species of vulture.

[2] K. von den Steinen, *Unter den Naturvölkern Zentral-Brasiliens* (Berlin, 1894), p. 377. The German name of *Canis vetulus* is *Kampfuchs*. The author refers to Brehm, *Säugetiere*, ii. 57, "*fängt Krebbse und Krabben.*"

The Tembes, an Indian tribe of north-eastern Brazil, in the province of Grao Para, say that fire was formerly in the possession of the king vulture; hence the Tembes had to dry in the sun such flesh as they wished to eat. So they resolved to steal fire from the vulture, and for that purpose they killed a tapir. They let it lie, and after three days it was rotten and full of maggots. The king vulture came down with his clan. They pulled off their garments of feathers and appeared in human form. They had brought a firebrand with them and kindled a great fire with it. They gathered the maggots, wrapped them in leaves, and roasted them. The Tembes, who had lain in ambush, rushed to the spot, but the vultures flew up and bore the fire to a place of safety. Thus the Indians exerted themselves for three days in vain. Then they built a hunting-lodge or shelter beside the carrion, and an old medicine-man hid himself in it. The vultures came again and kindled their fire close to the shelter. " This time," said the old man to himself, " if I jump on them quickly, I shall get a firebrand." So when the vultures had laid aside their feather garments and were roasting maggots, he jumped out. The vultures rushed towards their feather garments, and in the meantime the old man snatched a firebrand ; the birds gathered up the rest of the fire and flew away with it. The old man put the fire into all the trees from which the Indians now extract fire by friction.[1]

The Arekuna Indians of northern Brazil tell of a certain man named Makunaima, who lived with his brothers long ago before the great flood. They had as yet no fire and were obliged to eat all their food raw. So they sought for fire and found the little green bird called by the natives *mutug* (*Prionites momota*), which was said to be in possession of fire. The bird was in the act of fishing, and Makunaima tied a string to its tail without its knowledge. Then the bird took fright and flew high, dragging the string behind it. The string was very long, and following it up the brothers came to the bird's house, from which they carried away fire with

[1] Curt Nimuendajú, " Sagen der Tembé - Indianer," *Zeitschrift für Ethnologie*, xlvii. (1915) p. 289 ; Th. Koch-Grünberg, *Indianermärchen aus Südamerika* (Jena, 1920), No. 65, pp.

186 *sq.* The words (" *aus deren Holz man heute Feuer bohrt* ") seem to imply that these Indians kindle fire by the fire-drill.

them. Afterwards there came a great flood, and a certain
rodent, which the natives call *akuli* (*Dasyprocta Aguti*),
saved itself from drowning by creeping into a hole in a tree
and bunging up the hole. There in the hole it made fire,
but the fire caught the animal's hinder quarters and changed
into red hair, and the animal has red hair on that part of its
body to this day.[1]   In that way we may suppose, though we
are not expressly informed, that fire was preserved from
extinction during the great flood.

The Taulipang Indians, another tribe of northern Brazil,
say that in the olden time, when as yet men in general had no
fire, there lived a certain old woman named Pelenosamo, who
had fire in her body and produced it whenever she wished to
bake her manioc cakes. But other people had to bake their
manioc cakes in the sun. One day a girl saw how the old
woman produced fire from her body, and she told the people.
So they went to the old woman and begged her to give them
some fire. But she refused, saying that she had none.
Thereupon they seized her and tied her arms and legs
together ; and having collected much fuel, they set the old
woman against it and squeezed her body with their hands till
the fire spurted out. But the fire changed into the stones
called *wato*, which, on being struck, give forth fire.[2]

The Warrau Indians of British Guiana tell a story to
explain how it is that fire exists in wood and can be elicited
from it by friction. They say that two twin boys, named
Makunaima and Pia, were born of a mother who died just
before the birth took place. The infants were tenderly
nurtured by an old woman named Nanyobo, which means a
big kind of frog. When they grew bigger, the children used
to go to the waterside and shoot fish and game. Every time
they shot fish, the old woman would say to them, " You must
dry your fish in the sun, and never over a fire." But curiously
enough she would invariably send them to fetch firewood, and
by the time that they had returned with it, they would find
the fish nicely cooked and ready for them. The truth is that
she used to vomit fire out of her mouth, cook the victuals, and

[1] Theodor Koch-Grünberg, *Vom*
Roroima zum Orinoco (Berlin, 1916–
1917), ii. 33-36.

[2] Theodor Koch-Grünberg, *op. cit.*
ii. 76.

then lick up the fire before the boys returned, so that she never had a fire burning for them to see. When this happened day after day, the boys grew suspicious ; they could not understand how the old woman made her fire, and accordingly they determined to watch. So the next time they were sent to fetch firewood one of the twins changed himself into a lizard, and turning back he ran up into the roof, from which he could get a good view of everything that was going on. There he saw the old woman vomit out fire, use it, and lick it up again. Satisfied with what he had witnessed, he came down from the roof and ran after his brother. They discussed the matter carefully and decided to kill the old woman. So they cleared a large field, leaving in the middle of it a fine tree, to which they tied up their kind old foster-mother. Then surrounding her and the tree with stacks of timber, they set the whole on fire. As the ancient dame was gradually consumed in the blaze, the fire which used to be within her body passed into the surrounding faggots. These faggots were of the wood which the Indians call *hima-heru*, and from which they still elicit fire by rubbing two sticks of the wood together.[1]

Thus the Warrau Indians of Guiana explain the latent fire of wood by a mythical old woman who had fire in her body, just as the Taulipang Indians of northern Brazil explain the latent fire of stone by a similar fiction.

The Tarumas are an Arawak tribe of Indians who inhabit the forests in the south-eastern region of British Guiana. They subsist to some extent on fish, catching them in the perennial waters of the Essequibo River, which flows through their country ; they make more use of game and pay less attention to agriculture than other Arawak tribes, though they have fields of cassava and plant a little corn.[2] They say that in the beginning two brothers only lived on earth, Ajijeko the elder, and Duid the younger. There were no other men and no women. But the brothers suspected that there must be a woman somewhere, because at a certain rock near the river they often noticed scales and fragments of the

[1] W. E. Roth, " An Inquiry into the Animism and Folk-lore of the Guiana Indians," *Thirtieth Annual Report of the Bureau of American Ethnology* (Washington, 1915), p. 133.

[2] W. C. Farabee, *The Central Arawaks* (Philadelphia, 1918), p. 136 (*University of Pennsylvania, Anthropological Publications*, vol. ix.).

bones of fish. After making fruitless inquiries of a frog and an owl, they caught a female otter and compelled her to reveal to them the abode of the woman. They learned that the woman dwelt in a certain deep pool of the river, and that if they would get her they must fish for her. They did so, and for several days they continued to hook and land women's gear of various sorts, such as a basket and a hammock. At last the elder brother Ajijeko was tired and fell asleep, and while he slept, his younger brother Duid drew up the woman and took her to wife, and from that first couple the whole of mankind are descended.

After Duid's marriage the two brothers inhabited separate houses near each other in the same clearing. They had always eaten their food raw, but they noticed that the woman ate nothing raw except fruit, and they thought she must have some secret because she always ate alone. They tried to persuade her to tell them where her fire came from, and how it was made, but she refused to gratify their curiosity. Many years afterwards, when she was an old woman and had many children, the elder brother Ajijeko paid her and her husband a visit, and about sunset bade them good-bye and set off for home. They thought it strange that he had left his bag of trinkets behind. Presently he called to his sister-in-law to bring them over to him. She brought them, and standing at some distance said, " Here they are." But he said, " No, bring them here, up closer to me." She then came closer, holding them at arm's length, but he said, " No, bring them closer still, close up to me." She was frightened and said, " I am going to throw them to you." He said, " Do not do that ; they will break. Bring them right here where I am." She did so, and immediately he sprang up and seized her. He told her that he would embrace her if she did not reveal to him the secret of fire. After several evasions she consented to do so. She sat flat on the floor with legs wide apart. Taking hold of the upper part of her abdomen she gave it a good shake, and a ball of fire rolled out of the genital canal on the floor. This was not the fire that we know to-day ; it would not burn nor make things boil. These properties were lost when the woman gave it up. Ajijeko said, however, that he could remedy that ; so he gathered all the barks, fruits, and hot peppers which burn one, and with these and the woman's fire he made the fire which we now use. Now that the brothers had fire, all nature wanted it, and it was given to the woman's husband Duid to guard and protect it.

One day he was sitting on the bank of the river with the fire by his side, when an alligator snapped it up in his jaws and carried it off. However, the elder brother came, called up the alligator, and induced him to disgorge the fire. The fire itself was quite uninjured, but it had burned out the alligator's tongue, and he has been tongueless ever since.

Another day, soon afterwards, when Duid was looking after the fire, a maroudi picked it up and flew away with it. But when Ajijeko came to the house, Duid told him of the loss of the fire ; the bird was recalled, and she returned the fire as good as she got it, but her own neck was burned and has remained red to this day.

Another day Duid went away and left the fire all alone on the trail. In his absence a jaguar came along, and accidentally stepping on the fire he burned his feet so badly that he has never since been able to put them flat on the ground, but must walk on his toes. The tapir also came along and stepped on the fire, and he is so slow in his movements that his feet were very badly burned and he has had hoofs ever since.[1]

We are not told how the Tarumas, who tell this story of the origin of fire, produce fire at the present time ; but probably they make it by means of the fire-drill, for that method is employed by the Wapisianas, a kindred tribe of the same region. Among them, one man twirls the upright stick between the palms of his hands, while he holds down the horizontal stick at one end with his foot, the other end of the stick being kept in position by an assistant. Sometimes they rotate the upright stick by means of a bow instead of the palms of the hands.[2]

The Jibaros, an Indian tribe of eastern Ecuador, say that of old their ancestors did not know the use of fire and so dressed their victuals by warming meat under their armpits, by heating *yuca* (edible roots) in their jaws, and by cooking eggs in the burning rays of the sun. The only one

[1] W. C. Farabee, *op. cit.* pp. 143-147. [2] W. C. Farabee, *op. cit.* pp. 42 *sq.* with Plate vii.

who had fire was a certain Jibaro called Tacquea, who knew how to make fire by rubbing two sticks against each other, but being at enmity with the other Jibaros he would neither lend them fire nor teach them how to make it. Many Jibaros came flying (for in these early days it appears that the Jibaros were birds) and tried to steal fire from the house of Tacquea, but they could not. For the artful Tacquea kept his door a little ajar, and whenever a bird tried to fly in, he slammed the door and crushed the bird to death between the door and the jamb.

At last the little humming-bird up and said to the other birds, " I'll go and steal fire from the house of Tacquea." So he wetted his wings and dropped down on the middle of the path, pretending that he could not fly and shivering as if with cold. The wife of Tacquea, returning from her plantation, saw the wet bird and took it to her house that it might dry its dripping plumage at the fire, thinking to make a pet of it. After a short time the humming-bird, having dried itself a little, tried to rise and fly, but it could not. The wife of Tacquea took the bird up again and set it beside the fire. As the humming-bird, being very small, could not carry off a whole brand, he whisked his tail through the flames so that the feathers caught fire, and with his tail ablaze flew to a tall tree with very dry bark, which the Jibaros call *mukúna*. The bark of the tree in turn took fire, and with a little of the burning bark the humming-bird flew to a house, crying out to the others, " Here you have fire ! Take it quickly and carry it away, all of you. Now you can cook your food properly ; now you need not warm it under your arms."

When Tacquea saw that the humming-bird had escaped with the fire, he was vexed and reproached his family, saying, " Why did you let that bird enter to steal our fire ? Now the whole world must have fire. You others are responsible for this theft." Ever since that time the Jibaros have had fire, and they learned the art of kindling fire by rubbing two pieces of cotton-wood (*algodon, urúchi númi*) against each other.[1]

---

[1] Rafael Karsten, " Mitos de los indios jíbaros (Shuará) del Oriente del Ecuador," *Boletin de la Sociedad* *Equatoriana de Estudios Historicos Americanos*, ii. (1919) pp. 333 *sq.*

CHAPTER XII

THE Quichés of Guatemala tell of a time when their ancestors had no fire and suffered from cold. But the god Tohil was the creator of fire and had some in his possession ; so the Quichés in their need applied to him for fire and he furnished them with it. But shortly afterwards there fell a great rain, mingled with hail, which extinguished all the fires in the land. However, Tohil created fire again by stamping with his sandal. Several times the fire thus failed the Quichés, but Tohil always renewed it for them.[1]

The Cora Indians of Mexico tell how in former times the iguana, a species of lizard, was in possession of fire, and how, having quarrelled with his wife and his mother-in-law, he retired to the sky, taking the fire with him. Thus there was no more fire on earth, because the iguana had carried it all away and kept it hidden up aloft. So the people were much in want of fire, and they met in assembly to consult how they could get it. The old men and the young men, they met and deliberated for five days, neither eating nor drinking nor sleeping, but thinking hard all the time both by day and by night. At last after five days they knew where the fire was. " There in the sky," said they, " is the fire. The iguana hid it. Thither to the sky went he, there it is." Then they took counsel : " How is it possible for us to bring the fire hither ? " And they said, " Some one must go and ascend and bring the fire down." Then they commissioned the raven to attempt the task, and said to him, " Go to, raven, and try if you can climb up there to the sky." A cliff drew near to the spot, and

---

[1] H. H. Bancroft, *Native Races of the Pacific States* (London, 1875–1876), iii. 50 (following the *Popol Vuh*).

the raven went and clambered up the cliff. He mounted up and had clambered about half-way, when he slipped and fell back on the ground. There he lay flat and burst. The raven was shivered in pieces ; the raven had failed.

Then the people called another, they called the humming-bird, and he went. But neither could he do it. When he came to the middle, he fell. He fell and saved himself with difficulty. He too returned and descended to the ground. When he was come, he said to the elders, " It is impossible to mount up thither ; there is a waterfall there ; there is no access." Then another went. He started and went likewise, but he could not mount up. He too returned and descended to the earth. When he was come, he said to the elders, " It is impossible, there is no means of mounting up."

Thus all the birds tried, but none of them succeeded in ascending to the sky. Then they summoned the opossum. At first he would not, but when he had made up his mind to go, he said to them, " If it is possible to mount up, do as follows. If I am able to get up, look out. Watch when the fire comes down, which I will throw. Await it in your blankets, and when it comes down, let it not fall on the ground, lest the earth should be consumed by fire."

Then the opossum started, and climbed, and climbed, and came to the middle. There grew a *texcallame* tree, and there the opossum rested. Then he climbed farther up. The way was very smooth, and he came to the waterfall. Hardly did he extricate himself from it, and shaking himself pursue the upper way, drenched through and through. When he was up, he looked about him and saw the fire. He went up to it, and there beside the fire sat an old man. The opossum greeted him, " Good day, grandfather ! good day, grandfather ! " The old man arose and said, " Who speaks to me ? " The opossum answered, " I, your grandson," and asked for leave to warm himself. At first the man was unwilling, but the opossum pleaded, " I am very cold, I should like to warm myself." Then the man replied, " Warm yourself, but do not take the fire away." So the opossum sat down, and the old man lay down and fell asleep. While he slept, the opossum twined his tail round a brand and drew it gently out of the fire. At that the old man woke up. " You are taking away the fire, grandson," quoth he. " No, I am raking up the fire," replied the opossum. Again the old man fell asleep, and this time he slept sound. While he slept, the opossum arose softly, and seizing the firebrand began to drag it slowly away. Thus he had dragged it a good long way and was already near the abyss, when the old man awoke and saw it all. So up he got and gave chase. But the opossum had already reached the abyss and flung the fire down. When the old man came up with the opossum, he beat him black and blue with his stick and hurled him down to earth. And having done so, he went away, saying, " You don't take my fire from me, opossum."

Now the people on earth were looking for the fire, and down it came. They waited to catch it in their blankets, but it did not fall on them, it fell on the ground. They took the fire, and immediately the earth burned. While they were picking up the fire, the opossum came plump down and fell dead on the ground. Then they covered him up and wrapped him in their blankets. After a while he stirred under the blankets, he came to life, he rose with difficulty and sat upright. When he came to his senses, he asked, " Is the fire come ? I threw the fire down here. My grandfather killed me, he gave me such a drubbing ! " They answered him, " The fire fell here. Nobody caught it as it fell. It fell on the ground, and the earth is burning. How shall we now put it out ? It is quite impossible for us to put it out." Then they called on our Mother, the Earth Goddess, and she put out the fire with her milk. So they carried away the fire, and it remained there.[1]

In this Cora myth the iguana, after carrying off the fire from earth to the sky, disappears from the story and is replaced by an old man, the guardian of the heavenly fire. But the old man may be only the iguana in more or less human form ; for savages make no sharp distinction between animals and men. In a briefer version of the Cora myth the being from whom the opossum steals the heavenly fire is described as " the old vulture." [2]

---

[1] K. Th. Preuss, *Die Nayarit-Expedition*, i. (Leipsic, 1912) pp. 177-181.
[2] K. Th. Preuss, *op. cit.* i. 271 *sq.*

CHAPTER XIII

THE ORIGIN OF FIRE IN NORTH AMERICA

THE Sia Indians of New Mexico say that the Spider, whom they call Sussistinnako, was the creator of men, animals, birds, and all living things. He dwelt in a house underground, and there he made fire by rubbing a sharp-pointed stone on a round flat stone. But having kindled the fire he kept it in his house, setting a snake, a cougar, and a bear to guard the first, second, and third doors, that no one might enter and see the fire. So people on earth did not possess fire ; the secret of it was not yet brought to this upper world. In time they grew tired of browsing on grass like deer and other animals ; so they resolved to send the coyote to steal fire for them from the nether world. The coyote consented to undertake the task. When he came to the Spider's house in the middle of the night, he found the snake, who guarded the first door, sleeping at his post, so he slipped in past him. The cougar, who guarded the second door, was also asleep, and so was the bear who guarded the third door. Passing them, the coyote came to a fourth door, but the guardian there was likewise asleep ; so slipping past him the coyote entered the room. There he found Spider himself slumbering soundly ; so he hastened to the fire, lighted at it the cedar brand which was fastened to his tail, and then hurried away. The Spider awoke, rubbing his eyes, just in time to be aware that some one was leaving the room. " Who is there ? " he cried ; " some one has been here." But before he could rouse the sleeping guardians of the doors to stop the thief, the coyote was far on his way with the fire to the upper world.[1]

The Navahoes, or Navajoes, an Indian tribe of New

[1] Mrs. Matilda Coxe Stevenson, " The Sia," *Eleventh Annual Report* *of the Bureau of Ethnology* (Washington, 1894), pp. 26 *sq.*, 70, 72 *sq.*

Mexico, say that their first ancestors, six men and six women, came out of the earth in the middle of the lake, which is in the valley of Montezuma. In their ascent through the ground they were preceded by the locust and the badger; indeed, on arriving at the surface of the earth, they found the very same animals which now inhabit it, except the deer and the moose, which had not yet been created. Nay, the animals were in one respect better off than the human beings, for they were in possession of fire, whereas men and women were not. But among the animals the coyote, the bat, and the squirrel were the special friends of the Navahoes and they agreed to aid each other in procuring fire for them. So when the other animals were playing the moccasin or shoe game beside a fire, the coyote went to the scene of the sport with some splinters of resinous pine-wood tied to his tail ; and while the attention of the animals was absorbed in the play, he ran quickly through the fire, so that the splinters of pine were ignited. He then ran off, pursued by all the animals ; and when he was tired out, the bat, as had been previously arranged between them, relieved him by taking up both the fire and the running. Flying hither and thither, and dodging first to one side and then to another, the bat escaped his pursuers for a time, and when he was like to drop, he handed on the fire to the squirrel, who, by virtue of his great agility and endurance, contrived to carry the fire safe to the Navahoes.[1]

The Jicarilla Apaches of northern New Mexico say that when their ancestors first emerged from their abode in the nether world the trees could talk, but people could not burn them, because they contained no fire. However, mankind at last obtained fire through the exertions of the fox. For one day the fox went to visit the geese, wishing to learn to imitate their cackle. The geese promised to teach him, but told him that if he would learn the true cackle he must accompany them in their flights. For this purpose they gave him wings to fly with, but warned him that in flying he must not open his eyes. So when the geese spread their wings and soared aloft, the fox flew with them. As darkness fell, they

[1] Major E. Backus, " An Account of the Navajoes of New Mexico," in H. R. Schoolcraft's *Indian Tribes of* *the United States* (Philadelphia, 1853– 1856), iv. 218 *sq.*

passed over the walled enclosure where the fireflies lived. Some gleams from their flickering fires penetrated the closed eyelids of the fox and caused him to open his eyes. At once his wings failed him and he fell into the walled enclosure near the tents of the fireflies. Two of the flies went to see the fallen fox, and he gave each of them a necklace of juniper berries to induce them to tell him where he could pass the wall which surrounded them. The fireflies showed the fox a cedar tree which would bend down at command and assist anyone to pass over the wall. In the evening the fox went to the spring where the fireflies drew water and found there coloured earths suitable for paint, and with one of them he gave himself a coat of white. Returning to the camp, he told the fireflies that they ought to have a feast ; they should dance and make merry, and he would give them a new musical instrument. They agreed to his proposal, and gathered wood for a great camp-fire, which they ignited by their own glow. Before the ceremonies began, the fox tied shreds of cedar bark to his tail, and then made a drum, the first ever constructed, which he beat for some time. Tired of beating the drum, he gave it to one of the fireflies and edged nearer to the fire, finally thrusting his tail into it, though the fireflies about him warned him not to do so, saying that his tail would burn. " I am a medicine-man," replied the fox, " and my tail will not burn." However, he kept a close watch upon it, and when the bark was burning well, he said, " It is too warm here; stand aside and let me go where it is cooler." So saying, he ran away with his tail ablaze, followed by the fireflies, who cried, " Stop, you do not know the road ; come back ! " But the fox ran straight to the cedar tree and called, " Bend down to me, my tree, bend down ! " The tree lifted him out of the enclosure, and on he ran, still pursued by the fireflies. As he passed along, the bushes and trees on either side were kindled by the sparks which fell from the burning cedar, and thus fire was widely spread over the earth. Tired with running, the fox at last handed on the fire to the hawk, which carried it on and finally delivered it to the brown crane. The crane flew far southward with the fire, yet not so far but that one tree was not reached, and that tree will not burn to this day. But what is the name of the

incombustible tree, the Jicarilla Apaches do not know.   The
fireflies pursued the fox to his burrow, and informed him that
as a punishment for having stolen fire from them and spread
it abroad over the land, he should never be permitted to use
it himself.[1]

The Uintah Utes of north-eastern Utah tell a long story
about the origin, or rather the theft, of fire.   In a condensed
form the story runs as follows.   Coyote lived with the people
of whom he was chief.   They had no fire.   But one day,
lying on his bed in his tent, Coyote saw something fall down
before him.   It was a small piece of burnt rush which had
gone up with the smoke and had been carried by the wind.
Coyote picked it up and put it away, and then he called his
head men and asked them if they knew what it was and where
it came from.   But none of them knew.   Then Coyote
pointed to one of his men, the Owl.   " I select you," said he ;
" bring very many Owls."   He sent another to call the Eagle
people ;   another to bring the Crows, and others to bring the
Grouse, and the Sage-hens, and the Humming-bird tribes.
He also sent to the Hawk-moths and to all the kinds of birds.
They were to send runners to other tribes, and all were to
come to him quickly.

Then he said to one man, " My friend, go to the river and
get reeds.   Bring them here."   The man brought them, and
Coyote took a stick and crushed the reeds into shreds.   Thus
he had a heap of the shredded bark of the reeds.   When it
grew dark, he took dark blue paint and rubbed the paint and
the bark together till the bark grew blue ; but when he rubbed
them longer together, the bark grew black.   It was black like
human hair.   Next morning after sunrise he called his friends
to come.   He put the shredded bark on his head, and it was
like long hair reaching down to the ground.   When his
friends came, he did not look to them like Coyote but like
another person.   They did not know what to make of it.
Then he sent them home again, and taking off his bark hair,
he wrapped it up and put it away.

Now the various tribes which he had sent for began to
arrive.   They were all able men, not the entire people.   They

¹ Frank Russell, " Myths of the   *American Folk-lore*, xi. (1898) pp.
Jicarilla   Apaches,"   *Journal   of*   261 *sq.*

came towards his tent ; they sat in circles in several rows to
listen to Coyote.   He asked them all what it was, and whence
it came, and whether it came from above.   He handed it from
one man to another.   But nobody knew what it was.   Then
Coyote said, " I intend to hunt up this thing.   I shall find out
where it comes from, from what tribe it is, or whether it is
from the sky.   I want you to search, looking where each of
you thinks best.   That is why I called you.   We will start in
the morning."

So they all started, going westward ; for the wind blew
from the west, and Coyote thought that the mysterious thing
could have come from no other quarter.   Thus they travelled
up hill and down dale for several days.   One day Coyote sent
out a large Red-tailed Hawk to scout.   The Hawk flew high,
but came back very tired, saying that he had seen nothing.
Next Coyote despatched the Eagle.   The Eagle wheeled
about in circles till he was lost to sight, and he was away
longer than the Hawk.   But he too came back very tired,
saying that he had seen nothing, except that the earth looked
a little smoky.   Then the others thought the Humming-bird
was the best to go, and that Coyote ought to ask him.   " He
could do better than the Eagle," said they.   So Coyote sent
the Humming-bird.   Away flew the Humming-bird, and he
was away a long time, longer than either the Hawk or the
Eagle.   When he came back, he said, " At the edge of the
earth and the sky, where they meet, I saw something standing.
It was very far away.   It was a dark thing standing up, and
the top was bent over.   That was all I saw."   Coyote was
very glad to hear that.   He said, " That is what I thought one
of you would see.   That is what we are going for.   It is from
yonder thing that the thing came which I found."

So they travelled on, crossing mountain after mountain
and descending into the plain on the farther side.   When
they came to the foot of the last mountain, Coyote adorned
himself.   He took the bark and put it in his hair.   He spread
it all around like hair.   He parted it in the middle and
wrapped up two long strands of it that reached to his feet ;
he wrapped them with bark.   But before he had finished
decorating himself, he sent the Eagle up again.   The Eagle
went up, and when he came down, he said, " We are not very

far away now. I saw that which the Humming-bird saw.
We are near."

So they came near to a village on the top of a flat hill.
Then Coyote spoke to his friends. " We have burned nothing
heretofore. We have come to fire now. It is the fire for
which we have come. We will take it away from these people.
They will have none left here. Where the origin of the fire is,
there they will have no more fire. We will take it to the place
where we live, and we will possess it in our own land. I will
use this hair of mine to take it away from them. I will
deceive these people that have the fire."

Thereupon they all entered the village, and going to the
first tent Coyote inquired where the chief lived. The place
was pointed out to him, and he went and shook hands with
the chief. He told the chief that he had travelled very far
only to see him, and he desired that the chief would get up a
dance, for he and all his people would like to see it. The
chief consented and assembled his people for the dance ; all
the women and children came too, none were left in the
tents. At Coyote's proposal all the fires in the tents were
extinguished, and only one large fire was left burning in the
assembly. Then Coyote unwrapt the bark and put it on ;
the people thought that he was adorning himself for the dance.
He danced all night without stopping.

When it began to grow light, Coyote whooped as a signal
to his own people. Later, when the light grew brighter, he
moved close to the fire and whooped again, dancing about the
fire. His people now separated from the others ; they got
ready to start. Coyote now tore off his bark hair, and, seizing
it in his hands, he struck and extinguished the fire with it.
But the shredded bark caught fire, and carrying it with
him ablaze Coyote started to run. All Coyote's people ran
too. As for the people of the village, there was nothing
left for them ; all their fire was out. They now perceived the
treacherous intention with which the strangers had come, and
they gave chase, intending to kill them. As the fugitives ran,
Coyote passed the fire to the Eagle, saying, " You can run
fast ; take this, my friend." The Eagle took it and ran, but in
time he grew tired and passed the fire to the Humming-bird,
and when the Humming-bird was nearly exhausted, he handed

the fire to the Hawk-moth. Gradually the slow birds grew tired and, dropping out of the running, hid themselves as best they could ; only the best and fastest birds held on. But Coyote saw the pursuers drawing near, and he chose the Chicken-hawk as the swiftest bird and gave him the fire to carry. Afterwards Coyote took the fire himself and ran, telling all his people to run after him as hard as they could. Then the Humming-bird took it again from Coyote and flew ahead, but Coyote called after him, " Stop ! the fire is nearly out." That angered the Humming-bird, and he gave back the fire to Coyote, and he turned aside and hid, because he was angry with Coyote.

Of the fugitives only four were now left, and they were Coyote, the Eagle, the Chicken-hawk, and the Hawk-moth. All the rest were worn out and had scattered. At last even the Eagle, the Chicken-hawk, and the Hawk-moth gave out, and Coyote was left alone, running with the fire. The pursuers drew near, intending to kill him. He took refuge in a hole, closed the hole with a stone, and nursed the last spark of fire inside. Then he emerged from the hole and, changing his direction, cut away through a ravine, with the pursuers after him. But at last they gave up hope of catching him. They said, " Let him go. We will cause rain and then snow. We will make a hard storm and freeze him to death and put out the fire." So it rained till all the hollows were filled, and the valleys were nearly knee-deep with water. Coyote thought that the fire would soon be gone. He saw a small hill with a few cedars on it, and he thought that he might be safe there on the hill under the cedars, while the valleys below were flooded.

But before he reached the top of the hill, he saw a Black-tailed Rabbit sitting right in the water. Coyote gave him the fire to hold, and the Rabbit placed it right under himself. " Don't do that," said Coyote, " you are in the water; and you will put the fire out." So the Rabbit handed the fire back to Coyote,[1] and told him that there was a cave hard by in which he could find shelter. Entering the cave, Coyote

---

[1] This incident is probably intended to explain the black colour of the rabbit's tail, which was burned black in consequence of his sitting on the fire. But the explanation is not given in the tale as recorded.

found some dry sagebrush and dry cedar lying there. So he piled them up and lit them with the fire which he was carrying. He had been shivering before, but as the fire blazed up he felt warm and comfortable, though outside the snow was falling and it was bitter cold ; for his pursuers had thought to freeze him dead. In the morning the sky was clear and cloud-less, and everywhere there was ice. But the south wind blew, and the ice all melted away. Coming forth from the cave, Coyote saw the Rabbit sitting just where he had sat the night before. Coyote shot him and killed him. Then he went back to the cave, and took a piece of old dry sagebrush and bored a hole through it. He filled the hole with coals of fire and closed it up. He thought he could carry the fire safely thus.

Putting the fire, thus protected, under his belt, Coyote went away with it and returned home. There he laid down the tube of sagebrush containing the fire. He called together the few men who were left at home with the women and children. When they were come, he took the fire. It looked only like a stick. Then he whittled hard greasewood. " Now look, you people," said he. He told two men to hold the sagebrush firmly to the ground. Then he bored it with the greasewood, and picked up the borings and put them into dry grass. Blowing on the grass, he soon had a fire. " This dry pine-nut," said he, " will be burned. Dry cedar will also be burned. Take fire into all the tents. There will be fire in every house." Thus said Coyote. Now all the birds that had grown tired and hidden themselves in the pursuit arrived at the village. But they all flew back to the places from which they had come, and ever since they have been birds.[1]

This story is clearly told to explain the process of eliciting fire by rubbing the point of a piece of hard greasewood in the hole of a soft piece of sagebrush. Here, too, as in so many of these myths, the actors in the story are regarded, at one time, seemingly as men and women, at another time as animals and birds. The line between the two is drawn with a wavering and uncertain hand, because in the mind of the story-teller the two classes of beings melted into each other.

[1] A. L. Kroeber, " Ute Tales," *Journal of American Folk-lore*, xiv. (1901) pp. 252-260.

In some stories told by the Indian tribes which inhabit the south-eastern region of the United States the coyote is replaced by the rabbit as the thief of fire.   Thus the Creek Indians say that once upon a time all the people came together and said, " How shall we obtain fire ? "   It was agreed that Rabbit should try to get fire for the people.   He went across the great water to the east.   There he was received gladly, and a great dance was arranged.   Then Rabbit entered the dancing circle, gaily dressed and wearing a peculiar cap on his head into which he had stuck four sticks of rosin.   As the people danced they approached nearer and nearer the sacred fire in the centre of the circle, and the Rabbit also danced nearer and nearer the fire.   The dancers began to bow to the sacred fire, lower and lower, and Rabbit also bowed to the fire, lower and lower.   Suddenly, as he bowed very low the sticks of rosin in his cap caught fire, and his head was in a blaze of flame.   The people were amazed at the impious stranger who had dared to touch the sacred fire.   They ran at him in anger, and away ran Rabbit, the people hot foot after him.   He ran to the great water and plunged into it, while the people stopped on the shore.   Across the great water swam Rabbit with the flames flaring from his cap. He returned to his people, who thus obtained fire from the east.[1]

In this story " the great water to the east " is apparently the Atlantic Ocean.   The identification is confirmed by a somewhat fuller version of the same story which is told by the Koasati Indians.   They say that formerly there was no fire in their country ;   only on the other side of the great ocean was it to be found.   The people wanted fire, but the owners would not let them have it, so the Koasatis had to do without it.   Then Rabbit said, " I can bring away some fire."   A person who had many daughters sat among them and said, " Whoever goes over and brings back some fire shall be given one of these girls."   But Rabbit said, " One woman is not enough for me."   Big Man-eater said, " I can bring it," and the person replied, " All right, you go for it and bring it back."   Then Big Man-eater wanted a woman, so

---

[1] John R. Swanton, *Myths and Tales of the Southeastern Indians* (Washing-ton, 1929), p. 46 (*Bureau of American Ethnology, Bulletin* 88).

he started off. He plunged into the ocean and vanished and never came back.

Then Rabbit said, " No one else can win back. But I know how to win back." So the man sent for him, and Rabbit said, " All right, I will bring fire and sleep with all of the young girls." The person said, " All right." Then Rabbit started, and when he came to the water he took off his shirt and threw it down, placed wood on it, and sitting on it went across. In that way he got over the water. He travelled on. When he said he wanted fire and the people refused to give it, he seized some and ran away, and they pursued him. He ran with it through the woods. He came to the sea and stood by it. Then he rubbed pitch on the back of his head, and when one of the pursuers came up with him he jumped into the water and swam, holding the fire in one hand above the waves. After a time he grew tired and stuck the fire on the back of his head. The pitch took fire and he swam along with it blazing. So he crossed the ocean and came with the fire to the man who had sent him. The man said to him, " Now these young women are yours." And Rabbit remained there very happy.[1]

The Hitchiti Indians also relate how Rabbit stole the fire and distributed it to all the people. They tell of a time when fire was not, indeed, unknown, but when custom forbade to kindle it anywhere save on the ceremonial ground where sacred rites were celebrated and solemn dances performed. Now Rabbit knew that there was to be a dance on the ceremonial ground, and thinks he to himself, " I will run away with some fire." He thought over the matter and made up his mind how he was to do it. He had his head rubbed with pitch to make his hair bristle up. Then he set out. When he came to the holy ground, a great crowd was gathered there. People were dancing, and Rabbit sat down. Then they came to him and said that he must lead the dance. He agreed and got up. So he danced round the fire singing, and the people followed him. Faster and faster went the dance, and as Rabbit circled round the fire he would from time to time duck his head toward the flame as if he would

[1] John R. Swanton, *Myths and Tales of the Southeastern Indians,* pp. 203 *sq.*

take hold of it. But all that the people said was, " When Rabbit leads the dance, he always acts like that." At last he poked his head right into the flames and ran off with his head all ablaze. But the people made after him with a hue and cry of " Hulloa, catch him and throw him down ! " So away he tore with the people after him, but they could not catch him, and he vanished out of their sight. Then they made it rain for three whole days, and on the fourth day they said, " By now the rain must have put out the fire." So the rain stopped, the sun shone out once more, and the weather was fine. But Rabbit had built a fire in a hollow tree, and there he stayed while it rained, and when the sun shone he came out and brought forth his fires. But rain fell again and put out all the fires save the one which Rabbit kept burning in the hollow tree. This happened again and again. But though the rains were heavy they could not entirely extinguish the fires which in the intervals of sunshine Rabbit had brought out from the hollow tree. So the people came and took up the smouldering embers and carried them away. Thus Rabbit distributed the fire to all people.[1]

The Alabama Indians have a different myth of the origin of fire. They say that formerly the bears owned the fire and always took it about with them. Once on a time they set it down on the ground and went on farther, munching acorns. Thus left alone the fire almost went out, and in his distress he called aloud : " Feed me," cried he. Some human beings heard the cry and came to the rescue. They got a stick toward the north and laid it down upon the fire. They got another stick toward the west and laid it down upon it. They got a stick at the south and laid it down there. They got another at the east and laid it down, and the fire blazed up. When the bears came back to get their fire, the fire said to them, " I do not know you any more." So the bears did not get back the fire, and now it belongs to human beings.[2]

The Cheyenne Indians have a tradition that in the early ages of the world one of their ancestors named Sweet Root was taught by Thunder how to make fire by means of the

---

[1] John R. Swanton, *Myths and Tales of the Southeastern Indians*, pp. 102 *sq.*

[2] John R. Swanton, *Myths and Tales of the Southeastern Indians*, p. 122.

fire-drill. According to this tradition, Thunder obtained from Buffalo Bull a chip (of wood) from which fire could be elicited. Then, addressing Sweet Root, he said, " Get a stick ; I will teach you something by which your people can warm themselves, can cook food, and with which they can burn things." When Sweet Root had brought the stick, Thunder said to him, " Rest the point in the middle of the chip and hold it between your hands and twirl it fast." Sweet Root did so a few times and the chip caught fire. Thus through Thunder was given help to the people against Hō-ĭm′-ă-hā, who is commonly interpreted as " winter man " or " storm," the power that brings the cold and snow ; the people thereby got the means of warming themselves.[1]

The Sioux, Menomonis, Foxes, and several other Indian tribes inhabiting the valley of the Mississippi, have a tradition of a great flood in which all the inhabitants of the earth, except one man and one woman, were drowned. The solitary survivors escaped by taking refuge on a high mountain. Seeing that in their forlorn plight they had need of fire, the Master of Life sent a white raven to carry it to them. But the raven stopped by the way to devour carrion and allowed the fire to go out. He then returned to heaven to get more. But the Great Spirit drove him away and punished him by making him black instead of white. Then the Great Spirit sent the *erbette*, a little grey bird, as his messenger to carry fire to the man and woman. The bird did as he was bidden and returned to report to the Great Spirit, who rewarded him by giving him two little black bars on each side of his eyes. Hence the Indians regard the bird with great respect ; they never kill it themselves and they forbid their children to shoot it. Moreover, they imitate the bird by painting two little black bars on each side of their own eyes.[2]

The Omaha Indians say that in the olden time their ancestors had no fire and suffered from the cold. They thought, What shall we do ? A man found an elm root that was very dry, and he dug a hole in it, and put a stick in the hole, and rubbed it. Then smoke came. He smelled it.

[1] G. B. Grinnell, " Some early Cheyenne Tales," *Journal of American Folk-lore*, xx (1907) p. 171.

[2] Francois - Vincent Badin, in *Annales de l'Association de la Propagation de la Foi*, iv. (Lyons and Paris, 1830) pp. 537 *sq.*

Then the people smelled it and came near ; others helped him to rub. At last a spark leaped forth ; they blew it into a flame, and so fire came to warm the people and to cook their food.[1]

The Chippewa or Ojibway Indians, a large group of tribes belonging to the central Algonquian stock, say that in the beginning men were not wise ; they had no clothes and sat about doing nothing. The Spirit of the Creator sent a man to teach them. This man was called *ockabewis*, that is Messenger. Some of those ancient people lived in the south, where they did not need any clothing. But the people farther north were cold and began to be troubled about what they should do. The Messenger saw the southern people naked and homeless, and he left them to themselves. He came farther north where the people were suffering and in need of his help. He said, "Why are you sitting here with no clothing on ? " They answered, " Because we do not know what to do." The first thing he taught them was how to kindle a fire by means of a bow and stick and a bit of decayed wood ; and this method of making fire is still used by the Chippewas, or was so down to modern times. Afterwards the Messenger taught the people how to cook meat by the fire.[2]

The Cherokee Indians say that in the beginning there was no fire and the world was cold, until the thunders sent their lightning and put fire into the bottom of a hollow sycamore tree, which grew on an island. The animals knew that it was there, because they could see the fire coming out at the top, but they could not get to it on account of the water. So they held a council to decide what to do.

Every animal that could fly or swim was anxious to go after the fire. The raven offered to go, and because he was so large and strong they thought he could surely do the work ; so

[1] Alice C. Fletcher and Francis la Flesche, "The Omaha Tribe," *Twenty-seventh Annual Report of the Bureau of American Ethnology* (Washington, 1911), p. 70.

[2] Frances Densmore, *Chippewa Customs* (Washington, 1929), p. 98, and as to the mode of kindling the fire, *ib.* p. 142 (*Bureau of American Ethnology, Bulletin* 86). The mode of kindling fire in question is known as the bow-drill ; an upright shaft is made to revolve rapidly in a piece of soft wood by means of a string which is coiled round it and fastened to a bow. See Walter Hough, *Fire as an Agent in human Culture* (Washington, 1926), pp. 96-98 (*United States National Museum, Bulletin* 139).

he was sent first.   He flew high and far across the water and
lighted on the sycamore tree ; but the heat scorched all his
feathers black, and he was frightened and came back without
the fire.   The little screech-owl next volunteered to go, and
he reached the place safely ; but as he was peering down into
the hollow tree, a blast of hot air came up and nearly burned
out his eyes.   He made shift to fly home, but it was long,
long before he could see well, and his eyes are red to this
day.   Then the hooting-owl and the horned-owl went, but
by the time they got to the hollow tree the fire was burning so
fiercely that the smoke nearly blinded them, and the ashes
carried by the wind made white rings about their eyes.
They had to come home again without the fire, but rub as
they would they have never been able to rub off those white
rings.

Now no more of the birds would venture, so the little
uksuhi snake, the black racer, said that he would swim across
the water and bring back some fire.   So he swam to the island,
crawled through the grass to the tree, and entered it by a
small hole at the foot.   However, the heat and smoke were
too much for him also, and after dodging about blindly
among the ashes he was glad to get out again by the same
hole by which he had entered ; but his body was now scorched
black, and ever since it has been his habit to dart and double
on his tracks, as if he were trying to escape from something at
close quarters.   Afterwards the great black snake, which the
Indians call *gulegi* or " the climber," offered to go for fire.
He swam over to the island and climbed up the tree on the
outside, as the black snake always does ; but when he popped
his head into the hole, the smoke choked him so that he fell
into the burning stump, and before he could climb out again
he was as black as the little *uksuhi* snake.

Hereupon the animals held another council, for still there
was no fire, and the world was cold ; but birds, snakes, and
four-footed animals were now all afraid to venture near the
burning sycamore.   At last the water spider said that she
would go.   This is not the water spider that looks like a
mosquito, but the other one, with black downy hair and red
stripes on her body.   She can run on the top of the water or
dive to the bottom ; so it was easy enough for her to cross

over to the island, but how was she to bring back the fire ?
That was the rub. " I'll manage that," said the water
spider ; so she span a thread from her body and wove it
into a *tusti* bowl, which she fastened on her back. Then she
crossed over to the island and made her way through the
grass to the tree, where the fire was still burning. She put
one little coal of fire into her bowl, and came back with it ;
and ever since we have had fire, and the water spider still
keeps her *tusti* bowl.[1]

This myth appears to be intended primarily to explain the
peculiar appearance or gait of certain animals and birds ;
the explanation of the origin of fire is secondary, and no
attempt is made to solve the problem of the fire latent in
wood or stones.

The Karok Indians of California tell of a time in the early
ages of the world when their ancestors had no fire. For the
Creator, Kareya, who had made both men and animals, had
not given them fire ; on the contrary, he had hidden it in a
casket, which he gave to two old hags to keep, lest some
Karok should steal it. However, the coyote was friendly to
the Karok and promised to bring them some fire. So he
went and got together a great company of animals, one of
every kind from the lion [2] down to the frog. These he
stationed in a line all along the road, from the home of the
Karok to the far distant land where the fire was hidden.
The animals were arranged according to their strength, the
weakest nearest home, and the strongest near the fire. Then
he took an Indian with him, and hid him under a hill, and
went to the hut of the hags who kept the casket, and rapped
on the door. One of them came out, and he said, " Good
evening," and they replied, " Good evening." Then he said,
" It's a pretty cold night ; can you let me sit by your fire ? "
And they said, " Yes, come in." So he went in and stretched
himself out before the fire, and reached his snout out toward
the blaze, and sniffed the heat, and felt very snug and comfortable. Finally he stretched his nose out along his fore-
paws and pretended to go to sleep, though he kept the corner

[1] James Mooney, " Myths of the
Cherokee," *Nineteenth Annual Re-
port of the Bureau of American Ethno-* *logy*, Part i. (Washington, 1900) pp.
240-242.
[2] No doubt the puma is meant.

of one eye open, watching the old hags. But they never slept, day or night, and he spent the whole night watching and thinking to no purpose.

So next morning he went out and told the Indian whom he had hidden under the hill that he must make an attack on the hags' cabin, as if he were about to steal some fire, while he (the coyote) was in it. He then went back and asked the hags to let him in again, which they did, as they did not think a coyote could steal any fire. He stood close by the casket of fire, and when the Indian made a rush on the cabin, and the hags dashed out after him at one door, the coyote seized a brand in his teeth and ran out at the other door. He almost flew over the ground, but the hags saw the sparks flying and gave chase, and gained on him fast. But by the time he was out of breath he reached the lion, who took the brand and ran with it to the next animal, and so on, each animal barely having time to give it to the next before the hags came up.

The next to the last in the line was the ground-squirrel. He took the brand and ran so fast with it that his tail caught fire, and he curled it up over his back, and so burned the black spot which we see to this day just behind his fore-shoulders. The last in the line of animals was the frog, but he could not run at all ; so he opened his mouth wide, and the squirrel threw the fire into it, and the frog swallowed it down with a gulp. Then he turned and gave a great jump, but the hags were so close behind that one of them seized him by the tail (for he was a tadpole then) and tweaked it off, and that is the reason why frogs have no tails to this day. He swam under water as long as he could hold in his breath, then bobbed up and spat out the fire into a log of driftwood, and there it has stayed ever since, so that when an Indian rubs two pieces of wood together, the fire comes forth.[1]

The Tolowa Indians of California tell of a great flood in which all the Indians were drowned except a single pair who were saved by retreating to the top of the highest mountain. But when the waters subsided, the survivors had no fire, and though in time the earth was repeopled by their exertions,

[1] Stephen Powers, *Tribes of California* (Washington, 1877), pp. 38 *sq.* (*Contributions to North American Ethnology*, vol. iii.).

still men were destitute of fire, and they looked with envious
eyes on the moon, conceiving that it possessed the treasure
which was denied to them. Accordingly the Spider Indians
and the Snake Indians together hatched a plot for stealing
fire from the moon. To put it in practice the Spider Indians
wove a gossamer.balloon and fastened it to the earth by a long
rope, which they paid out as they mounted in the balloon
towards the lunar orb. In time they reached their destination,
but the Moon Indians looked askance at them, divining
their errand. The Spiders, however, contrived to persuade
the inhabitants of the moon that they had only come to
gamble. At that the Moon Indians were much pleased and
proposed to start the game forthwith. But while they sat
gambling by the fire, a Snake Indian, who had climbed up the
long rope, arrived on the scene, and darting through the fire
made good his escape before the Moon Indians had recovered
from their surprise. On his return to earth it became in-
cumbent on him to travel over every rock, stick, and tree ;
everything he touched from that time forth contained fire,
and the hearts of the Indians were glad. As the fire has
remained constant ever since, the Snake Indians congratulate
themselves on their success.[1]

The Paom Pomo Indians of California believe that lightning was the source of fire on earth ; they think that the
primordial bolt which fell from heaven deposited the spark in
the wood, so that it now comes forth when two pieces of wood
are rubbed together.[2]

The Gallinomero Indians of California are of opinion that
it was the coyote who first produced fire by rubbing two
pieces of wood together in his paws, and that the sagacious
animal has preserved the sacred spark in the tree-trunks to
this day.[3]

The Achomâwi Indians of California think that our earth
was created by the coyote and the eagle, or rather that the
coyote began and the eagle completed it. Last of all the
coyote brought fire into the world, for the Indians were
freezing. He journeyed far to the west, to a place where
there was fire, stole some of it, and brought it home in his

---

[1] S. Powers, *op. cit.* pp. 70 *sq.*   [2] S. Powers, *op. cit.* p. 161.
[3] S. Powers, *op. cit.* p. 182.

ears. He kindled a fire in the mountains, and the Indians saw the smoke of it, and went up and got fire ; so they were warmed and comforted and have kept it ever since.[1]

The Nishinam Indians of California say that after the coyote had created the world and its inhabitants, one thing still was lacking, and that was fire   In the western country there was plenty of it, but nobody could get it, for it was far away and closely hidden. So the bat proposed to the lizard that he should go and steal some. This the lizard did, and he got a good coal of it, but found it very hard to bring home, because everybody wanted to steal it from him. At length he reached the western edge of the Sacramento Valley, and he had to be very careful in crossing the valley with the fire, lest he should set the country ablaze. To keep the dry grass from catching fire, and to prevent thieves from stealing the precious element, he was forced to travel by night. One night when he had nearly reached the hills on the eastern side of the valley, he was so unlucky as to light upon a company of sand-hill cranes, who were sitting up all night gambling. He crept slyly along on the side of a log, holding the fire in his hand, but they discovered him and gave chase. The legs of the cranes were so long that he had no hope of escape, so he was obliged to set fire to the grass and to let it burn into the mountains. Thus he soon had a roaring fire, but he had to run at the top of his speed to keep ahead of it. When the bat saw the fire coming, being unused to it, he was half-blinded and had sharp pains in his eyes. He cried out to the lizard that his eyes would be put out, and asked him to cover them up with pitch. The lizard complied, but rubbed the pitch on so thick that the bat could see nothing at all. Thus blinded, the bat hopped, jumped, and fluttered ; he flew this way, he flew that way ; he burnt his head, he burnt his tail. Then he flew towards the west and cried out loud, " Blow, O wind ! " The wind heard him and blew in his eyes, but he could not blow off all the pitch, and that is why the bat is so blear-sighted to this day. And because he was in the fire he is so black and looks as if he had been singed.[2]

The Maidu Indians of California say that at one time

[1] S. Powers, *op. cit.* p. 273.   [2] S. Powers, *op. cit.* pp. 343 *sq.*

people had found fire and were going to use it ; but Thunder wanted to take it away from them, as he desired to be the only one who should have fire. He thought that if he could do this, he would be able to kill all the people. After a time he succeeded, and carried the fire home with him, far to the south. He put Woswosim (a small bird) to guard the fire and see that no one should steal it. Thunder thought that people would die after he had stolen their fire, for they would not be able to cook their food ; but the people contrived to scrape along somehow. They ate most of their food raw, and sometimes they got Toyeskom (another small bird) to look for a long time at a piece of meat, because he had a very red eye, which, by looking at the meat long enough, cooked it almost as well as a fire. But only the chiefs had their food cooked in that way.

All the people lived together in a big sweat-house. The house was as big as a mountain. Among the people was Lizard and his brother ; they were always the first in the morning to go outside and sun themselves on the roof of the sweat-house. One morning as they lay there sunning themselves, they looked west, toward the Coast Range, and saw smoke. They called to all the other people, saying that they had seen smoke far away to the west. The people, however, would not believe them ; and Coyote came out and threw a lot of dust and dirt over the two. But one of the other people did not like this, and he remonstrated with Coyote on his unmannerly behaviour. Then the other people felt sorry. They asked the two Lizards about what they had seen, and requested them to point out the smoke. The Lizards did so, and all could see the thin column rising up far to the west. One person said, " How shall we get that fire back ? How shall we get it away from Thunder ? He is a bad man. I don't know whether we had better try to get it or not." Then the chief said, " The best one among you had better try to get it. Even if Thunder is a bad man, we must try to get the fire." Mouse, Deer, Dog, and Coyote were the ones who were to try, but all the other people went too. They took a flute with them, for they meant to put the fire in it.

They travelled a long time and at last came near to Thunder's house, where was the fire. Woswosim, who was supposed to guard the fire in the house, began to sing, " I am the man who never sleeps. I am the man who never sleeps." Thunder had paid him for his work in beads, and he wore them about his neck and his waist. He sat on the top of the sweat-house, by the smoke-hole. After a while Mouse was sent up to see whether he could get in. He crept up slowly till he got close to Woswosim, and then saw that his eyes were shut. He was asleep, in spite of the song that he sang. When Mouse saw that the watcher was asleep, he crawled to the opening and went in. Now Thunder had several daughters, and they were lying there asleep. Mouse stole up quietly and untied the waist-string of each one's apron, so that should the alarm be given and the girls jump up, these aprons or skirts would fall off and they would have to stop to fasten them. That done, Mouse took the flute, filled it with fire, then crept out, and rejoined the other people who were waiting outside. Some of the fire was taken out and put in Dog's ear, while the rest of the fire in the flute was given to the swiftest runner to carry. However, Deer took a little of it and carried it on the hock of his leg, where there is a reddish spot to this day.

For a while all went well, but when they were about half-way back, Thunder woke up, and, suspecting that something was wrong, asked, " What is the matter with my fire ? " Then he jumped up with a roar of thunder, and his daughters also jumped up ; but their aprons fell off as they did so, and they had to sit down again to put them on. When they were all ready, they went out with Thunder to give chase. They carried with them a heavy wind and a great rain and a hail-storm, so that they might put out any fire the people had. Thunder and his daughters hurried along, and soon overtook the fugitives, but Skunk shot at Thunder and killed him. Then Skunk called out, " After this you must never try to follow and kill people. You must stay up in the sky and be the thunder. That is what you will be." The daughters of Thunder did not follow any farther ; so the people went on safely, and got home with their fire, and people have had it ever since.[1]

[1] Roland   B.   Dixon,   " Maidu   *Museum of Natural History*, xvii. Myths," *Bulletin of the American*   Part ii. (New York, 1902) pp. 65-67.

The Indian tribes who live, or used to live, on the north-western coast of Washington State, the adjoining coast of British Columbia, and the south-western end of Vancouver Island are, or were, known by the national name of Whulle-mooch. Among them the old people used to tell of a time long ago when their ancestors had no fire and were obliged to eat their food raw and to pass their evenings in the dark. One day as they sat on the grass eating raw flesh, a pretty bird with a shining tail came and hovered around them. After admiring its beautiful plumage, some one said, " Pretty bird, what do you want ? Pretty bird, where do you come from ? " " I come," replied the bird, " from a beautiful country far away, bringing you all the blessings of fire (*hieuc*). That which you see about my tail is fire. I have come to give it to the children of the Whullemooch conditionally. First, you must, in order to value it, earn it. Again, no one who has been guilty of a bad deed or of a mean action need try for it. To-day, get ready, each of you, some pitch-pine (*chummuch*). To-morrow morning I shall be here with you." When the bird came next morning, it said, " Have all of you got some pitch-pine ? " " Yes," said all. " I go," said the bird, " and whoever catches me and puts his pitch-pine on my tail shall obtain a blessing, a something whereby to warm himself or herself, cook his food, and do many a service to himself and to the children of the Whullemooch for ever. I go." It went ; and every man and woman, boy and girl of the tribe followed helter-skelter. Some who lacked persever-ance turned back and went home ; all were growing tired and hungry, when one of the men came near the bird and tried to catch it, but the bird eluded his grasp—" You can never get the prize : you are too selfish." With that away flew the bird, and another man took up the chase. But the bird refused to let itself be caught by him, because he had stolen his neighbour's wife. Then, passing a woman who was nursing a sick old man, the bird said to her, " Good woman, you are always doing good, thinking it only your duty. Bring your wood, put it on my tail, and take the fire. It is justly yours." When the wood was laid on the bird's tail, it blazed up. All the others brought their pitch-pine and got fire from her. From that time till now the Indians have

never been without fire.   But as for the bird that brought the
fire, it flew away and was never seen again.[1]

The Nootka or Aht Indians, on the western coast of
Vancouver Island, tell a story of the origin of fire, of which at
least three different versions have been recorded by inde-
pendent inquirers.   It may not be uninstructive to report
and compare the three.   The earliest of these versions is the
one published by Mr. G. M. Sproat, who lived long among
these Indians and knew them intimately.   He resided at
Alberni, on Barclay Sound, then the only civilized settlement
on the western coast of the island.   The surrounding country
is rocky, mountainous, and covered with thick forests of pine ;
the condition of the native Indians, when Mr. Sproat first
settled among them, was almost or quite unknown.   Their
story of the origin of fire, as he has recorded it, runs thus :

" *How Fire was obtained.*—Quawteaht made the earth,
and also all the animals, but had not given them fire, which
burned only in the dwelling of the cuttle-fish (Telhoop), who
could live both on land and in the sea.   All the beasts of the
forest went in a body in search of the necessary element (for
in those days the beasts required fire, having the Indians in
their bodies), which was finally discovered and stolen from
the house of Telhoop by the deer (Moouch), who carried it
away, as the natives curiously describe it, both by words and
signs, in the joint of his hind leg.   The narrators vary slightly
in this legend ; some asserting that the fire was stolen from
the cuttle-fish, others that it was taken from Quawteaht.   All
agree that it was not bestowed as a gift, but was surreptitiously
obtained." [2]

[1] James Deans, " How the Whulle-mooch got Fire," *The American
Antiquarian and Oriental Journal*,
viii. (Chicago, 1886) pp. 41-43.   The
same story, in an abridged form, is
said to be told by the Songhie tribe.
See M. Macfie, *Vancouver Island and
British Columbia* (London, 1865), p.
456.   Mr. Macfie seems to have derived the story from Mr. James Deans,
to whom he acknowledges his obliga-
tions (p. 455).

[2] G. M. Sproat, *Scenes and Studies
of Savage Life* (London, 1868), pp.
178 *sq.*   Mr. Sproat was the first
European to plant a settlement on
Barclay Sound, displacing an Indian
camp from the site which he proposed
to occupy.   For a description of the
wild and rugged character of the
scenery, see his book, pp. 1 *sq.*, 11 *sqq.*
The fire-myths found among the
Indian tribes of North-western
America have been briefly analysed
and compared by Dr. Franz Boas.
He enumerates twenty versions of the
myth.   See Franz Boas, " Tsimshian
Mythology," *Thirty-first Annual Report of the Bureau of American Ethnology* (Washington, 1916), pp. 660-663.

Another version of the Nootka story is reported by the eminent American ethnologist, Dr. Franz Boas, as follows :

In the beginning the Wolves alone possessed fire. The other animals and birds wished very much to get it. After they had made various vain attempts, the Woodpecker, who was Chief, said to the Deer, " Go into the house of the Wolf and dance. We will all sing for you. Tie cedar-bark to your tail, and when you approach the fire, the bark will ignite." So the Deer ran forthwith to the house of the Wolf and danced there till the bark on his tail caught fire. He would have leaped out, but the Wolves caught him before he could escape and wrested the fire from him. Then Woodpecker sent the bird Tsatsiskums and said, " The whole tribe shall sing for you, and you will get fire." So all the animals and birds went to the house of the Wolves, led by Woodpecker and Kwotiath. Before they entered the house they sang a song, and they sang a different song when they had entered it. There they danced round, while the Wolves lay by the fire and watched them. Some of the birds danced aloft on the rafters, but the Wolves did not notice it, so intent were they on watching the dance by the fire. At last the birds on the rafters lighted on the apparatus for making fire, which was kept there. They took it, danced back and gave it to Woodpecker and Kwotiath, and the other animals and birds continued to dance in the house until Woodpecker and Kwotiath had reached home safely. When Kwotiath came home, he worked the apparatus for making fire by friction until sparks flew out. Then he put it to his cheek and burned it. Since then he has had a hole in his cheek. When the dancers in the house of the Wolves knew that Kwotiath had returned home, they gave a shriek and fled from the house. Thus the Wolves lost the fire.[1]

A fuller version of the Nootka myth has been recorded by Mr. George Hunt as follows :

Once upon a time there lived Woodpecker, a chief of the

---

[1] Franz Boas, *Indianische Sagen von der Nord-Pacifischen Küste Amerikas* (Berlin, 1895), p. 102. Kwotiath seems to be a bird or beast, but Dr. Boas gives no explanation. The collective name applied to birds and beasts in this story is *Kyaimimit*, which is the term applied to the birds and other animals in the beginning, before they were transformed into human beings. See F. Boas, *op. cit.* p. 98.

Wolves, who had a slave named Kwatiyat.   He was the only
one in the world who had fire in his house ; even his own
people did not have fire.   The wise chief Ebewayak, chief of
the Mowatcath tribe, his rival, did not know how to get fire
from Woodpecker, the chief of the Wolves.

One day the Mowatcath tribe had a secret meeting, for
they heard that a winter ceremony was going to take place in
the house of Woodpecker.   They decided that they would go
into Woodpecker's house, where the fire was.   Woodpecker
had many sharp-pointed sticks put on the floor near the door,
so that the people could not run out without hurting their
feet.   Chief Ebewayak spoke in the meeting, saying, " My
people, who among you will try to steal fire from Woodpecker ? "   The Deer said, " I will get fire for you."   Then
the chief took some hair-oil in a seaweed bottle, saying,
" Take this with you, and also this comb, and this piece of
stone.   When you get the fire, you must run away ; and when
the Wolves pursue you, throw the stone between you and the
Wolves, and there shall be a large mountain ; and when they
come near again, throw the comb behind you, and it will be
transformed into thick bushes.   When they get through the
thick bushes, they will run after you again ; and when they
come near you, you must throw down the hair-oil, and it will
turn into a large lake.   Then you must run.   You will see
Periwinkle Shell on the road ; to him you must give the fire,
and then you must run to save your life.   Now let me dress
you up with soft cedar-bark to catch the fire with."   He took
the soft cedar-bark and tied a bunch of it on each of Deer's
elbows, telling him that he must stand up and dance round
the fire during one song.   He continued, " When that song is
ended, ask them to open the smoke-hole, because you need
fresh air ; and when they have opened the hole, we will sing
the second song, and in the middle of it you must touch the
fire with your elbow and jump through the smoke-hole.   Now
I will put these hard black stones on your feet, so that they
will not be hurt by the sharp-pointed sticks on the floor of the
chief's house."   So saying he rubbed the stones on Deer's
feet.

By the time the council ended it was dark ; and the people
of the Mowatcath tribe sang as they were going toward the

dancing-house of the Wolves. Deer was dancing in front of them. Before they came to the door of the house, Wood-pecker, the chief of the Wolves, said to his people, " We will not let the Mowatcath in, for they might try to steal our fire." But his daughter said, " I want to see the dance, for I am told that Deer dances well ; you never let me go out to see a dance." Then her father said, " Open the door, and let them come in ; but keep close watch on Deer, and do not let him dance too near the fire. When they are inside, shut the door and put a bar across it, so that he cannot run out." Thus the chief spoke to his people.

So the Wolves opened the door and called the people in. They entered singing ; and after they were in, the chief warriors of the Wolves shut the door, put a bar across it, and stood in front of it. The Mowatcath began to sing Deer's first dancing-song ; and he began to dance round the fire weakly. At the end of the first song, he said, " It is very hot in here. Will you please open the smoke-hole to let the fresh air come in and cool me, for I am sweating ? " Woodpecker, the chief of the Wolves, said, " He cannot jump so high. Go and open the smoke-hole, for it is hot in here." One of his people opened the smoke-hole. Meanwhile the visitors kept quiet and gave Deer a good rest.

After the smoke-hole was wide open, the song-leader of the visitors began to sing ; and Deer began to dance round the fire. Sometimes he would go near the fire. Whenever the chief saw him go near the fire, he would send one of his warriors to tell him to keep away. When the song was about half ended, Deer jumped up through the smoke-hole and ran into the woods, and all the warrior Wolves pursued him. When he came to the foot of a large mountain, he saw the Wolves close behind. Therefore he took the small stone and threw it behind him, and it turned into a large mountain, which detained the Wolves. He ran a long way. Again the Wolves drew near, and he threw the comb backward. It turned into thorny bushes, and the Wolves were kept back on the other side of it. Thus Deer gained another long lead over the Wolves. After a while they made their way through the thorny bushes, and ran after him again. They saw Deer running ahead ; and when they drew near, he poured the hair-oil on the ground.   All of a sudden there was a great lake between Deer and his pursuers ; and while he ran on, the Wolves had to swim across the lake.   Now Deer drew near to the beach ;   there he saw Periwinkle and said to him, " Periwinkle, open your mouth, take this fire into it, and hide it from the Wolves, for I have stolen it from Chief Woodpecker's house.   Do not tell them which way I went."   Periwinkle took the fire in his mouth and hid it ;   and Deer ran on ahead.

After a while the Wolves came and saw Periwinkle sitting down on the roadside.   They asked him if he knew which way Deer had gone ;   but he could not answer, for he could not open his mouth.   He only said, with his mouth shut, " Ho, ho, ho ! " pointing here and there ;   so the Wolves lost track of Deer and went home without catching him.   Ever since the fire has been spread all round the world.[1]

In this last version it is implied that the fire which Deer stole from the Wolves was caught and carried off by him in the bunches of cedar-bark which his chief had tied to his elbows for that purpose.   Mr. Hunt's version differs from that of Dr. Boas in representing Woodpecker as the owner instead of the thief of fire ;   and the Kwatiyat of the one story is probably the same person with the Kwotiath of the other, though in the one story Kwatiyat is the slave of the owner of the fire, whereas in the other Kwotiath is an accomplice in the theft of the fire.   Mr. Hunt's version agrees with that of Mr. Sproat in representing Deer as the thief of the fire ;   whereas in Dr. Boas's version Deer fails in the attempt to steal it and the actual theft is perpetrated by Woodpecker and his accomplice.

The Catloltq, an Indian tribe of Vancouver Island, to the north of the Nootka, say that long ago men had no fire.   But an old man had a daughter, who possessed a wonderful bow and arrows, with which she could hit and bring down whatever she chose.   But she was very lazy and slept constantly. Therefore her father was angry and said to her, " Sleep not always, but take your bow and shoot into the navel of the ocean, that we may get fire."   Now the navel of the ocean

<hr />

[1] George Hunt, " Myths of the Nootka," in " Tsimshian Mythology," by Franz Boas, *Thirty-first Annual*   *Report of the Bureau of American Ethnology* (Washington, 1916), pp. 894-896.

was a huge whirlpool, in which sticks for the making of fire by friction were drifting about. The girl took her bow and shot into the navel of the ocean, and the apparatus for the making of fire by friction sprang ashore. The old man was very glad. He kindled a great fire, and as he wished to keep it to himself, he built a house with a single door, which opened and shut with a snap like a mouth and killed everybody who tried to enter. But people knew that he had fire in his possession, and the Deer resolved to steal it for them. So he took resinous wood, split it, and stuck the splinters in his hair. Then he lashed two boats together, decked them over, and danced and sang on the deck, while he sailed towards the house of the old man. He sang, " Oh, I am going to fetch the fire." The old man's daughter heard him singing and said to her father, " Oh, let the stranger enter the house ; he sings and dances so beautifully." Meantime Deer landed and approached the door, singing and dancing. He leaped up to the door as if he would enter. Then the door closed with a snap, and when it opened again, Deer jumped into the house. There he sat down by the fire, as if he would dry himself, and continued to sing. At the same time he stooped his head over the fire, till it grew quite sooty and the splinters in his hair ignited. Then he sprang out of the house, ran away, and brought the fire to men.[1]

The Tlatlasikoala, a tribe of Kwakiutl Indians who formerly inhabited the north-eastern end of Vancouver Island,[2] similarly tell how in the early days the first fire was stolen by the Deer and brought to men. They say that formerly there was no fire, because Natlibikaq had hidden it. Then Kutena (*Glaucionetla langula Americana*) sent Lelekoista to fetch it. The messenger took up a glowing coal in his mouth and was making off with it, when Natlibikaq observed him and asked him, " What is that which you have in your mouth ? " As the thief could not answer, the owner of the fire struck him on the mouth, and out tumbled the fire. Next Kutena sent the Deer to fetch fire. So the Deer stuck dry wood in his hair

---

[1] Franz Boas, *Indianische Sagen von der Nord-Pacifischen Küste Amerikas*, pp. 80 *sq.*

[2] F. W. Hodge, *Handbook of American Indians North of Mexico* (Washington, 1907–1910), ii. 763.

and ran to Natlibikaq's house, and standing before the door sang, " I come to fetch the fire. I come to fetch the fire." Then he walked into the house, and after dancing round the fire thrust his head into it, so that the wood which he had stuck in his hair caught fire. Then he ran away, and Natlibikaq pursued him to recover the stolen fire. But Deer had foreseen and provided for this contingency ; and when Natlibikaq had almost overtaken him, he took some fat and threw it behind him on the ground. The fat was immediately turned into a great lake, which obliged the pursuer to take a long roundabout road. Yet the pursuer persevered, and when he was almost up with the fugitive, Deer flung some hairs behind him on the earth. The hairs were at once transformed into a dense forest of young trees, which Natlibikaq could not penetrate, and therefore was forced to make a long circuit, thus letting Deer get a long start. Once more the pursuer had almost caught him, when Deer threw behind him four stones, which were changed into four high mountains ; and before Natlibikaq could cross them, Deer had reached Kutena's house. Natlibikaq stood before the door and begged, saying, " O give me at least the half of my fire back " ; but Kutena would not listen to him, so Natlibikaq had to return without his fire. Then Kutena gave the fire to men.[1]

The Kwakiutl Indians, who inhabit the north-eastern coast of Vancouver Island and the opposite coast of British Columbia, across Queen Charlotte Sound, in like manner relate how the Deer, or a hero who assumed the form of a deer, procured the first fire for men. As told by those of the tribe who inhabit Vancouver Island the story runs thus : It was Kani-ke-laq who stole fire and gave it to the Indians. The chief who possessed fire lived at " the edge of the day," that is, at the rising of the sun. When the friends of this chief were dancing round the fire, Kani-ke-laq appeared in the form of a deer, and, with a bunch of resinous wood between his antlers, joined the dancers. At a given signal from his friends outside, he dipped his head and the sticks on it ignited. He leaped across the fire and rushed from

---

[1] Franz Boas, *Indianische Sagen von der Nord-Pacifischen Küste Amerikas*, p. 187.

the house, scattering the stolen fire everywhere. He was pursued, but his friends had placed halibut on his track, which caused his pursuers to trip up. This accounts for the short black tail of the deer, which was burnt by the fire.[1]

Another version of the Kwakiutl myth represents not the deer but the mink as the animal which first procured fire for men. They say that Mink went out to fight the Ghosts (*Lalenoq*). He stole quietly into the house of the chief of the Ghosts and carried off the chief's child from the cradle. When the chief perceived his loss he gave chase, but did not come up with the fugitive until Mink had reached his own house and barred it. The chief of the Ghosts besought Mink, saying, " Oh ! give me my child back " ; but Mink refused until the chief gave him fire as a recompense. Thus men got fire.[2]

The Awikenoq, an Indian tribe who inhabit the coast of British Columbia to the north of the Kwakiutl, agree with the Nootka and Kwakiutl of Vancouver Island in attributing the first theft of fire to the Deer. They say that after the Raven had set free the imprisoned sun, two beings named Noakaua (" the Wise ") and Masamasalaniq came down from heaven to make everything good and beautiful on earth. At the desire of Noakaua, his companion Masamasalaniq separated the land from the water, created that fat fish, the oolachan,[3] and fashioned men and women by carving them out of cedar wood. Afterwards Noakaua thought, " Oh that Masamasalaniq would fetch the fire ! " But Masamasalaniq could not. So Noakaua sent first the Ermine to the house of the man who guarded the fire. The Ermine took up surreptitiously the fire in his mouth and was making off with it, when the owner of the fire asked him, " Where are you off to ? " But Ermine could not answer because he had the fire in his mouth. Then the owner gave him a slap on the side of his head

---

[1] George M. Dawson, " Notes and Observations on the Kwakiool People of Vancouver Island," *Transactions of the Royal Society of Canada*, vol. v. section ii. (1887) p. 22.

[2] Franz Boas, *Indianische Sagen von der Nord-Pacifischen Küste Amerikas*, p. 158.

[3] The oolachan or oulachan is the candle-fish (*Thaleichthys pacificus*) of north-western America.

which made him drop the fire. As the mission of Ermine thus proved unsuccessful, Noakaua despatched the Deer on the same errand. The Deer went first to Masamasalaniq to have his legs made slim and fleet. And Noakaua thought, " Oh that Masamasalaniq would stick fir-wood in the Deer's tail ! " So Masamasalaniq stuck fir-wood in the Deer's tail. Swiftly now ran the Deer from there. He came to the house where was the fire, and danced round the fire, singing, " I should like to find the light ! " Suddenly he turned his back to the flames, so that the wood on his tail caught fire. Then he ran away, and everywhere the fire of the burning wood fell from his tail on the ground, and men carefully preserved it. And the Deer as he ran cried to the wood which he passed, " Hide the fire " ; and the wood received the fire and has been combustible ever since.[1]

Here, as in many other myths, the story of the theft of fire is employed to explain how it comes about that fire can be produced by the friction of wood.

Among the Heiltsuk, another Indian tribe on the coast of British Columbia, to the north of the Awikenoq, the Deer is said, as a man, to have been called by a name which means Torch-bearer, because he stole the fire by means of the wood which he tied to his tail.[2]

Substantially the same myth to account for the origin of fire among men is told by the Tsimshian, another tribe on the coast of British Columbia, to the north of the Heiltsuk. They say that in the early days of the world there was a certain marvellous being called Txamsem or Giant, who did great wonders, as for instance by procuring daylight at the time when the world was still plunged in darkness. From his father he had received a raven blanket or skin, and whenever he put it on he could fly like a raven through the air. Indeed, we may conclude that Giant was no other than Raven himself, who, as we shall see presently, plays a great part in the fire-myths of the more northerly Indians. Be that as it may, the Tsimshian tell how, when people

[1] Franz Boas, *Indianische Sagen von der Nord-Pacifischen Küste Amerikas*, pp. 213 *sq.*

[2] Franz Boas, *Indianische Sagen von der Nord-Pacifischen Küste Amerikas*, p. 241.

began to multiply on the earth, they were distressed because they had no fire with which to cook their food and to warm themselves in winter. Thereupon Giant remembered that the animals had fire in their village, and he tried to fetch it for the people. So he put on his raven blanket and went to the village, but the people of the village refused to let him have fire and sent him away from their town. He tried in every way to get fire, but he failed, for the people would not let him have it.

Finally, he sent one of his attendants, the Sea-gull, to carry a message to the people ; and this is the message the Sea-gull carried : " A good-looking young chief will come soon to the people to have a dance in your chief's house." Then the whole tribe made ready to welcome the young chief. Now Giant caught a deer and skinned it. At that time the deer had a long tail, like a wolf's tail. Giant tied pitch-wood to the long tail of the deer. He borrowed the canoe of the great Shark, and they came to the village, where the chief had a large fire in his house. The big Shark's canoe was full of crows and sea-gulls ; and Giant sat in the middle of the canoe, dressed in his deer-skin. Then all the people entered. They built a large fire, larger than it had been before, and the great house of the chief was full of his tribesmen Then all the new-comers were seated on one side of the large house, ready to sing. Soon the young chief began to dance, and all his companions beat time with their sticks, and one had a drum. They all sang a song together, and some of the birds clapped their hands

The Deer entered at the door. He looked around and entered, leaping and dancing, and went round the large fire. Then all the people were well pleased to see him dance. Finally, he whisked his tail over the fire, and the pitch-wood on his tail caught fire. He ran out with the firebrand at his tail and swam on the water. Then all his companions flew away out of the house. The great Shark canoe also left. The people tried to catch the Deer, intending to kill him. He jumped and swam quickly, and the pitch-wood at his tail was burning. When he arrived at one of the islands, he went ashore quickly, struck a fir-tree with his

tail, and said, " You shall burn as long as the years last."
For that reason the deer has a short black tail.[1]

In this story we may perhaps detect a fusion of two
different versions of the fire-myth, in one of which the fire
was stolen by the Deer and in the other by the Raven ; for
while the narrator expressly tells us that the fire was stolen
by the dancing Deer, he had previously told us that the
dancer was really Giant wrapt for the occasion in a deer-skin,
though usually he wore a raven blanket or skin. Such a
fusion of the two versions may be explained by the geographical situation of the Tsimshian ; for they occupy a
territory on the coast intermediate between the territories
of the Southern Indians (the Nootka, Kwakiutl, and so on)
and of the Northern Indians (the Haida, Tlingit, and
Tinneh) ; and whereas among the Southern Indians the
usual hero of the fire-myth is the Deer, among the Northern
Indians he is the Raven. Thus in the Tsimshian story
we can see a meeting of the two distinct versions and an
attempt to harmonize them.

Before we pass to a consideration of the fire-myths of the
Northern Indians, it remains to relate the fire-myths of the
Southern Indians of British Columbia, who for the most
part inhabit the interior of the country and belong to the
Salish stock. We shall begin with that branch of the Salish
stock who are commonly known as the Thompson Indians,
because they inhabit the valley of the Thompson River.

The Thompson Indians say that in the beginning the
people were without fire and had to depend altogether on the
sun for cooking their food. At that time the sun was very
much hotter than it is now, and people were able to cook their
food by holding it up to the sun or by spreading it under the
sun's rays. This, however, was not so good as fire ; and
Beaver and Eagle determined they would find out if there was
any fire in the world, and obtain it, if possible, for the people.
They trained themselves in the mountains until they became
full of " mystery," and through their magic were able to look

---

[1] Franz Boas, " Tsimshian Mythology," *Thirty-first Annual Report of
the Bureau of American Ethnology*
(Washington, 1916), p. 63. As to
Giant, his raven blanket or skin, and
his creation of daylight, see *ib.* pp.
58 *sqq.*

over all the world, even to its edges. They discovered that there was fire in a lodge at Lytton, so they laid their plans accordingly. They left their home at the mouth of the Fraser, and journeyed up that river until they arrived at Lytton.[1] The Eagle soared away through the air, and at last discovered the shell of a fresh-water clam, of which he took possession. The Beaver appeared at the place where the people drew water out of the creek. They lived in an underground lodge. Some young girls, going down to the creek for water in the morning, came back running, with the intelligence that there was a beaver at the watering-place. Some young men ran out with bows and arrows, shot him, and brought him up to the house. They began to skin him. In the meanwhile the Beaver thought, " Oh, my elder brother ! He is long in coming. I am nearly done for." Just then the Eagle perched on the top of the ladder, and at once attracted the people's attention, so that they forgot all about the Beaver in their anxiety to shoot the Eagle, which they could not kill, though they shot arrows at him. Meanwhile the Beaver caused the house to be flooded with water. In the confusion the Eagle dropped the clam-shell down into the fire. The Beaver immediately filled it with fire, put it under his armpit, and made off in the water. He spread the fire over the whole country. After that the Indians could make fire out of trees. Some say that the Beaver put fire into all wood and trees which grow near his haunts, whilst the Eagle put it into the trees which grow in high or distant parts of the country, away from the watercourses and lakes.[2]

Another version of the Thompson story, differing only in details from the first, runs as follows : The people of Nicola and Spences Bridge had no fire, and no means of procuring it, for wood did not burn in those days. Of all people, only those at Lytton had fire. Beaver, Weasel, and Eagle agreed that they would try to steal fire from the Lytton people, who were living at a little spring near the mouth of the Thompson

[1] James Teit, " Mythology of the Thompson Indians," *The Jesup North Pacific Expedition*, vol. viii. Part ii. (Leyden and New York, 1912) pp. 229 *sq.* (*Memoir of the American Museum of Natural History*).

[2] James Teit, *Traditions of the Thompson River Indians of British Columbia* (Boston and New York, 1898), pp. 56 *sq.*, with note [181] on p. 112.

River. Beaver went there first, and began to dam up the water, while Eagle and Weasel went into training in the mountains. The fourth day, when they were sweat-bathing, Weasel's guardian spirit appeared in the form of a weasel, and entered into his sweat-house. Here it cut itself open, and Weasel, entering its body, assumed animal form. Eagle's guardian spirit came to his sweat-house in the form of an eagle. He also let Eagle enter his body, so that he assumed the form of a bird.

Eagle said, " I will fly far up, and watch brother Beaver." And Weasel said, " I will run along the high mountain ridges, and see what brother Beaver is doing." When they came within sight of Lytton, they saw that they had no time to lose, for Beaver was already a prisoner in the hands of the people, who were making ready to cut him up. Eagle swooped down and perched on the top of the ladder of the underground house, while Weasel busied himself making a hole at the base of the house that the water might flood it. The people were so anxious to shoot Eagle that they forgot all about Beaver, and never saw Weasel. They could not hit Eagle, however, and were angry at one another for missing. Meanwhile the water which Beaver had dammed up began to pour in through the hole which Weasel had made, and, in the confusion, Beaver snatched up a firebrand, put it in a clam-shell, ran off with it, and escaped.

When the three reached home, Beaver made a fire for the people. Eagle showed them how to cook, and how to roast food ; and Weasel showed them how to boil food with stones. They threw some of the fire at each of the different kinds of wood, and since that time all kinds of wood burn.[1]

In this version we can detect an attempt to rationalize the myth by explaining that the Eagle and Weasel, who figure in it, were not a real eagle and a real weasel, but merely men named Eagle and Weasel respectively, who temporarily assumed the forms of an eagle and a weasel for the purpose of stealing fire. Such an interpretation of the old story betrays a later stage of reflection, at which men begin to doubt the possibility of animals using or kindling fire.

---

[1] James Teit, " Mythology of the Thompson Indians," *The Jesup North*　*Pacific Expedition,* vol. viii. Part ii. pp. 338 *sq.*

The Thompson Indians have also a tradition that formerly their ancestors procured fire from the Sun. They say that long ago, before Beaver and Eagle stole the fire, and before there was any fire in wood, the people could not make fire. When they were very cold, they sent messengers to the Sun to procure fire. The messengers had to travel a long way. When the fire brought by the messengers was used up, and they wanted more, they sent for some more from the Sun. Some say that the messengers carried the fire between shells, or enclosed in some other way. The fire fetched from the Sun gave a strong heat. Some men are said to have had the power of bringing down sun-heat and fire without having to go to the Sun for it. They drew down the sunbeams.[1]

Again, the Thompson Indians tell a fire-myth of a different sort, in which the Coyote is represented as the first thief of fire. The story is as follows : From the top of a mountain Coyote saw a light far away to the south. At first he did not know what it was, but by a process of divination he learned that it was fire. He made up his mind to go and get it. Many people accompanied him. Fox, Wolf, Antelope, and all the good runners went with him. After travelling a long way, they reached the house of the Fire people. They told them, " We have come to visit you, to dance, to play, and to gamble." They prepared for a dance that night. Coyote made a head-dress of pitchy yellow-pine shavings, with long fringes of cedar-bark reaching to the ground. The Fire people danced first. The fire was very low. Then Coyote and his people danced in a circle round the fire. They complained that they could not see. Then the Fire people made a large fire. Coyote complained four times, and finally they let the fire blaze up high. Coyote's people pretended to be very hot, and went out to cool themselves. They took up positions for running. Only Coyote was left. He danced about wildly until his head-dress took fire. He pretended to be afraid, and requested the Fire people to put it out. They warned him not to dance so close to the fire. When he came

---

[1] James A. Teit, " Thompson Tales," in *Folk-tales of Salishan and Sahaptin Tribes*, edited by Franz Boas (Lancaster, Pa., and New York, 1917), pp. 20 *sq.* (*Memoirs of the American Folk-lore Society*, vol. xi.).

near the door, he swung the long fringes of his head-dress across the fire and ran out. The Fire people pursued him. He gave his head-band to Antelope, who ran and passed it on to the next runner. Thus they carried it in relays. The Fire people caught up with the animals and killed them one by one. Only Coyote was left. They nearly caught him, but he ran behind a tree and gave the fire to it. The Fire people looked for him, but could not find him. They caused the wind to rise, and the burning fragments of bark that had fallen here and there set fire to the grass. They said, " Coyote will now burn up." A heavy smoke arose, and Coyote escaped. The fire spread all over the country, and burned up many people. Coyote caused a heavy rainfall and a flood, which put out the fire. After that, the fire was in the trees, and grass and trees could be used for making fire. For that reason dry cedar-bark carries fire and can be used for slow matches. For the same reason, too, pitch-wood ignites easily and is used for starting fires. Since then there have been smoke and fire in the world, and the two are inseparable.[1]

This story clearly belongs to the same class of myths of which we have found examples much farther south, among the Indians of New Mexico, Utah, and California. The characteristic features of this type of myth are that the thief of fire is the coyote, and that he passes the stolen fire down a long line of animal runners, who relieve each other, each of them taking up the fire and the running as his predecessor is exhausted.[2]

The Lillooet Indians, whose country borders that of the Thompson Indians on the west, tell a story of the origin of fire which agrees closely with one of the fire-myths told by the Thompson Indians.[3] Nor is this resemblance between the stories surprising, since the Lillooet are not only the immediate neighbours of the Thompsons, but belong to the same Salish stock and speak a closely related language.[4] Their version of the myth runs as follows :

---

[1] James A. Teit, "Thompson Tales," in *Folk-tales of Salishan and Sahaptin Tribes*, edited by Franz Boas, p. 2.

[2] See above, pp. 139 *sq.*, 142 *sqq.*, 153 *sq.*

[3] See above, pp. 170-172.

[4] James Teit, " The Lillooet Indians," *The Jesup North Pacific Expedition*, vol. ii. Part v. (Leyden and New York, 1906) p. 195 (*Memoir of the American Museum of Natural History*).

Beaver and Eagle lived with their sister in the Lillooet country. They had no fire and ate their food raw. The sister cried and complained constantly, because she had no fire at which to roast her dried salmon-skins. At last the brothers took pity on her because she cried so much, and said, " Don't cry any more ! We will procure fire for you. We will train ourselves for a long time, and during our absence you must be very careful not to cry or complain ; for, if you do, we shall fail in our object, and our training will be fruitless."

Leaving their sister, the brothers repaired to the mountains, where they spent four years training themselves. At the end of that time, they returned to their sister, who had never cried during their absence, and told her that they would go to fetch fire, as they now knew where it could be found, and how they could obtain it.

After five days' journeying, they arrived at the house [1] of the people who possessed fire. Then one brother drew over himself an eagle's body, and the other one a beaver's body. The brother who was disguised as a Beaver dammed the stream near by, and that night he made a hole underneath the people's house. Next morning he swam about in the water made by the dam, and an old man saw him and shot him. He took Beaver into the house, and, laying him beside the fire, told the people to skin him. While they were skinning him, they came on something hard underneath his armpit. This was a clam-shell, which Beaver had hidden there. Just then the people saw a very large and fine-looking eagle perch on a tree near by. They were anxious to kill him to get his plumes ; so they all ran out and began to shoot at him, but none of them could hit him. When they were thus engaged, Beaver, who was now left alone, put some of the fire in his clam-shell, and escaped through the hole he had made. He soon reached the water, which was now almost at the house, and swam away with his prize.

As soon as Eagle saw that his brother was safe, he flew away and joined him. They continued their journey home, Eagle resting on Beaver's back when he grew tired. Thus

[1] Most Indian informants agree that the house was an underground house, and according to some it was near the sea.

they brought fire home, and gave it to their sister, who now became very happy and contented.[1]

A different story of the origin of fire is told by the Lillooet as follows : They say that Raven and Sea-gull were friends and lived in the Lillooet country. Raven had four servants, namely, Worm, Flea, Louse, and Little Louse. It was dark all over the world at that time, because Sea-gull owned the daylight and kept it in a box, never letting any of it out except when he needed it for his own private use. However, Raven contrived by guile to break the box and let the daylight spread over the world. Thus Raven had light, but he had not yet got fire.

At last, looking out from the roof of his house, he saw smoke rising far away in the south, on the shore of the sea. Next day he embarked with all his servants in Little Louse's canoe ; but it was too small, and they were swamped. Next day he tried Big Louse's canoe ; but it also was too small. Thus he tried all his servants' canoes, but with the same result. Now he told his wife to go and ask the loan of Sea-gull's large canoe, as he intended to go and get fire. The following day, after he had obtained the canoe, he embarked with his servants, and, after four days' paddling down stream, they arrived close to the house of the people who possessed fire.

Now Raven asked his servants which of them was willing to go and steal the baby-girl of these people. Little Louse offered to go ; but the others said, " You will make too much noise and wake the people." Big Louse offered himself, but they had the same objections to him. Then Flea said, " I will go. In one jump I will reach and snatch the baby, and with another jump I will be out again. The people won't be able to catch me." But the others said, " You will make a noise, and we don't want the people to know." Worm now spoke, saying, " I will go slowly and quietly, and will bore a hole underground. I will come out underneath where the baby hangs in its cradle, steal it, and return without any one hearing me." They all thought this was the best proposal, and assented to Worm's plan. So that night Worm bored a

---

[1] James Teit, " Traditions of the Lillooet Indians of British Columbia," *Journal of American Folk-lore,* xxv. (1912) pp. 299 *sq.*

hole underground and stole the baby. As soon as he returned with it, they put it in their canoe and paddled rapidly away toward home.

Early the next morning the people missed the baby, and the wise ones knew what had happened. They gave chase, but could neither discover nor overtake Raven and his servants. Sturgeon, Whale, and Seal searched long and far, but at last gave it up and returned home. Only one small fish[1] found the course the canoe had taken, and overtook it. It tried to retard the canoe's progress by sticking to the paddles, but at last it grew tired and returned home. The mother of the child caused a heavy rain to fall (some say by her weeping), thinking that the rain would stop the thieves, but all in vain. Raven reached his own country with the child, and the child's kinsfolk, hearing where it had been taken to, came to Raven's house with many presents ; but Raven said the presents were not what he wanted, so the baby's kinsfolk went home without the child.

Twice again they visited Raven with presents, but with the same result. On their fourth visit, too, Raven refused their presents, although each time they brought more valuable gifts than the time before. Then they asked him what he wanted, and he said, " Fire." They answered, " Why did not you say that before ? " and they were glad, because they had plenty of fire and deemed it of little value. So they went and brought him fire, and he gave them back the baby. The Fish people showed Raven how to make fire with dry cottonwood roots. Raven was glad, and said to Sea-gull, " If I had not stolen light from you, I could not have seen where fire was kept. Now we have fire and light, and both are benefited." Thereafter Raven sold fire to every family that wished it, and each family that bought it paid him a young girl. Thus Raven became possessed of many wives.[2]

We have seen that in a Kwakiutl story the Mink similarly obtained the coveted fire by stealing a baby and then swapping it for fire.[3]

---

[1] Said to be a small, very spiny fish inhabiting the sea.

[2] James Teit, " Traditions of the Lillooet Indians of British Columbia,"

Journal of American Folk-lore, xxv. (1912) pp. 300-303.

[3] See above, p. 167.

Another Lillooet story, recorded by Dr. Boas on the Lower Fraser River, relates how fire was procured by a different application of the same principle of barter. The story is as follows :

The Beaver gave fire to the Ghosts. Men did not know how to procure it, and at last they sent the Little Otter [1] to fetch it. The Little Otter borrowed his grandmother's knife, hid it under his cloak, and set off for the home of the Ghosts. On reaching their house, he went in and saw them dancing. When the dance was over, the Ghosts wished to bathe and wash. " Hold on," said Little Otter, " I will fetch you water." He took a bucket and went down to the bank of the river. When he came back with the bucket full, and was passing one of the fires that were burning in the house, he pretended to stumble, and in so doing poured the water on the fire, so that it went out. " Oh," cried he, " I stumbled," and so saying he went back to the water to fill his bucket. When he returned to the house and was passing the other fire he poured water on it also and put it out. It was now quite dark in the house. Then Little Otter whipped out his knife and cut off the head of the chief of the Ghosts. After that he strewed dust on the severed neck of the decapitated chief to prevent it from bleeding, and made off with the head. But even before the Ghosts could relight the fire, the dust was soaked with blood. The chief's mother perceived it, and as soon as they had made up the fire again, they saw that the head of their chief had been cut off. Then the mother of the dead chief spoke, saying, " Go to-morrow to Little Otter and ransom the head from him." They did so and came to Little Otter's house. Now Little Otter had built ten houses for himself, and had caused his grandmother to make him ten different suits of clothes. So when the Ghosts arrived, Little Otter appeared on the roof now of one house and now of another, and always in a different suit of clothes ; so the Ghosts thought that there were many people there. When the Ghosts were come, they spoke to Little Otter's grandmother, saying, " We will give you robes in exchange for the head of our chief." But she answered, " My grandson does not want robes." Then they offered a bow and arrows, but the

[1] *Kaig*, in German *Nerz*

grandmother rejected these also. Then the Ghosts wept and the trees wept with them, so sorrowful were they ; and the tears of the trees were rain. At last the Ghosts offered Little Otter the fire-drill. The grandmother accepted it, and gave them back the head. Since then men have had fire.[1]

The Snanaimuq or Nanaimo, a tribe of the Salish stock who inhabit a district about Nanaimo Harbour and Nanaimo Lake in the south-eastern part of Vancouver Island,[2] tell similarly how fire was procured in exchange for an infant. They say that long ago men had no fire. The Mink desired to fetch fire, and for that purpose he repaired with his grandmother to the chief who kept the fire. They landed unobserved, and Mink stole by night into the house, while the chief and his wife were sleeping. But the bird Tegya was rocking the baby in the cradle. Mink set the door ajar. When the bird heard the creaking of the door, it cried " Pq ! pq ! " to waken the chief. But Mink whispered, " Sleep ! Sleep ! " and the bird fell asleep. Mink now entered the house and stole the chief's child from the cradle. Then he went quickly to his boat, in which his grandmother was waiting for him, and together they sailed or paddled home. Every time they passed a village the grandmother had to pinch the brat to make it squall. At last they reached Tlaltq (Gabriola Island, opposite Nanaimo), where Mink had a large house, in which he and his grandmother dwelt alone.

Next morning the chief missed his child and was very sad. He paddled out in his canoe to seek it, and when he came to a village, he asked, " Have you not seen my child ? Somebody has stolen it from me." The people answered, " Last night Mink passed by here, and a child squalled in his canoe." So at the end the chief found his way to Tlaltq. Mink had expected him, and when he saw him coming afar off, he clapped one of his many hats on his head, and going out he danced in front of the house, while his grandmother beat time and sang. Then he rushed back into the house, clapped a second hat on his head, and appeared at another

---

[1] Franz Boas, *Indianische Sagen von der Nord-Pacifischen Küste Amerikas*, pp. 43 *sq.*

[2] F. W. Hodge, *Handbook of American Indians*, ii. 23.

door in a different guise. At last he stepped out of the middle door, carrying the chief's child on his arm. The chief did not dare to attack Mink because he thought that there were many people in the house. He said, " Give me my child back. I will give you many plates of copper." [1] But Mink's grandmother called out to him, " Don't accept them." At last the chief offered him the fire-drill, and Mink accepted it on his grandmother's advice. The chief got his child and went home, and Mink made a great fire. Thus men received the boon of fire.[2] This story is substantially identical with the one reported in a briefer form among the Kwakiutl.[3]

A story of the origin of fire is told by the Okanaken Indians, who form the easternmost division of the Salish stock in British Columbia. But they are not confined to that province, for they extend southward into the United States, the boundary between the two countries separating them into two fairly equal divisions.[4] Their story of the origin of fire runs thus :

Once there was no fire, so all the people met together to discuss the problem of procuring the fire. They wondered how they could best ascend into the upper world. At last they resolved to make a chain of arrows. Accordingly they shot an arrow into the sky, but it would not stick fast. They all tried, one after another, to make their arrows stick, but they all failed. At last a certain bird (*tsiskakena*) shot his arrows home, and left his last arrow suspended in such a way that the others could attach theirs to it. Presently the chain of arrows was complete and they all climbed up. They now consulted as to the best method of procuring the fire. It was determined that Beaver should go into the water and be caught by the Fire people, who were fishing at that time close by ; and that when Beaver was being skinned by them, the Eagle should fly over and attract the

---

[1] Plates of copper are, or used to be, highly valued by the Indians of North-western America.

[2] Franz Boas, *Indianische Sagen von der Nord-Pacifischen Küste Amerikas*, p. 54. Dr. Boas records a second and almost identical version of the myth (pp. 54 *sq.*).

[3] See above, p. 167.

[4] C. Hill Tout, " Report on the Ethnology of the Okanaken of British Columbia," *Journal of the Royal Anthropological Institute*, xli. (1911) p. 130.

people's attention and draw them away from Beaver, who was then to seize a portion of the fire and make off with it. Accordingly Beaver entered the stream where the Fire people were fishing, and he allowed himself to be caught by them. They immediately took him home and began to skin him. They had just cut open the skin at the breast, when Eagle flew over and attracted their attention. Everybody seized his bow and arrows and, giving chase to Eagle, tried to bring him down. Seizing the opportunity, Beaver jumped up, and placing some of the fire inside his skin, where it had been cut open, made off to his companions, where he was presently joined by the Eagle. There was great excitement now at the top of the ladder as to who should go down first. In their pushing and striving the chain of arrows broke before they all got down, and some of them had to jump for it. Catfish fell into a hole and broke his jaw all to pieces. The Sucker struck his head and smashed all the bones in it, in consequence of which all the other animals had each to contribute a bone to give him a new head. That is why the Catfish has so peculiar a mouth, and the Sucker so peculiar a head.[1]

The same story is told, with trifling variations, by the Sanpoil Indians, who belong to the Salish stock and live on the San Poil River and the Columbia River, below Big Bend, in the State of Washington.[2] They say that once upon a time it rained until all the fires on earth were extinguished. The animals held a council and decided to make war on the sky in order to bring back the fire. In spring the people began, and tried to shoot their arrows up to the sky. Coyote tried first, but did not succeed. Finally the Chickadee contrived to shoot an arrow which stuck in the sky. He continued to shoot, making a chain of arrows by means of which the animals climbed up. The last to climb was the Grizzly Bear, but under his weight the chain of arrows broke down, and he could not join the other animals in the sky.

[1] C. Hill Tout, "Report on the Ethnology of the Okanaken of British Columbia," *Journal of the Royal Anthropological Institute*, xli. (1911) p. 146.

[2] F. W. Hodge, *Handbook of American Indians*, ii. 451.

When the rest of the animals reached the sky, they found themselves in a valley near a lake, where the people of the sky were fishing. Coyote wished to act as scout, but was captured. Then the Musk-rat dug holes along the shore of the lake, and Beaver and Eagle set out to obtain the fire. Beaver entered one of the fish-traps and pretended to be dead. They carried him to the chief's house, where the people began to skin him. Just then the Eagle perched on a tree near the tent. When the people saw the Eagle, they ran out, and at once Beaver took a clam-shell full of glowing coals and ran away. He jumped into the lake and people tried to catch him in nets ; but the water drained away through the holes which Musk-rat had made. The animals ran back to the chain of arrows, but found it broken. Then each bird took a quadruped on its back and flew down with it. Only Coyote and the Sucker were left aloft. Coyote tied a piece of buffalo robe to each paw and jumped down. He sailed down on the skin, and finally landed on a pine-tree. Next morning he showed off his wings, but he could not take them off again, and was transformed into a bat. The Sucker had to jump down, and was broken to pieces. The animals fitted his bones together ; and, since some were missing, they put pine-needles into its tail. Therefore the Sucker has many bones.[1]

We now leave the tribes of the Salish stock, who inhabit the southern part of British Columbia, and pass to the more northerly tribes, who belong to the great Athapascan family. Among these are the Chilcotin or Tsilkotin, who inhabit the valley of the river to which they have given their name. Their territory thus lies in the interior of British Columbia, at about latitude 52° north.[2] Their story of the origin of fire runs as follows :

In the old days there was no fire in the world except at the house of one man, and he would not give it to the other people. So one day Raven resolved to steal it, and

[1] Marian K. Gould, " Sanpoil Tales," in *Folk-tales of Salishan and Sahaptin Tribes*, edited by Franz Boas, pp. 107 *sq.*

[2] Livingston Farrand, " Traditions of the Chilcotin Indians," *The Jesup* *North Pacific Expedition*, vol. ii. Part i. (New York, 1900) p. 3 (*Memoir of the American Museum of Natural History*) ; F. W. Hodge, *Handbook of American Indians*, i. 109.

he gathered his brothers and friends and went to the house of the fire-man. The fire was burning at one side of the house, and the owner sat beside it to guard it. As soon as Raven and his friends came in, they all started to dance. Now, Raven had tied shavings of pitch-wood in his hair; and as he danced, he would come near the fire, so that the shavings would almost ignite; but the fire-man kept a sharp watch that it should not happen. So they danced and danced, until one after another grew tired and dropped out, but Raven kept on. And Raven danced all that day and all that night and all the next day, until even the fire-man was worn out with watching and fell asleep. As soon as Raven saw that, he put his head so that the pitch-wood caught fire, and, dashing out of the house, ran about over the country, starting fires in different spots. The fire-man awoke, and, seeing smoke all about, knew at once what had happened, and ran about trying his best to get his fire back, but could not, because it was burning in so many places; and since that time people have always had fire. Now, when the woods began to burn, the animals started to run; and they all escaped except the rabbit, who did not run fast enough, and so was caught in the fire and burnt his feet. And that is why rabbits have black spots on the soles of their feet to-day. After the trees had caught fire, the fire remained in the wood; and that is why wood burns to-day, and you can get fire by rubbing two sticks together.[1]

The Kaska Indians, another tribe of the Athapascan family, occupy a territory in the northern interior of British Columbia, on the Arctic slope of the mountains, farther north than the territory of the Chilcotin Indians.[2] They tell a story of the origin of fire, which runs thus:

Long ago the people had no fire. Of all the people, only Bear had fire. He had a fire-stone, with which he could make fire at any time. He jealously guarded this stone, and always kept it tied to his belt. One day he was lying down by the fire in his lodge, when a little bird came in and approached the fire. Bear said, " What do you want? " and the bird answered, " I am nearly frozen, and

---

[1] Livingston Farrand, op. cit. p. 15. *Journal of American Folk-lore*, xxx.
[2] James A. Teit, " Kaska Tales," (1917) pp. 427 *sq.*

have come in to warm myself." Bear told it to come and
pick his lice. The little bird assented, and began to hop
all over Bear, picking his lice. While it did this, it also
picked the string which fastened the fire-stone to Bear's
belt. When the string was quite picked asunder, the bird
suddenly snatched the stone and flew off with it. Now
the animals had already arranged for the stealing of the
fire, and waited in line, one behind another. Bear chased
the bird, and caught it up just as it reached the first animal
of the line. As it threw the fire to him, he ran with it ;
and, as Bear in turn overtook him, he passed it on to the
next, and so on. At last the fire was passed to Fox, who
ran up a high mountain with it. Bear was now so exhausted
that he could not follow Fox, and turned back. Fox broke
up the fire-stone on the top of the mountain, and threw a
fragment of it to each tribe. Thus the many tribes all over
the earth obtained fire ; and that is why there is fire in the
rocks and woods everywhere now.[1]

The Babine Indians, another tribe of the Athapascan
stock, who inhabit the country about Babine Lake, in the
northern interior of British Columbia, have also a story of
the origin of fire. They say that long ago the only fire in
the world was in the possession of an old chief, who kept it all
to himself in his lodge and would not share it with anybody.
So all men shivered with cold, except this one old man ; and
as he remained deaf to their prayers for fire, they resolved to
wrest it from him by stratagem. Accordingly they applied
to the Caribou and the Musk-rat. They provided the
Caribou with a head-dress of resinous wood with shavings
attached to it ; and they dressed up the Musk-rat in an apron
of marmot skin. Then they entered the lodge of the old
chief who owned the fire, and as they entered they sang.
The Caribou and the Musk-rat took up position at either side
of the hearth, over which the master of the lodge kept
vigilant watch. Then the two animals began to dance. As
they danced, the Caribou, by shaking his head from side to
side in his usual fashion, contrived to kindle his head-dress of
resinous wood at the flames of the hearth ; but the wary old

[1] James A. Teit, " Kaska Tales," *Journal of American Folk-lore,* xxx.
(1917) p. 443.

man at once extinguished the incipient fire. A little afterwards, amid the noisy songs with which the assembly accompanied the dance, the Caribou succeeded in setting fire to his
head-dress again, and this time the old man had great trouble
in putting it out. While he was thus occupied, the cunning
Musk-rat, who had had long practice in burrowing through
the earth and was only biding his time, seized furtively a
little of the glowing embers and disappeared with it under
ground. Some time later a column of smoke was seen rising
from a mountain on the horizon. The smoke was soon
followed by tongues of fire, and thus men learned that the
Musk-rat had succeeded in procuring fire for them.[1]

The story that men first learned of the boon of fire by
observing smoke and flames issuing from a mountain is
significant. It suggests that these Indians obtained, or rather
believed themselves to have obtained, the first fire from one of
the active volcanoes which exist in this part of America.

The Haida Indians of Queen Charlotte Islands say that
very long ago there was a great flood by which all men and
animals were destroyed, with the exception of a single raven.
This creature, however, was not exactly an ordinary bird, but,
like all animals in the old Indian stories, possessed the attributes of a human being to a great extent. His coat of feathers,
for example, he could put on or off at will, like a garment. It
is even related in one version of the story that he was born of a
woman who had no husband, and that she made bows and
arrows for him. After the destruction of mankind in the
great flood this remarkable Raven married a cockle, which
bore him a female child ; and by taking this child to wife he
at last repeopled the earth.

But still the people, his descendants, had many wants,
for as yet they had neither fire, nor daylight, nor fresh water,
nor the oolachan fish. These things were all in the possession
of a great chief or deity called Setlin-ki-jash, who lived where
the Nasse River now is. All these good things, however,
the cunning Raven contrived to steal from their owner and to

---

[1] Le R. P. Morice, *Au pays de
l'Ours noir, chez les Sauvages de la
Colombie Britannique* (Paris and
Lyons, 1897), pp. 151-153. According
to the writer (p. 150), the same myth
is found among the Carrier or Takulli
Indians, an Athapascan tribe of which
the Babine Indians are a branch.
Compare F. W. Hodge, *Handbook of
American Indians*, i. 123, ii. 675.

bestow upon mankind.   The way in which he succeeded in
stealing fire was this.   He did not dare to appear in the
chief's house ;   but, assuming the form of a single needle-like
leaf of the spruce-tree, he floated on the water near the house.
Now the chief had a daughter, and when she went down to
draw water, she drew up the leaf along with the water in
her vessel, and then drinking of the water she swallowed the
leaf without noticing it.   Shortly afterwards she conceived
and bore a child, who was no other than the subtle Raven.
Thus Raven gained an entry into the lodge.   Watching his
opportunity, he one day picked up a burning brand, and,
donning his coat of feathers, flew out of the smoke-hole at the
top of the lodge, carrying the fire with him and spreading it
wherever he went.   One of the first places to which he set
fire was near the north end of Vancouver Island, and that is
the reason why so many of the trees there have black bark.[1]

Another Haida version of the myth, taken down in the
Masset dialect, is as follows :

At that time, when Raven was on his travels, there was no
fire to be seen, and people did not know of it.   Then Raven
went northward upon the surface of the sea.   And far out at
sea a big kelp was growing out of the water.   And the kelp-
head was gone, and many sparks came out of it.   This was
the first time that Raven saw fire.   And he went to it along
the bottom of the ocean.   Then the big fishes wanted to kill
him as he went along—black whale, devil-fish, sculpin, and
the rest.   Owner-of-the-Fire was the one to whom Raven
went.

And when he entered the house, Owner-of-the-Fire said
to him, " Come and sit here, chief."   Then Raven said to
him, " Will the chief give me fire ? "   The chief gave it to
him as he had desired.   And when he gave it to him, he gave
it to him in a stone tray, and a cover was over it.   Then
Raven went away from him with it.   And after he had gone
up to the shore, he put a fragment of live coal into a cedar
standing there.   Then he entered the house in which his
sister lived.   Butterfly was also there with her.   Then he
lighted a fire in his house.   Because he put a piece of fire

---

[1] George M. Dawson, *Report on*   (Montreal, 1880), pp.   149B - 151B
the Queen Charlotte Islands, 1878   (*Geological Survey of Canada*).

into the cedar, when people try to light a fire with cedar by means of a fire-drill, fire comes from it.[1]

The Tlingit Indians of Alaska also tell of the wonderful doings of Raven in the early days of the world. They say that at that time fire did not yet exist on the earth, but only on an island in the sea. Raven flew thither, and picking up a firebrand in his bill returned in swift flight. But so great was the distance that when he came to land the brand was almost consumed, and even Raven's bill was half burnt off. As soon as he reached the shore he dropped the glowing embers on the ground, and the scattered sparks fell on stones and wood. And that, the Tlingit say, is the reason why both stones and wood still contain fire ; for you can strike sparks from stones by knocking them with steel, and you can produce fire from wood by rubbing two sticks together.[2]

Another Tlingit version of the myth is as follows :

In the beginning men had no fire. But Raven (*Yetl*) knew that the Snow-owl, who lived far out in the ocean, guarded the fire He commanded all men, who in those days still had the form of animals, to go, one after the other, to fetch fire ; but none of them succeeded in bringing it. At last the Deer, who then had a long tail, said, " I will take fir-wood and tie it to my tail. With that I will fetch the fire." He did as he had said, ran to the house of the Snow-owl, danced round the fire, and at last whisked his tail close to the flames. Then the wood on his tail caught fire, and he ran away. Thus it came about that his tail was burnt off, and since that time the Deer has had only a stumpy tail.[3]

In this Tlingit version of the story it is not Raven himself but Deer who steals the fire by dancing round it with combustible wood tied to his tail. We have seen that precisely

[1] John R. Swanton, " Haida texts— Masset dialect," *The Jesup North Pacific Expedition*, vol. x. Part ii. (Leyden and New York, 1908) pp. 315 *sq.* (*Memoir of the American Museum of Natural History, New York*).

[2] H. J. Holmberg, " Über die Völker des Russischen Amerika," *Acta Societatis Scientiarum Fennicae*, iv. (Helsingfors, 1856) p. 339 ; Alph.

Pinart, " Notes sur les Koloches," *Bulletins de la Société d'Anthropologie de Paris*, IIme Série, vii. (1872) pp. 798 *sq.* ; Aurel Krause, *Die Tlinkit-Indianer* (Jena, 1885), p. 263. The authority for the myth seems to be the old Russian missionary Veniaminov, to whom Krause refers.

[3] Franz Boas, *Indianische Sagen von der Nord-Pacifischen Küste Amerikas*, p. 314.

the same story is told by the Nootka, Kwakiutl, and other southerly tribes of British Columbia.[1]

A third Tlingit version of the myth is reported, in which neither the Raven nor the Deer figures as the thief of fire. The Tlingit say that on his travels Raven came to a place where he saw something floating not far from shore, though it never came any nearer. He assembled all kinds of fowl. Toward evening he looked at the thing and saw that it resembled fire. So he told a Chicken-hawk, which had a very long bill, to fly out to it, saying, " Be very brave. If you get some of that fire, do not let go of it." The Chicken-hawk reached the place, seized some fire, and started back as fast as it could fly, but by the time it brought the fire to Raven, its bill was burnt off. That is why the bill of the Chicken-hawk is short. Then Raven took some red cedar and some white stones, which are found on the beach ; and he put fire into them, so that it could be found ever afterwards all over the world.[2]

Still farther to the north, among the Eskimo who inhabit the bleak shores of Bering Strait, the Raven plays a great part in the myths told to account for the origins of all things.[3] These Eskimo say that soon after the appearance of the first men on earth the Raven taught them to make a fire-drill and bow from a piece of dry wood and a cord, taking the wood from the bushes and small trees which he, the Raven, had caused to grow in hollows and sheltered places on the hillside. Also he showed them how to make fire with the fire-drill, and to place the spark of tinder in a bunch of dry grass, and to wave it about till it blazed, and then to lay dry wood on the burning grass.[4] The fire-making apparatus which the Raven is here said to have revealed to the Eskimo is clearly the bow-drill, in which the bowstring is wound round the drill and, being stretched by the bow, causes the drill to revolve much more rapidly than when a simple string is employed and its two ends are pulled by the operator's

[1] See above, pp. 161-170.

[2] John R. Swanton, *Tlingit Myths and Texts* (Washington, 1909), p. 11 (*Bureau of American Ethnology, Bulletin* No. 39).

[3] E. W. Nelson, " The Eskimo about Bering Strait," *Eighteenth Annual Report of the Bureau of American Ethnology*, Part i. (Washington, 1899) pp. 452 *sqq.*

[4] E. W. Nelson, *op. cit.* p. 456.

hands.[1] This improved form of the fire-drill is actually used by the Eskimo of Bering Strait,[2] and indeed by the whole Eskimo race,[3] as well as by some tribes of North American Indians.[4]

[1] E. B. Tylor, *Researches into the Early History of Mankind*, p. 246.

[2] E. W. Nelson, *op. cit.* pp. 75 *sq.*, with plate xxxiv. fig. 2.

[3] W. Hough, " Fire-making Apparatus in the United States National Museum," *Report of the National Museum*, 1887–1888 (Washington, 1890), pp. 555 *sqq.* ; *id., Fire as an Agent in Human Culture*, pp. 96 *sq.*

[4] E. B. Tylor, *Researches into the Early History of Mankind*, p. 246 ; W. Hough, *Fire as an Agent in Human Culture*, pp. 97 *sq.*

CHAPTER XIV

THE ORIGIN OF FIRE IN EUROPE

THE following story of the origin of fire is told in Normandy:

Long, long ago there was no more fire on earth and people did not know how to get it. They agreed that it was necessary to go and fetch it from the good God. But the good God is far away. Who will undertake the journey? They applied to the big birds, but the big birds refused, and so did the middle-sized birds, even the lark. While they were consulting, the little wren (*rebette*) listened. " Since nobody else will go, I will go myself." "But you are so small!" they said. "Your wings are so short! You will die of weariness before you get there." "I will try," quoth she; " if I die on the way, so much the worse."

So away she flew, and so well did she fly that she reached the good God. The good God was very much surprised to see her. He made her rest on his knees. But he hesitated to give her the fire. " You will burn yourself," said he, " before you reach the earth." But the wren insisted. " Very well," said the good God at last, " I will give you what you ask of me. But take your time, do not fly too fast. If you fly too fast, you will set your feathers on fire."

The wren promised to be prudent, and flew away joyously toward the earth. While she was far off, she restrained herself and did not hurry; but when she drew near and saw them all looking and waiting for her and calling to her, she involuntarily quickened her speed. Then it happened as the good God had told her. She brought the fire, and people soon got possession of it; but the poor wren had not a feather left—all had been burnt! The birds gathered

eagerly about her.   Each of them tore a feather from itself
to make a garment for the wren without delay.   Since that
time the wren's plumage has been speckled.   There was
only one rascally bird that would give nothing, and that
was the screech-owl.   All the birds rushed at him to punish
him for his hardness of heart, and he was forced to hide
himself.   That is why he only comes out at night, and why,
if he comes out by day, all the birds fly at him and force him
to return into his hole.[1]   To this day any bad boy who
should kill a wren or rob its nest would draw down the fire
of heaven on his own house.   As a punishment for his
misdeed he might perhaps remain an orphan and homeless.[2]
In more general terms we read that in Normandy the wren
(*rebet*) " is much respected because he is said to have brought
fire from the sky, and people are convinced that some mis-
fortune would befall him who should kill the bird." [3]

The same story is told about the wren in Upper Brittany ;
there too he is said to have brought fire from heaven and
to have received a feather in return from every bird except
the screech-owl, who declared that his feathers were far
too fine to be burned ; that is why the other birds, and
especially the magpie, are always after him.   Hence in
Brittany they say that you should not hurt wrens, because
it was they who brought fire down to earth.   In the neighbourhood of Dol it is believed that if anybody robs a wren's
nest, the fingers of the hand which stole the eggs or the
young will be crippled.   At Saint Donan they say that if
little children touch a wren's young ones, they will catch
St. Lawrence's fire, that is, they will suffer from pimples
or pustules on the face, legs, and other parts of the body.[4]
In the neighbourhood of Lorient the story runs that the
wren went to fetch fire, not in heaven but in hell, and that
he scorched his plumes in passing through the keyhole.[5]

[1] Jean Fleury, *Littérature orale de
la Basse-Normandie* (Paris, 1883),
pp. 108 *sq.*   The story is told in substantially the same form by Amélie
Bosquet, *La Normandie romanesque
et merveilleuse* (Paris and Rouen,
1845), pp. 220 *sq.*

[2] Amélie Bosquet, *op. cit.* p. 221.

[3] Alfred de Nore, *Coutumes, Mythes,*
et Traditions des Provinces de France
(Paris and Lyons, 1846), p. 271.

[4] P. Sébillot, *Traditions et Superstitions de la Haute-Bretagne* (Paris,
1882), ii. 214 *sq.*

[5] E. Rolland, *Faune populaire de la
France,* ii. (Paris, 1879) p. 294 ; P.
Sébillot, *Le Folk-lore de France* (Paris,
1904–1907), iii. 157.

But in some parts of Brittany the fire-myth is told, not of the wren, but of the robin-redbreast. They say that robin-redbreast went to fetch fire, and that in so doing he burnt all his feathers. Then the birds took pity on him and resolved to clothe him afresh by each one giving him a feather. Only the screech-owl, a proud and hard-hearted bird, refused to lend a feather. That is why, when he shows himself by day, all the little birds cry out on him, especially the robin-redbreast, who by his note upbraids the screech-owl with his pride.[1] However, in Brittany an attempt is made to reconcile the claims of the two rival birds to the honour of having brought the fire ; for in one version of the story it is said that while it was the robin who went to fetch the fire, it was the wren who lit it.[2]

In Guernsey the robin-redbreast is said to have been the first who brought fire to the island ; while he was crossing the water, the fire singed his feathers, and hence his breast has been red ever since. An old woman, a native of the island, who told the tale, added, " My mother had a great veneration for the robin, for what should we have done without fire ? "[3]

At Le Charme, in the Département of Loiret, the story goes that the wren stole the fire of heaven, and was descending with it to earth, but his wings caught fire, and he was obliged to entrust his precious burden to robin-redbreast ; but robin burned his breast by hugging the fire to it, hence he in his turn had to resign the office of fire-bearer ; then the lark took up the sacred fire and, carrying it safe to earth, delivered the treasure to mankind.[4] This story resembles many fire-myths of the American Indians, in which the stolen fire is said to have been passed on from one to another along a line of animal runners.[5]

In Germany the myth of the wren as the first bringer of fire appears to be unknown.[6]

[1] P. Sébillot, *Traditions et Superstitions de la Haute-Bretagne*, ii. 209.q.

[2] P. Sébillot, *Traditions et Superstitions de la Haute-Bretagne*, ii. 214.

[3] Charles Swainson, *The Folk-lore and Provincial Names of British Birds* (London, 1886), p. 16.

[4] E. Rolland, *Faune populaire de la France*, ii. 294 ; P. Sébillot, *Le Folk-lore de France*, iii. 156.

[5] See above, p. 174.

[6] J. W. Wolf, *Beiträge zur deutschen Mythologie* (Göttingen, 1852–1857), ii. 438.

CHAPTER XV

THE ORIGIN OF FIRE IN ANCIENT GREECE

In ancient Greece the common story ran that the great sky-god Zeus hid fire from men, but that the crafty hero Prometheus, son of the Titan Iapetus, stole fire from the deity in heaven and brought it down to men on earth, concealed in a stalk of fennel. For this theft Zeus punished Prometheus by nailing or chaining him to a peak in the Caucasus and sending an eagle which devoured the hero's liver or heart by day perpetually; for by night the organ recovered all that it had lost by day. This torture Prometheus endured for thirty or for thirty thousand years, until he was at last released by Hercules.[1]

However, according to Plato, it was not from Zeus in heaven but from the workshop of the fire-god Hephaestus and Athena, the goddess of the arts, that Prometheus stole the fire which he bestowed on men. The philosopher tells us that the gods fashioned all mortal creatures, including men and beasts, underneath the ground, compounding their bodies out of earth and fire. When the time came to bring up these newly fashioned creatures to the surface of the ground, the gods assigned to Prometheus and his brother Epimetheus the duty of equipping men and animals and assigning to each species its proper function and powers. But the foolish Epimetheus persuaded his wise brother to leave the delicate task to him, and he bungled it badly; for he bestowed all

---

[1] Hesiod, *Works and Days*, 47 *sqq.*, *Theog.* 561 *sqq.*; Aeschylus, *Prometheus Vinctus*, 107 *sqq.*; Hyginus, *Fab.* 144, *Astronom.* ii. 15; Horace, *Odes*, i. 3. 25 *sqq.*; Juvenal, xv. 84-86; Servius, on Virgil, *Ecl.* vi. 42.

In one passage (*Fab.* 144) Hyginus puts the period of Prometheus's sufferings at thirty, in another (*Astronom.* ii. 15) at thirty thousand years, citing Aeschylus as his authority for the longer period of penal servitude.

the best gifts on the animals and left man naked and defence-less. Prometheus, the friend of the human race, was sore puzzled how to remedy these defects, especially as the day decreed by fate was close at hand when mankind should issue from the bowels of the earth. In his perplexity he bethought him of bestowing the gift of fire on his favourites, calculating that its use in the mechanical arts would com-pensate mankind for the want of the precious gifts which his thoughtless brother had lavished on the brutes. But Prometheus might not enter the citadel of Zeus to bring down fire from heaven, for it was guarded by dreadful warders ; so he made his way secretly into the workshop where Hephaestus and Athena laboured in common, and stealing the fire of Hephaestus and the mechanical skill of Athena he bestowed both these valuable possessions on mankind.[1] This Platonic version of the myth was known to Lucian, for he represents Hephaestus upbraiding Pro-metheus with filching his fire and leaving his forge cold.[2] Cicero speaks of the Lemnian theft for which Prometheus was punished so grievously,[3] which implies that the fire was stolen from the forge of Hephaestus in Lemnos, the island on which Hephaestus fell when he was hurled from heaven by Zeus.[4] Perhaps another myth may have explained the origin of fire on earth by this fall of Hephaestus, who may have been supposed to carry fire with him in his descent from heaven, and to have used it to kindle the furnace of his smithy in the island.

According to one account, Prometheus obtained the celestial fire by ascending up to heaven and kindling a torch at the sun's fiery wheel.[5] The rationalistic Greek historian Diodorus Siculus explained the myth of Prometheus and his theft of fire by supposing that Prometheus invented the fire-sticks, by the friction of which against each other fire is elicited ;[6] but Greek tradition ascribed the invention of the fire-sticks to Hermes.[7] Lucretius conjectured that men may

---

[1] Plato, *Protagoras*, ii. pp. 320 D-321 E.

[2] Lucian, *Prometheus*, 5.

[3] Cicero, *Tusculan Disput.* ii. 10. 23.

[4] Homer, *Iliad*, i. 590 *sqq.* ; Apol-lodorus, i. 3. 5 ; Lucian, *De sacri-ficiis*, 6.

[5] Servius, on Virgil, *Ecl.* vi. 42.

[6] Diodorus Siculus, v. 67. 2.

[7] *Homeric Hymns*, iv. *To Hermes*, 111.

have learned to kindle fire by observing how branches take
fire by rubbing against each other in the wind ; or again
our rude forefathers may have got their first fire from a
conflagration set up by lightning.[1]

The plant (*narthex*) in which Prometheus carried the
stolen fire is commonly identified with the giant fennel
(*Ferula communis*),[2] which grows in all parts of Greece and
may be seen in particular abundance at Phalerum, near
Athens.[3] The French traveller Tournefort found this fennel
growing rank in Skinosa, the ancient Schinussa, a small
deserted island south of Naxos.[4] He describes the stalk as
about five feet high and three inches thick, with knots and
branches at intervals of about ten inches, the whole being
covered with a tolerably hard rind. " This stalk is filled with
a white pith, which, being very dry, catches fire just like a
wick ; the fire keeps alight perfectly in the stalk and con-
sumes the pith only gradually, without damaging the rind ;
hence people use this plant to carry fire from one place to
another ; our sailors laid in a supply of it. This custom is of
great antiquity, and may serve to explain a passage in Hesiod,
who, speaking of the fire which Prometheus stole from
heaven, says that he carried it away in a stalk of fennel." [5]
In Naxos the English traveller J. T. Bent saw orange gardens
divided by hedges of tall reeds, and he adds: " In Lesbos this
reed is still called νάρθηκα (νάρθηξ), a survival of the old word
for the reed by which Prometheus brought down fire from
heaven. One can understand the idea well : a peasant to-day
who wishes to carry a light from one house to another will put
it into one of these reeds to prevent its being blown out." [6]
Apparently Mr. Bent mistook the giant fennel for a reed.

The Argives denied that Prometheus had given fire to
men ; they ascribed the honour of having discovered fire to
their ancient king Phoroneus,[7] at whose grave they continued
to offer sacrifices down at least to the second century of our

[1] Lucretius, *De rerum natura*, v.
1091-1101.
[2] L. Whibley, *Companion to Greek
Studies*[3] (Cambridge, 1916), p. 67.
[3] W. G. Clark, *Peloponnesus*
(London, 1858), p. 111 ; J. Murr,
*Die Pflanzenwelt in der griechischen
Mythologie* (Innsbruck, 1890), p. 231.

[4] Pliny, *Nat. Hist.* iv. 68.
[5] P. de Tournefort, *Relation d'un
Voyage du Levant* (Amsterdam, 1718),
i. 93.
[6] J. Theodore Bent, *The Cyclades*
(London, 1885), p. 365.
[7] Pausanias, ii. 19. 5.

era.[1] In the great sanctuary of Wolfish (*Lykios*) Apollo at
Argos a fire was kept burning, which the Argives called the
fire of Phoroneus.[2] On the subject of Phoroneus there was an
ancient epic poem called the *Phoronis*, but only a few verses
of it have survived.[3] In the poem the story of its hero's discovery of fire was probably told at large. Some eminent
philologists would derive the name Phoroneus from the verb
pherein, " to bear or bring " ;[4] if they are right, we might
be tempted to interpret the name of Phoroneus as " the
bringer " of fire. Adalbert Kuhn would identify the name
Phoroneus with the Sanscrit *bhuraṇya*, a standing epithet
of the Vedic fire-god Agni, which is said to be derived from
the Sanscrit verb *bhar*, answering to the Greek verb *pherein*,
" to bear or bring." [5] But in mythology comparisons based
on etymology are very precarious, and in general they are
best eschewed.

This last observation applies to a more famous etymology
proposed by the same learned and ingenious scholar. Kuhn
argued that the name Prometheus is derived from *pramantha*,
the Sanscrit name for the upper part of the fire-drill ; thus
he would interpret Prometheus as a personification of that
primitive implement for the production of fire.[6] But to
this derivation of the name weighty objections have been
raised.[7] For neither Prometheus nor his Indian counterpart
Mâtariṣvan is commonly associated with the fire-drill, the
invention of which was ascribed in Greek mythology to
Hermes, though Diodorus Siculus, as we saw, would father
it on Prometheus ;[8] and there seems to be no sufficient reason
for abandoning the obvious sense of the " Fore-thinker,"
which the Greeks themselves took to be the meaning of Prometheus in opposition to the " After-thinker," Epimetheus,

---

[1] Pausanias, ii. 20. 3.

[2] Pausanias, ii. 19. 5.

[3] *Epicorum Graecorum Fragmenta*,
ed. G. Kinkel (Lipsiae, 1887), pp.
209-212.

[4] Adalbert Kuhn, *Die Herabkunft
des Feuers und des Göttertranks*[2]
(Gütersloh, 1886), p. 27.

[5] Adalbert Kuhn, *Die Herabkunft
des Feuers und des Göttertranks*,[2]
pp. 27 *sq.*

[6] Adalbert Kuhn, *op. cit.* pp. 14-
20, 35.

[7] K. Bapp, *s.v.* " Prometheus " in
W. H. Roscher's *Lexikon der grie-
chischen und römischen Mythologie*, iii.
(Leipzig, 1897-1909) coll. 3033-3034;
E. E. Sikes, " The Fire-Bringer," in
his edition of Aeschylus, *Prometheus
Vinctus* (London, 1912), pp. xiii-xiv.

[8] See above, p. 194.

thus contrasting the wise with the foolish brother, the sage with the dunce.

On the analogy of savage myths, which, as we have seen, often relate how the first fire was procured for man by a bird, Salomon Reinach would explain Prometheus as originally an eagle which brought down the first fire from heaven, but which, through a later misunderstanding of the primitive myth, was transformed into a minister of vengeance for the punishment of the trespass which himself had committed. The theory is more ingenious than probable; indeed, its learned author, comparing his hypothesis to a house of cards, candidly confessed the weakness of the foundation on which it rests.[1]

---

[1] Salomon Reinach, " Aetos Prometheus," *Cultes, Mythes et Religions*, iii. (Paris, 1908) pp. 68-91.

CHAPTER XVI

THE ORIGIN OF FIRE IN ANCIENT INDIA

In Vedic mythology fire is said to have been brought down from heaven by Mâtariṣvan, who so far answers to the Greek Prometheus. He was the messenger of Vivasvant, the first sacrificer, and he fetched the fire for the purpose of being used in sacrifice ; for in the opinion of the Vedic poets the prime utility of fire is not to warm man and to cook his food, but to consume the sacrifice offered to the gods.[1] Thus in a hymn of the *Rigveda* addressed jointly to Agni (the deified fire) and Soma (the deified plant, source of an intoxicant drink), it is said :

" Agni and Soma, joined in operation ye have set up the shining lights in heaven.
From curse and from reproach, Agni and Soma, ye freed the rivers that were bound in fetters.
One of you (that is, Agni) Mâtariṣvan brought from heaven, the Falcon rent the other (that is, Soma) from the mountain." [2]

Again, in a hymn addressed to Agni alone, we read that :

" Him wandering at his own free will, Agni here hidden from our view, Him Mâtariṣvan brought to us from far away produced by friction, from the Gods." [3]

Again, in another hymn addressed to Agni alone, it is written :

" The Mighty seized him in the bosom of the floods : the people waited on the King who should be praised.
As envoy of Vivasvân Mâtariṣvan brought Agni Vaiṣvânara hither from far away." [4]

[1] H. Oldenberg, *Die Religion des Veda* (Berlin, 1894), pp. 122 *sq.*

[2] *Hymns of the Rigveda*, translated with a popular Commentary by Ralph T. H. Griffith, Second Edition (Benares, 1896–1897), vol. i. p. 120, Hymn, i. 93. 5-6.

[3] *Rigveda*, Hymn iii. 9. 5 (Griffith's translation, vol. i. p. 329).

[4] *Rigveda*, Hymn vi. 8. 4 (Griffith's translation, vol. i. p. 563).

Again, in another hymn addressed to Agni alone, it is said:

" That Mâtariṣvan rich in wealth and treasure, light-winner, finds a
   pathway for his offspring.
Guard of our folk, Father of earth and heaven.   The gods possessed
   the wealth-bestowing Agni." [1]

Again, in another hymn addressed to Agni alone, we read:

" As great as is the fair-winged Morning's presence to him who dwells
   beside us, Mâtariṣvan !
Is what the Brâhman does when he approaches to sacrifice and sits
   below the Hotar." [2]

Again, in a hymn addressed to the Viṣvedevas, it is said :

" Two perfect springs of heat pervade the Threefold, and come for their
   delight is Mâtariṣvan.
Craving the milk of heaven the Gods are present : well do they know
   the praise-song and the Sâman." [3]

In the references of the Vedic poets to Mâtariṣvan his
personality is ill-defined ; but, like his Greek counterpart
Prometheus, he would seem to have been conceived, not as a
human sage who revealed fire to his rude fellow-men, but as a
demi-god who brought it down to them from heaven, though
in his legend there is no hint that he stole it from the gods.[4]
Sometimes in the *Rigveda* he appears to be identified with
Agni, that is, with the fire from which he is elsewhere distinguished.[5]   In the *Atharvaveda*, the *Brahmanas*, and all
later literature the name Mâtariṣvan is, by a curious change
of meaning, a designation of wind (Vayu) ; but in this sense
the word seems never to occur in the *Rigveda*.[6]

---

[1] *Rigveda*, Hymn i. 96. 4 (Griffith's
translation, vol. i. p. 126). On this
passage Mr. Griffith has a note :
" *Mâtariṣvan* : usually the name of
the divine being who brought Agni
from heaven, said by Sâyana to mean
in this place Agni himself."

[2] *Rigveda*, x. 88. 19 (Griffith's
translation, vol. ii. p. 515). The Hotar
is the priest who recited or sang the
hymns ; in early times he also com-
posed them. See H. Oldenberg, *Die
Religion des Veda*, pp. 129 *sq.* ; H. D.
Griswold, *The Religion of the Rigveda*
(Oxford University Press, 1923), p. 48.

[3] *Rigveda*, Hymn x. 114. 1
(Griffith's translation, vol. ii. p. 557).

[4] J. Muir, *Original Sanskrit Texts,
collected, translated and illustrated*,
vol. v. (London, 1872) pp. 204 *sq.*

[5] A. A. Macdonell, *Vedic Mythology* (Strassburg, 1897), p. 71 ; Roth,
quoted by J. Muir, *Original Sanskrit
Texts*, v. 205 ; H. Oldenberg, *Die
Religion des Veda*, p. 122 note (who
rejects the theory of the identity of
Mâtariṣvan and Agni).

[6] J. Muir, *Original Sanskrit Texts*,
vol. v. pp. 204 *sq.* ; H. Oldenberg,
Die Religion des Veda, p. 122 note [1];
A. A. Macdonell, *Vedic Mythology*,
p. 72 ; H. D. Griswold, *The Religion
of the Rigveda*, p. 163.

If we ask to what natural phenomenon Mâtariṣvan corresponds, the most probable answer seems to be that he was in origin a personification of the lightning-flash which, descending from heaven, kindles fire on earth. This view is accepted by some good scholars.[1] Perhaps the Greek legend of the fall of Hephaestus from heaven[2] may have been a mythical expression of the same natural and often repeated phenomenon. If that were so, we might expect to find Hephaestus figuring in Greek mythology as the first bringer of fire to men ; but no such Greek myth, so far as I know, has come down to us, though according to Plato, as we have seen, it was from the forge of Hephaestus that Prometheus stole the fire which he bestowed on men.[3]

[1] A. A. Macdonell, *Vedic Mythology*, p. 72 ; H. D. Griswold, *The Religion of the Rigveda*, pp. 163 *sq.* As to Mâtariṣvan compare A. Kuhn, *Die Herabkunft des Feuers*[2] (Güters-loh, 1886), pp. 8 *sqq.*, who held that Mâtariṣvan was originally the fire.

[2] See above, p. 194.

[3] See above, p. 193 *sq.*

CHAPTER XVII

§ 1. *The Three Ages*

THE narratives which we have passed in review suffice to prove that the problem of the discovery of fire and of the modes of kindling it have excited the curiosity and exercised the ingenuity of men in various ages and in many parts of the world. Taken altogether, they appear to indicate a general belief that with regard to fire mankind in the course of evolution has passed through three phases : in the first of these they were ignorant of the use or even of the existence of fire ; in the second, they had become acquainted with fire and used it to warm themselves and cook their food, but were still ignorant of all modes of kindling it ; in the third, they had discovered and regularly employed means of kindling it by one or more of the methods which are still, or which were till lately, in vogue among the more backward races of men. Corresponding to these three phases of culture the narratives implicitly assume three successive ages, which we may call the Fireless Age, the Age of Fire Used, and the Age of Fire Kindled. However these conclusions may have been reached, whether by speculation or by actual reminiscence orally transmitted, it seems highly probable that they are substantially correct ; for if, as is now generally believed, mankind has been gradually evolved from much lower forms of animal life, it is certain that our animal ancestors must have been as ignorant of the use of fire as all animals but man are to this day ; and even when the race had attained a stage which deserves to be called human, it is likely that men long remained ignorant both of the use of fire and of the methods of kindling it. Thus we conclude that the myths of the origin of fire which we have reviewed, despite the extravagant and fanciful features which adorn or disfigure many of them, contain a substantial element of truth. It may therefore be worth while to examine them a little more closely in the character of professedly historical documents.

§ 2. *The Fireless Age*

Many races of men, as we have seen, believe that of old their ancestors, or even the whole of mankind, were entirely without the use of fire and consequently suffered hardships from cold and from the lack of means of cooking their food, which they were obliged to consume raw. Thus the aborigines of Victoria told of a time when their forefathers had no fire and were in sad distress, because they had no means of cooking their food and there was no camp fire at which they could warm themselves when the weather was cold.[1] The Masingara people in British New Guinea say that in former times they had no fire, and that their only food consisted of ripe bananas and fish dried in the sun : of this monotonous and insipid diet they grew tired.[2] The natives of Yap, one of the Caroline Islands, affirm that of old they had yams and taro, but as yet there was no fire to cook them ; so they baked their yams and taro by means of the sun's heat playing on the sand, but they suffered grievously from gripes.[3] The Kachins of Burma have a tradition that in the beginning men had no fire ; hence they ate their food raw, and they were cold and lean.[4] To the same effect the Buriats of Siberia say that formerly men knew not fire, and therefore they could not dress their victuals and went about hungry and cold.[5] So, too, the Wachagga of East Africa allege that in the olden time men were ignorant of fire and were forced to eat their food raw, even bananas, just like the baboons.[6] According to the Shilluk of the White Nile, there was a time when nobody knew of fire. In those days people used to warm their victuals in the sun, and the upper part of the food, which was thus partially cooked, was consumed by the men, while the under part, which remained raw, was

---

[1] Above, p. 5. [3] Above, p. 90. [5] Above, p. 105.
[2] Above, p. 35. [4] Above, p. 103. [6] Above, p. 120.

eaten by the women.[1]   The Jibaros of Ecuador, in South America, say that of old their ancestors did not know the use of fire and so dressed their food by warming meat under their armpits, by heating edible roots in their mouths, and by cooking eggs in the burning rays of the sun.[2]   The Sia Indians of New Mexico affirm that in the beginning people on earth did not possess fire and grew tired of browsing on grass like deer and other animals.[3]   The Ojibway Indians say that at first men were not wise ; they had neither clothes nor fire, and while people in the south made shift to do without garments, the naked folk in the north suffered from the cold.[4]   Once more, among the Whullemooch Indians of Washington State and British Columbia the old people used to tell of a time when their ancestors had no fire and were obliged to eat their food raw and to pass their evenings in the dark.[5]

Some peoples, without dwelling on the other hardships of the Fireless Age, single out the necessity of warming their food in the sun as if it were the sorest to bear of the privations which the want of fire entailed on the community.[6]   The insistence on this particular hardship suggests that the craving for hot food is a natural instinct of the human organism, for which physiological causes may probably be assigned by science.

§ 3   *The Age of Fire Used*

If we may trust the traditions of some peoples, the Fireless Age was succeeded by an Age in which men were acquainted with fire and made use of it for the purposes of daily life, but were still ignorant of all modes of kindling it.   Thus some natives of Queensland relate how a tribe of blacks accidentally acquired fire for the first time from a conflagration kindled by lightning ;   how they gave the precious element in charge to an old woman with strict

---

[1] Above, pp. 121 *sq.*

[2] Above, p. 134.

[3] Above, p. 139.

[4] Above, p. 151.

[5] Above, p. 159.

[6] Pp. 30 (Kiwai), 31 (Badu Island), 35 (Kiwai), 38 (the Motu of British New Guinea), 43 (Wagawaga in British New Guinea), 130 (the Tembes of Brazil), 170 (the Thompson Indians of British Columbia).

injunctions not to let the fire go out ; how she kept it burning for years but finally let it go out one wet night, and how she wandered long in the wilderness searching for fire, but all in vain, till one day, losing patience, she broke off two sticks from a tree and vented her rage by rubbing them violently together, with the unforeseen consequence that fire was produced by the friction.[1]

Again, the inhabitants of Mangaia, in the Pacific, say that their ancestors in like manner obtained fire from a great conflagration and used it to cook their food, but when it went out they did not know how to kindle it afresh.[2] The Toradyas of Central Celebes relate that in the beginning the Creator gave fire to the first man and woman, but he did not teach them how to make it ; so in those early days people were very careful not to let the fire go out on the hearth, and when it was through carelessness extinguished, they were at a loss how to boil their rice.[3] Again, the Bushongo, a nation in the valley of the Congo, have a tradition that in the olden times their ancestors obtained fire from conflagrations kindled by lightning, but did not know how to make it for themselves.[4]

To the question, How did men first get fire ? an answer is supplied by the foregoing narratives : they got it from conflagrations kindled by lightning. Similarly the Bakongo, in the lower valley of the Congo, say that fire came first from above by means of lightning, which struck a tree and set it on fire.[5] It may well be that this answer is true for many tribes or races of men ; for when we reflect how often in the immeasurable past of humanity trees, shrubs, and grass must have been ignited by lightning, we can hardly avoid concluding that this has been a source from which men have frequently derived fire long before they were able to kindle it for themselves.

Even when men have long been in possession of fire, they are apt to regard with peculiar awe and veneration a fire which has been kindled by a flash of lightning. Thus the Oraons of Chota Nagpur in India, though they do not ordinarily consider fire as sacred, esteem " lightning fire " (*bajar khatarka chich*) as " sent by Heaven." Not very many years

---

[1] Above, p. 21.   [3] Above, p. 93.   [5] Above, p. 117.
[2] Above, p. 79.   [4] Above, p. 114.

ago, at the village of Haril, a tree, on the branches of which an Oraon cultivator had stacked his straw, was struck by lightning and the tree caught fire. Thereupon all the Oraons of the village assembled and decided that, since God had sent this " lightning fire," all existing fire in the village should be extinguished, and a portion of this " Heaven-sent fire " should be taken and carefully preserved in every house and should be used for all purposes. And this was accordingly done.[1] Yet these same Oraons had long been familiar with fire, and before the introduction of lucifer matches they used to produce it by the fire-drill ; indeed, when a man goes into the jungle, he will sometimes do so still, using for the purpose two pieces of easily inflammable wood ; one of the two he lays on the ground and steadies with his feet, while he fixes the other perpendicularly in a notch of the former, and twirls it till the sawdust thus produced ignites and sets fire to a tinder of dry leaves or rag placed underneath.[2]

Another natural source from which some people claim to have derived their fire is the rubbing of branches against each other in the wind. Thus the natives of Nukufetau or De Peyster's Island in the Pacific say that men discovered fire by seeing smoke rising from the friction of two crossed branches, which rubbed against each other in the wind.[3] The Kiau Dusuns of North Borneo say that, rubbing against each other in the wind, two growing bamboos caught fire, and that a dog passing by seized one of the burning pieces and carried it home to its master's house, which soon blazed up, and that the fire not only roasted some cobs of maize which were in the house but also boiled some potatoes which had been left to soak. Thus at a single stroke the Dusuns learned both how to make fire and how to cook their food.[4]

As we have seen,[5] Lucretius suggested that man may have obtained his first fire from a conflagration kindled by lightning, and that he may have learned how to make fire by observing the ignition of branches rubbing against each other in the wind. Thus both the poet's suggestions are confirmed by the testimony of savages. Some years ago, when I had the

[1] Sarat Chandra Roy, *The Orāons of Chōtā-Nāgpur* (Ranchi, 1915), pp. 170 *sq.*

[2] Sarat Chandra Roy, *op. cit.* p. 472 note.

[3] Above, p. 88.

[4] Above, pp. 95 *sq.*

[5] Above, pp. 194 *sq.*

privilege of discussing primitive fire-making with Mr. Henry Balfour at the Pitt-Rivers Museum, Oxford, he told me that fire is undoubtedly sometimes produced, without human agency, through the friction of two branches in the wind ; the fact, he said, has been repeatedly observed and described.

Other natural sources from which some people suppose that man may have originally procured his fire are the sun, the moon, and the stars. Thus certain natives of Victoria relate that once upon a time a man threw a spear, with a string attached to it, at the clouds ; the spear stuck in the clouds, the man climbed up the string, and brought down fire from the sun to the earth.[1] A tribe in Queensland told how men obtained fire from the sun in a different fashion. They went westward to the setting sun, and just as the glowing orb was sinking beneath the horizon they adroitly chipped a piece off it and bore back the burning fragment to their camp.[2] The Gilbert Islanders say that fire was procured from a sunbeam which a man or hero caught in his mouth.[3] The Thompson Indians of British Columbia have it that long ago they could not make fire and they were very cold. So they sent messengers to the sun to procure fire, and when the supply was exhausted they dispatched more messengers and received a fresh supply. The messengers had to travel a long way, and some say that they brought back the fire between shells.[4] According to one account, Prometheus procured fire for men by lighting a torch at the sun's fiery wheel.[5] The Tolowa Indians of California allege that after the great flood, which extinguished all fires on earth, they obtained fresh fire from the moon, to which they mounted in a gossamer balloon attached to the earth by a long rope.[6]

Other myths connect the origin of fire with the stars rather than with the sun or moon. The Tasmanians appear to have identified the makers of the first fire on earth with the twin stars, Castor and Pollux.[7] The Bunarong tribe of Victoria traced their possession of fire to the good offices of a man who dwelt in the sky, and as a reward for his services was transformed into the planet Mars.[8] The Wurunjerri tribe of

---

[1] Above, p. 20.   [4] Above, p. 173.   [7] Above, pp. 3 *sq.*

[2] Above, p. 20.   [5] Above, p. 194.   [8] Above, pp. 16 *sq.*

[3] Above, p. 88.   [6] Above, pp. 154 *sq.*

Victoria thought that the women who first procured fire were carried up to heaven and changed into the Pleiades.[1] The Boorong tribe of north-western Victoria alleged that fire was first given to the natives by a crow, whom they identified with the star Canopus.[2]

This last legend introduces us to a large class of myths in which the first fire is said to have been given to men by a bird or beast. For, curiously enough, many savages appear to believe that fire was in the possession of animals before it was discovered and used by man. Thus the Tsimshian Indians of British Columbia say that when men began to multiply on earth they were distressed because they had no fire with which to cook their food and to warm themselves in winter, but the animals had fire in their village.[3] Oftener, however, fire is said to have been in the possession, not of animals in general, but of a particular species of animals or of a single individual of the species. Thus some of the aborigines of Victoria had a tradition that in the olden time fire belonged exclusively to the crows inhabiting the Grampian Mountains, and that the birds would not allow any other animals to get a light.[4] Elsewhere in Australia the natives said that long ago a little bandicoot was the sole owner of a firebrand, which he cherished with the greatest jealousy, carrying it about with him wherever he went and never lending it to anybody.[5] Some tribes of New South Wales thought that a water-rat and a cod-fish were formerly the sole possessors of fire, which they jealously guarded in an open space among the reed-beds of the Murray River.[6] According to the Kabi tribe of Queensland, the deaf adder of old had sole possession of fire and kept it securely in his inside.[7] The Booandik tribe of South Australia had a tradition that fire originated in the red crest of a cockatoo, and that the bird who was the fortunate owner of this valuable possession kept it for his sole benefit and would not even communicate it to the other cockatoos, who were angry with him for his selfishness.[8] The Arunta of Central Australia say that in the far distant time, to which they give the name of Alcheringa, a gigantic euro

---

[1] Above, p. 17.
[2] Above, p. 20.
[3] Above, pp. 168 *sq*.

[4] Above, p. 5.
[5] Above, p. 7.
[6] Above, p. 8.

[7] Above, pp. 8 *sq*.
[8] Above, pp. 10 *sq*.

carried fire in its body, while a hunter who pursued the animal had none ; however, he killed the euro and extracted the fire from its body.[1] In Badu Island, Torres Straits, they tell of a crocodile which had fire at one end of the island, while a man at the other end of the island had none.[2]

The Tapietes, a South American tribe of the Gran Chaco, say that in former days their ancestors had no fire, but the black vulture possessed it, having obtained the precious element by means of lightning.[3] According to the Matacos Indians of the Gran Chaco, the jaguar was in possession of fire and guarded it before man had procured it for himself.[4] The Bakairi Indians of Central Brazil allege that in the early days of the world the Lord of Fire was the animal which naturalists call *Canis vetulus*.[5] The Tembes, an Indian tribe of north-eastern Brazil, say that fire was formerly in possession of the king vultures, and that for want of it their ancestors had to dry in the sun such flesh as they wished to eat.[6] According to the Arekuna Indians of northern Brazil, there was a time before the great flood when their ancestors had no fire and were obliged·to eat all their food raw, but fire was in the possession of a little green bird, which naturalists call *Prionites momota*.[7] The Cora Indians of Mexico tell how in days of old the iguana, a species of lizard, was in possession of fire, and how, having quarrelled with his wife and his mother-in-law, he retired in dudgeon to the sky, taking the fire with him, so that no more fire was left on earth.[8] The Jicarilla Apaches of New Mexico say that, when their ancestors first emerged from their abode in the nether world, they were destitute of fire, but the fire-flies were in possession of it.[9] The Nootka or Aht Indians of Vancouver Island affirm, according to one account, that soon after the creation fire burned only in the dwelling of the cuttle-fish ; but according to another version of their myth it was the wolves who in the beginning possessed fire.[10]

But while in some myths fire is represented as in the sole possession of certain animals who keep it jealously to them-selves, in many other stories an animal or bird is the agent

[1] Above, pp. 21 *sq.*   [5] Above, p. 129.   [8] Above, p. 136.
[2] Above, p. 31.   [6] Above, p. 130.   [9] Above, pp. 140 *sq.*
[3] Above, p. 125.   [7] Above, p. 130.   [10] Above, pp. 160, 161.
[4] Above, p. 125.

to whom men are indebted for the knowledge and use of fire, the creature having stolen or otherwise procured it from the original owner, whether beast or bird or supernatural being, and thereafter having bestowed it on mankind, or at all events having made such use of it that men were able to partake of the boon. Thus, according to some aborigines of Victoria, it was a small bird, variously described as the fire-tail wren and the fire-tail finch, which first brought fire to men, either having fetched it from the sky or stolen it from the crows, which alone possessed it ; but the bird has still a red patch on its back where the fire burned it.[1] In some Australian myths it is the hawk who, in one way or another, is the agent in procuring for mankind the boon of fire ; [2] in others the same part is played by the cockatoo.[3] According to the Boorong tribe of Victoria, it was the crow who gave the first fire to men ; [4] and the same bird figures in other Australian stories of the origin of fire.[5]

In the island of Kiwai, off New Guinea, the natives say that the first fire was brought to them by the black cockatoo, and that the red streak round the bird's mouth still shows where it was burned by the glowing fire-stick which it carried in its beak.[6] However, in other parts of British New Guinea the dog is said to figure in most stories as the animal which brought the first fire to men.[7] The inhabitants of Wagifa, a small island of the D'Entrecasteaux Archipelago, aver that fire was brought to them by a dog, which swam across the strait with a burning fire-stick tied to its tail.[8] In a myth told by the Andaman Islanders the kingfisher is said to have stolen fire from a mythical being called Bilik and to have brought it to mankind ; but Bilik threw a brand at the thief and hit him on the back of his neck, and the patch of bright red feathers on the kingfisher's neck still marks the place where the fire burned him.[9] But in another Andaman myth it is the bronze-winged dove that stole the fire from Biliku (*sic*) and gave it to the people.[10] The Menri of the Malay Peninsula say that the first fire was brought to them by a woodpecker ; hence they will not kill the woodpecker

[1] Above, pp. 5 *sq.*
[2] Above, pp. 7, 8, 9, 10.
[3] Above, pp. 10 *sqq.*
[4] Above, p. 20.
[5] Above, pp. 15 *sqq.*
[6] Above, pp. 29 *sqq.*
[7] Above, pp. 38 *sqq.*
[8] Above, pp. 49 *sq.*
[9] Above, p. 98.
[10] Above, p. 99.

because the bird bestowed on them fire for warmth and cooking.[1]   Some of the Semang of the Malay Peninsula believe that the coconut monkey stole fire from the Supreme Being who lives in the sky and makes the thunder ; with this stolen fire the monkey ignited the savannah grass, thus putting fire within the reach of mankind, but in fleeing from the conflagration the ancestors of the dwarf tribes were overtaken by the flames, which singed their hair, and that is the reason why the dwarfs have curly hair down to this day.[2]   According to the Buriats of Siberia, a swallow stole fire from Tengri, who is the Sky, and brought it to men. But Tengri was angry and shot at the bird with his bow ; the arrow pierced the bird's tail, and that is why the swallow's tail is still cleft in two.[3]   In Ceylon the story runs that the blue-black swallow-tailed fly-catcher brought down fire from heaven for the benefit of man.[4]

The Bakongo of West Africa say that, when as yet there was no fire on earth, a man sent a jackal to fetch fire from the setting sun, but the animal never came back.[5]   The Shilluk of the White Nile relate how, in the days when they had no fire, they swathed the tail of a dog in straw and sent him to fetch fire from the land of the Great Spirit; the dog returned with his tail ablaze, and ever since the Shilluk have had fire.[6]

The Chiriguanos of Bolivia allege that after the great flood, when all the other fire on earth was extinguished, people got a light from a toad, which before the water rose had hidden in a hole, taking with him some live coals which he kept alight all the time of the deluge by blowing on them with his breath.[7]   The Choroti Indians of the Gran Chaco say that, when they were in a similar plight after the great flood, they got fire from a black vulture who had preserved the element in his nest above the reach of the water.[8]   The Tapiete Indians, another tribe of the Gran Chaco, aver that when the black vulture had fire and they themselves had none, a frog took pity on them, stole some of the fire at which the black vulture was warming himself, and brought it to the Indians in his mouth.[9]   The Matacos Indians,

[1] Above, p. 100.   [4] Above, pp. 106 *sq.*   [7] Above, p. 126.
[2] Above, p. 101.   [5] Above, p. 117.   [8] Above, pp. 124 *sq.*
[3] Above, p. 105.   [6] Above, pp. 121 *sq.*   [9] Above, p. 125.

another tribe of the Gran Chaco, say that they owe the possession of fire to a guinea-pig, who stole it from a jaguar, who possessed and used fire before the human race had procured it for themselves ; not that the guinea-pig communicated the precious gift to mankind, but that in using it to cook his own food he inadvertently set fire to the grass, and from the conflagration thus accidentally kindled the Matacos got their first fire.[1] The Bakairi of central Brazil allege that the first fire was procured for mankind by a fish and a snail, or rather by two great twin brothers who had temporarily assumed the form of these creatures, and in that guise stole it from the animal (*Canis vetulus*) who in the early days of the world was Lord of Fire.[2] According to the Jibaros of Ecuador the first fire was brought to them by a humming-bird, who stole it from a man who alone possessed it and kept it strictly to himself.[3]

The Sia Indians of New Mexico say that they procured fire from the coyote, who stole it for them from the spider, who lived in a house underground and set a snake, a cougar, and a bear to guard the fire against all comers ; but the coyote found the sentinels and the spider himself fast asleep, and before the sleepers were wide awake, the coyote was up and away with the fire.[4] In some stories told by the Indian tribes who inhabit the south-eastern part of the United States, the rabbit is said to be the animal which procured the first fire for men.[5] The Sioux and other Indian tribes of the Mississippi have a tradition that after the great flood the man and woman who alone survived the catastrophe received fire from a little grey bird which the Great Spirit in mercy sent to them with the priceless boon. Hence the Indians respect that species of bird and never kill it, and they paint two little black bars on either side of their eyes in imitation of the bars on the bird.[6] According to the Nootka or Aht Indians of Vancouver Island, the first fire was stolen by the deer from the cuttle-fish or the wolves, who in the early days of the world alone possessed it.[7] And in other Indian legends of North-West America the deer similarly figures as

---

[1] Above, p. 125. [4] Above, p. 139. [6] Above, p. 150.
[2] Above, p. 129. [5] Above, pp. 147 *sqq.* [7] Above, pp. 160 *sqq.*
[3] Above, pp. 134 *sq.*

the creature who first stole fire and brought it to men ; and still the deer has a stumpy black tail because the fire burned it.[1] Among the Indians who tell this story of the deer are the Kwakiutl of Vancouver Island, but in another version of the tale they say that it was the mink which procured fire for men by stealing a child from the Chief of the Ghosts and inducing the Chief to give him fire in exchange for the infant.[2] A similar tale is told by the Nanaimo tribe of Vancouver Island.[3] Among some of the Indians of British Columbia and Alaska the bringer of the first fire is the raven, a bird which plays a great part in the mythology of these northern tribes, and the mode in which he contrived to purloin the precious element is the theme of more than one marvellous tale.[4] The Eskimo of Bering Strait similarly profess to have learned the art of fire-making from the raven.[5]

In France it is the wren or the robin-redbreast which is said to have brought the first fire from heaven to earth, and the red feathers on the robin's breast are explained to be the mark burned by the fire on his plumage.[6]

But in many myths the first fire is said to have been brought, not by a single bird or beast, but by the joint efforts of a number of animals, which range themselves in a line and pass the fire from one to the other as each becomes exhausted in the race. Or again, we are told that a number of animals attempt the arduous task, but that only one succeeds in performing it. Thus to illustrate these myths of co-operative fire-bringing, as we may call them, in one Australian myth the hawk and the pigeon co-operate in stealing fire from the bandicoot.[7] In a myth told by the islanders of Torres Straits the snake, the frog, and various species of lizards attempt to steal the fire, and finally the big long-necked lizard succeeds and swims with it in his mouth to the island, his long neck enabling him to hold his head above the water.[8] A similar story is told by the Masingara of British New Guinea.[9] In Kiwai, an island off the coast of New Guinea, they tell how the animals, one after the other, attempted to bring fire from

[1] Above, pp. 165 *sqq.*
[2] Above, pp. 166 *sq.*
[3] Above, p. 179.
[4] Above, pp. 167, 176 *sq.*, 182 *sq.*, 185 *sqq.*
[5] Above, p. 188.
[6] Above, pp. 190 *sqq.*
[7] Above, p. 7.
[8] Above, pp. 25 *sq.*
[9] Above, p. 35.

the mainland ; the crocodile, the cassowary, and the dog all failed, then the birds tried in their turn, and finally the black cockatoo succeeded, but to this very day he bears round his mouth the red streak where the fire seared it.[1] In a myth told to the same effect by the Motu tribe of British New Guinea the snake, the bandicoot, the kangaroo, and a bird fail in the attempt, and the dog succeeds.[2] The Tsuwo, a tribe of mountaineers in Formosa, tell a similar story to explain how their ancestors obtained fire after the great flood : the goat was drowned in a gallant attempt to fetch fire to them, but the *taoron* brought it safe to land, and in their joy the people patted him, which is the reason why the animal has such a shiny skin and so tiny a body down to this day.[3] The Thay of Siam relate how after the great flood their ancestors were in the usual difficulty of recovering the lost fire, and how they dispatched the owl and the serpent to fetch it ; but these creatures loitered by the way and never reached their destination. After that, the gad-fly flew up to heaven and brought down from it, not indeed fire, but the secret of kindling it, having cunningly peeped at the Lord of Heaven in the act of making it with His own divine hands.[4]

The Admiralty Islanders have a story to the effect that, when there was no fire on earth, a woman sent the sea-eagle and the starling to fetch it from heaven. The two birds flew up to the sky and the fish-eagle took the fire ; but in returning to earth the fish-eagle shifted the fire to the starling, which carried it on the back of its neck, and the fire singed the bird.[5]

The Ba-ila of Northern Rhodesia tell how, when there was no fire on earth, the vulture, the fish-eagle, the crow, and the mason-wasp made up their minds to fetch it from God, who then resided somewhere in the sky. So up they flew, but after some days only the dead bones of the vulture, the fish-eagle, and the crow dropped down to earth, and mason-wasp was left to pursue his perilous path alone. Arrived in heaven he had a friendly interview with the Deity, who gave him His blessing and also, presumably, the fire.[6]

The Cora Indians of Mexico relate how fire was formerly

[1] Above, pp. 29 *sq.*
[2] Above, p. 38.
[3] Above, pp. 96 *sq.* I do not know what sort of creature a *taoron* is.
[4] Above, pp. 101 *sq.*
[5] Above, p. 48.
[6] Above, pp. 112 *sq.*

in the sole possession of the iguana, and how, in consequence
of a painful difference with his wife and his mother-in-law,
the animal removed it all to the sky, so people on earth were
left destitute of this necessity of life. In this emergency they
appealed to the birds and animals to fetch it down for them
from the sky. The heroic raven sacrificed his life in the vain
attempt ; the humming-bird failed, and so did all the other
birds, one after the other. At last the opossum succeeded in
climbing up to the sky and stealing fire from an old man
while he slept.[1] The Navahoes of New Mexico say that in
the days when animals had fire and men had none, the coyote,
the bat, and the squirrel agreed to aid each other in procuring
fire for their friends, the Indians. So, while the other animals
were playing about a fire, the coyote contrived to steal some
glowing embers and scudded away with them, pursued by all
the animals hot-foot. When he was tired out, he passed the
fire to the bat, and when the bat was like to drop he passed
it on to the squirrel, who, by reason of his great agility and
endurance, managed to carry the fire safe to the Navahoes.[2]
This myth of fire carried by relays of animal runners appears
to be widespread among the Indians of North America : it
meets us again, with variations of detail, among the Utes of
Utah,[3] among the Karok Indians of California,[4] among the
Thompson Indians of British Columbia,[5] and farther north
among the Kaska Indians, also of British Columbia, on the
Arctic slope of the mountains.[6] This type of myth has its
analogue in the French story, which tells how the wren,
having stolen fire from heaven, was compelled to pass on
his precious burden to robin - redbreast, who in his turn
resigned it to the lark, who brought it safe to earth.[7]

A myth of the co-operative type, without the relays of
runners, is told by the Cherokee Indians. They say that
in the beginning the only fire on earth was deposited in a
hollow sycamore tree, which grew on an island. So the
animals, who in those days needed fire as much as men,
laid their heads together to devise means of obtaining it.
The raven flew across the water to the tree, but as he was

---

[1] Above, pp. 136 *sqq.*
[2] Above, pp. 139 *sq.*
[3] Above, pp. 142 *sqq.*
[4] Above, pp. 153 *sq.*
[5] Above, pp. 173 *sq.*
[6] Above, pp. 183 *sq.*
[7] Above, p. 192.

fluttering over it, the heat scorched all his feathers black. The little screech-owl next attempted the enterprise, but as he peered down into the hollow tree, a blast of hot air nearly blinded him, and his eyes have been red ever since. The next to follow were the hooting-owl and the horned-owl, but they fared no better, for the smoke from the burning tree almost deprived them of sight, and round their eyes the ashes made white rings which they have never been able to rub off from that day to this. When the birds had done their best, but all in vain, the little black snake and the big black snake, one after the other, plunged into the hollow of the burning tree ; but the smoke choked them and the flames scorched them black, and black they have remained ever since. At last the water-spider, running on the surface of the water, crossed over to the island and brought back the fire in a bowl woven of a thread which she span out of her own body.[1]

The Nishinam Indians of California tell how, when all the fire in the world was hidden away somewhere far in the west, the bat proposed to the lizard that he should go and steal it. The lizard fell in with the proposal and stole the fire, but in carrying it he set the grass ablaze and had to run for dear life ; and a righteous retribution overtook the bat who had bespoken the theft, for the fire almost blinded him, and though the lizard applied a plaster of pitch to his eyes, the remedy had little effect, and the bat has been blear-sighted to this day, and he is still so black that you have only to look at him to see that he was singed by the fire.[2] The Maidu Indians of California relate how the mouse, the deer, the dog, and the coyote contrived to steal fire from Thunder, who kept it somewhere away in the west. The theft was successfully perpetrated ; the dog concealed some of the fire in his ear, while the deer carried some of it on his hock, where there is a reddish spot to this day, no doubt where the fire seared it.[3]

If we ask why in these myths the procuring of the first fire is so often fathered on animals or birds, which even the savage must perceive to be entirely destitute of it at the present time, the most probable answer seems to be that these stories are primarily intended to account for certain colours

[1] Above, pp. 151 *sqq.*   [2] Above, p. 156.   [3] Above, pp. 157 *sq.*

or other characteristics of animals, which primitive man attributed to the action of fire, and that they are only secondarily meant to explain the origin or discovery of fire. If this view is correct, the myths in question are rather zoological than physical. And in regard to them we should bear in mind that the savage, to whose crude philosophy these myths must be referred, is very far from discriminating sharply between man and the lower animals ; on the contrary, he commonly attributes to them a life and intelligence closely resembling his own ; hence he sees nothing incongruous or absurd in the notion that animals possess and use fire, nay even that they owned it before man and were indeed the agents by whose instrumentality he first acquired it.

We might naturally suppose that among the sources from which primitive man obtained fire before he learned to make it for himself would be volcanoes, but in the myths of the origin of fire there appear to be few references or allusions to volcanic agency. The principal exception to this general rule is probably furnished by the Polynesian myth, which regularly represents the first fire as fetched by a great hero from the nether world, where he has an encounter with a formidable being, the god or goddess of fire ; in the Samoan version of the myth, as we have seen, this subterranean fire-god is also the earthquake-god, and the account, how he suddenly blew up his oven and scattered the stones all about, may well be a mythical description of a volcanic eruption.[1] In this connexion we must remember that Hawaii is the seat of one of the most tremendous volcanoes in the world ; it would be no wonder if the people, who lived under its shadow and witnessed its terrific explosions, associated their stories of the origin of fire with the burning mountain and its huge cauldron of boiling lava.

Again, in a myth of the origin of fire told by the Babine Indians, who inhabit the northern interior of British Columbia, mention is made of a column of smoke which was seen rising from a mountain, followed by tongues of fire.[2] This, as I have already suggested, may be a reminiscence of the smoke and flame shot up by one of the volcanoes which exist in North-Western America.

[1] Above, pp. 72-74.   [2] Above, p. 185.

The curious notion that fire came originally from the sea, which meets us in the two parallel myths from Ontong Java and the Gilbert Islands,[1] may have been suggested by the wonderful and impressive spectacle of a tropical sea ablaze far and wide with the shimmering glow of phosphorescent light ; and as the spectacle is by no means confined to the tropics, it may also be the source both of the Nootka myth, that fire originally burned only in the house of the cuttle-fish,[2] and of the Haida myth, that raven brought the first fire to land from the depths of the sea, where he was exposed to the attacks of dangerous fish.[3]

§ 4. *The Age of Fire Kindled*

The myths of the origin of fire relate, as we have seen, how men, after obtaining and using fire, probably for long ages, without knowing how to produce it, at last discovered one or more of the methods by which savages kindle it to this day, or at all events used to kindle it before their primitive methods were superseded by more refined processes introduced by civilization. Of primitive ways of kindling fire the two commonest are by the friction of wood and the percussion of stone, and both of them are noticed in the myths of the origin of fire. Of the two processes the friction of wood is much the more commonly employed, and it is oftenest mentioned in the myths. Accordingly we may consider it first.

The friction of wood is applied to the production of fire in a variety of ways, of which three are commonly distinguished and named the fire-drill, the fire-saw, and the fire-plough (or stick-and-groove). Of these three the fire-drill is by far the most widely diffused among the backward races of men ; we need not wonder, therefore, that it is also oftenest mentioned in the myths.[4]

---

[1] Above, pp. 53 *sq.*, 88 *sqq.*
[2] Above, p. 160.
[3] Above, p. 186.
[4] See the Index, *s.v.* " Fire-drill." On primitive modes of making fire in general, see E. B. Tylor, *Researches into the Early History of Mankind*[2] (London, 1870), pp. 238 *sqq.* ; W. Hough, " Fire-making Apparatus in the United States National Museum," *Smithsonian Institution, Report* 1887–1888 (Washington, 1890), pp. 531-587 ; *id., Fire as an Agent in Human Culture* (Washington, 1926), pp. 84 *sqq.* ; A. E. Crawley, *s.v.* " Fire, Fire-Gods," in J. Hastings's

In its simplest form the fire-drill consists of two sticks, one of which is pointed and held upright with its point pressing on the other, which is laid flat on the ground; the upright stick, or drill proper, is twirled rapidly between the palms of the hands till the point bores a hole in the other stick and the continued friction generates first heat and then fire, which is caught and nursed into a flame by tinder of various sorts.

In this its simplest form, or improved by various mechanical devices, such as a cord or thong wound about the drill and pulled at both ends to increase the rapidity of the rotation, the fire-drill has had an immense range among the peoples of the world, having been used not only by the savage and barbarous tribes of Tasmania, Australia, New Guinea, Africa, America, and Asia, but also by the civilized races of antiquity, and even of modern times in Egypt, India, Japan, and Europe.[1]

Encyclopaedia of Religion and Ethics, vol. vi. (Edinburgh, 1913) pp. 26-27. I have collected a good deal of evidence on the subject, but the bulk of it must be reserved for another occasion.

[1] E. B. Tylor, *Researches into the Early History of Mankind*,[2] pp. 240 *sqq.*; W. Hough, " Fire-making Apparatus in the United States National Museum," *Smithsonian Institution, Report* 1887-1888, pp. 531 *sqq*; *id.*, *Fire as an Agent in Human Culture*, pp. 84-103. A Tasmanian fire-drill is in the Pitt-Rivers Museum at Oxford, where it was pointed out to me by Mr. Henry Balfour (19th August 1921); he told me that the late Lord Avebury possessed another example from Tasmania. As to the fire-drill in New Guinea, see R. Neuhauss, *Deutsch-Neu-Guinea* (Berlin, 1911), i. 257, iii. 24; A. F. R. Wollaston, *Pygmies and Papuans* (London, 1912), pp. 200-202; W. N. Beaver, *Unexplored New Guinea* (London, 1920), pp. 68 *sq.* For some evidence of the widespread use of the fire-drill in Africa, see F. Fülleborn, *Das deutsche Njassa- und Ruwuma Gebiet* (Berlin, 1906), p. 91 ; H. Rehse, *Kiziba, Land und Leute* (Stuttgart, 1910), pp. 19 *sq.*; G. St. J. Orde Browne, *The Vanishing Tribes of Kenya* (London, 1925), pp. 120 *sq.*;

C. K. Meek, *The Northern Tribes of Nigeria* (Oxford University Press, 1925), i. 172 ; S. S. Dornan, *Pygmies and Bushmen of the Kalahari* (London, 1925), pp. 116 *sq.* ; E. W. Smith and A. M. Dale, *The Ila-speaking Peoples of Northern Rhodesia* (London, 1920), i. 143 ; F. H. Melland, *In Witch-bound Africa* (London, 1923), p. 159 ; J. A. Massam, *The Cliff-dwellers of Kenya* (London, 1927), pp. 96 *sq.* ; Henri A. Junod, *The Life of a South African Tribe*, Second Edition (London, 1927), ii. 34 *sq.* My friend, Professor Alexandre Moret of the Collège de France, informed me at Paris that the ancient Egyptians made fire by means of the fire-drill. The process, he told me, is not mentioned in any Egyptian text, but the drills have been found, the lower stick showing traces of fire in the charred hollow. Compare A. Erman, *Ägypten und ägyptisches Leben im Altertum*, neu bearbeitet von H. Ranke (Tübingen, 1923), p. 217. As to the fire-drill in ancient India, see Adalbert Kuhn, *Die Herabkunft des Feuers und des Göttertranks*[2] (Gütersloh, 1886), pp. 14 *sqq.*, 64 *sqq.* The same ancient apparatus is still employed by the Brahmans in kindling the sacred fire. See W. Crooke, *Religion and Folklore of Northern*

If we ask, How did mankind discover the mode of producing fire by means of the fire-drill ? a simple and probable answer is supplied by one of the myths of the origin of fire. As we have seen, the Basongo Meno, a group of African tribes in the valley of the Congo, say that from the earliest times they made their fishing-traps out of the ribs of the raphia palm. One day a man, constructing such a trap, wished to bore a hole in the end of one of the ribs, and he used a small pointed stick for the purpose. In the process of boring the hole fire was elicited, and thus the people discovered the mode of producing it.[1] When we consider how often, before the discovery of metals, man must have used one piece of wood to bore a hole in another, we shall probably be disposed to admit that in this way the mode of kindling fire by the fire-drill may have been accidentally discovered, not once but many times in the history of mankind, and that consequently many peoples may have hit on it independently ; so that we need not have recourse to the hypothesis of a single discoverer, a solitary Prometheus, from whom the whole human race received the inestimable boon.

It is possible that the use of the fire-drill may explain certain peculiar features in some myths of the origin of fire. Thus in some of them fire is variously said to have been drawn from a sixth finger of a woman's right hand,[2] from between the finger and thumb of a woman's right hand,[3] from between the thumb and forefinger of the left hand,[4] from between the thumb and forefinger of a woman's right hand,[5] from between the thumb and forefinger of a man's right hand,[6] from the end of the forefinger of a boy's right hand,[7] from the nails of the fingers and toes of the fire-goddess,[8] and from the fingers of the fire-deity.[9] Perhaps the notion that fire could thus be elicited

India (Oxford University Press, 1926), pp. 335 *sq.* As to the fire-drill in ancient Greece and Rome, see A. Kuhn, *op. cit.* pp. 35-39 ; M. H. Morgan, " De ignis eliciendi modis apud antiquos," *Harvard Studies in Classical Philology,* i. (1890) pp. 13-34. As to the fire-drill in modern Europe, see J. Loewenthal und B. Mattlatzki, " Die europäischen Feuerbohrer," *Zeitschrift für Ethnologie,* xlviii. (1916) pp. 349-369 ; J. Loewenthal, " Über

einige altertümliche Feuerbohrer aus Schweden," *Zeitschrift für Ethnologie,* l. (1918) pp. 198-203.

[1] Above, p. 116.
[2] Above, pp. 25-27.
[3] Above, p. 27.
[4] Above, p. 28.
[5] Above, p. 31.
[6] Above, p. 32.
[7] Above, p. 34.
[8] Above, pp. 56 *sq.*
[9] Above, p. 58.

from the hand was suggested by the drill twirled between the palms of the hand and producing fire from its point, which might possibly be interpreted as a fiery finger ; while the idea of fire spurting out from the space between the thumb and forefinger may have been arrived at from the observation of the drill revolving in a position which might, without too great a stretch of imagination, be described as between the thumb and forefinger.

Further, the notion that fire was elicited from a woman's body, and particularly from her genital organ,[1] finds a ready explanation in the analogy which, as we have seen,[2] many savages trace between the working of the fire-drill on the one hand and the intercourse of the sexes on the other. In all such cases the horizontal stick, which the drill perforates, is regarded as female, while the upright stick or drill proper is considered as male ; so that on this analogy fire elicited by the fire-drill may be said to be produced from the body of a woman, and particularly from her genital organ, which in the fire-drill is represented by the hollow in which the drill revolves. This analogy is clearly recognized, and carried out practically in the ritual by which to this day the Brahman fire-priest (*Agnihotra*) and his wife between them kindle the sacred fire by means of the fire-drill. On the night before fire is made, the plunger or upper part of the fire-drill (*arani*) is put in charge of the priest and the lower part is put in charge of his wife, and husband and wife sleep with these parts at night, " the process of fire-making symbolizing coition." Next morning they together kindle the sacred fire ; the man holds the plunger firmly so that the point cannot leave the hole in the base-board, while his wife causes it to revolve by pulling the cord wound about it until fire is produced and communicated to the tinder. Both husband and wife are subject to special taboos while they are engaged in the performance of this sacred duty.[3]

The same analogy may possibly also explain why in the myths women are sometimes represented as in possession of fire before men.[4] For the fire which is extracted from the

---

[1] Above, pp. 23 *sq.*, 43, 45, 49, 85, 131, 131 *sq.*, 133.

[2] Above, p. 46.

[3] W. Crooke, *Religion and Folklore* *of Northern India* (Oxford University Press, 1926), p. 336.

[4] Above, pp. 5, 15, 23, 25, 27, 42, 43 *sq.*, 44 *sq.*, 49, 90 *sq.*, 131, 131 *sq.*, 133

board by the revolution of the drill is naturally interpreted by the savage as existing in the board before its extraction by the drill, or, in mythical language, as inherent in the female before it is drawn out by the male ; just as the savage imagines fire to be stored up in all the trees from whose wood he elicits it by friction. Thus to primitive thought it might seem natural to conclude that fire was owned by women before it came into the possession of men.

But the fire-drill, though the commonest, is by no means the only implement which savages have employed to produce fire by the friction of wood. Another is the fire-saw, of which there are two different sorts, the rigid and the flexible. The rigid fire-saw consists of a piece of wood or bamboo which is rubbed rapidly to and fro, with a sawing motion, across a piece of wood or bamboo till the friction elicits fire. In this apparatus the material usually employed is bamboo, the siliceous coating of which readily lends itself to the production of fire by friction. A sharpened piece of bamboo is drawn rapidly over a convex piece of bamboo, which is thus sawn through, while the sawdust falls on tinder placed below. Mr. Henry Balfour informed me that this is the easiest of all primitive methods of making fire ; he himself has thus produced fire in forty seconds. The apparatus is, or has been, employed by the natives of various parts of the Malay Archipelago, the Philippine Islands, the Nicobar Islands, Burma, India, and some regions of Europe.[1] The late William Crooke suggested that " the production of fire by means of friction would naturally occur to jungle races, who must have constantly seen it occur by the ignition of the bamboo stalks rubbed together by the blasts of summer. From this would easily be developed the very primitive fire-drill or Asgara, used to this day by the Cheros, Korwas, Bhuiyas, and other Dravidian dwellers in the jungle. These people even to the present day habitually produce fire in this way. A small round cavity is made in a dry piece of bamboo, in which two men alternately with their open hands revolve a second pointed piece of the wood of the same tree. Smoke and finally

---

[1] E. B. Tylor, *Researches into the Early History of Mankind*,[2] p. 240 ; W. Hough, *Fire as an Agent in Human Culture*, pp. 104-106 ; H. Balfour, " Frictional Fire-making with a flexible sawing-thong," *Journal of the Royal Anthropological Institute*, xliv. (1914) p. 32.

fire are rapidly produced in this way, and the sparks are received on a dry leaf or other suitable tinder." [1]

The flexible fire-saw consists of a pliable strip of cane, liana, or other suitable material, which is drawn backwards and forwards, with a sawing motion, across a piece of bamboo or wood, detaching in the process a fine sawdust and generating sufficient heat to ignite the sawdust and cause it to smoulder. From the smouldering sawdust a flame can readily be educed with the help of dry grass or other suitable tinder.   The geographical diffusion of this mode of kindling fire has been carefully studied by Mr. Henry Balfour.   He traces it from the Naga Hills in Assam through the Chittagong Hills, Annam, and the Malay Peninsula to Borneo and New Guinea, and he notes its employment in Europe, particularly in Sweden, Germany, and Russia, for the ceremonial production of a new fire commonly known as need-fire. [2]

Both the flexible and the rigid fire-saw are mentioned in myths of the origin of fire. Thus the flexible fire-saw meets us in a Kiwai story, which relates how in a dream a spirit taught a man to make fire by sawing a piece of wood with his bowstring ; [3] and another Kiwai story similarly sets forth how a boy accidentally discovered the method of kindling fire by sawing a billet of wood in two with a bamboo rope. [4] On the other hand, the rigid fire-saw occurs in a story told by the Toradyas of Celebes which relates how the Lord of Heaven made fire by rubbing two bamboos together, [5] and a similar story is current among the Thay or Tai of Siam. [6] Again, the Kachins of Burma say that in the early days of the world a spirit taught men how to produce fire by setting a

---

[1] W. Crooke, *Popular Religion and Folk-lore of Northern India* (Westminster, 1896), ii. 194. However, the apparatus described by Crooke in this passage is the fire-drill, not the fire-saw.

[2] Henry Balfour, " Frictional Fire-making with a flexible sawing-thong," *Journal of the Royal Anthropological Institute*, xliv. (1914) pp. 32-64. Mr. Balfour has also published a valuable memoir on the mode of making fire by compressed air in a piston, which is used by some backward peoples in

Burma, the Malay Peninsula, Sumatra, Borneo, Java, and the Philippine Islands ; but as it appears not to be noticed in any of the myths of the origin of fire, it does not concern us here. See Henry Balfour, " The Fire-piston," in *Anthropological Essays presented to Edward Burnett Tylor* (Oxford, 1907), pp. 17-49.

[3] Above, pp. 36 *sq.*

[4] Above, p. 37.

[5] Above, p. 94.

[6] Above, pp. 101-103.

man and woman to rub two pieces of bamboo together.[1] According to the Kiau Dusuns of North Borneo, the first fire was produced spontaneously by the friction of two growing bamboos rubbing against each other in the wind,[2] and, as we have seen, this spontaneous ignition of bamboos is said to happen constantly in the jungle.[3] Hence it appears to be perfectly possible that in many cases this may have been really the source from which the savage procured his first fire and learned the mode of kindling it. If that was so, the area within which fire was thus obtained must have been within the habitat of the bamboo, and therefore within the tropics.

Another mode in which many savages make fire by the friction of wood is known as the fire-plough or stick-and-groove. It consists in rubbing the point of one stick in the groove of another until the friction produces heat and then flame. This simple apparatus is met with most commonly among the islanders of the Pacific, especially in Polynesia, but also in Melanesia, New Guinea, and Borneo.[4] Much more rarely it occurs in some parts of Africa[5] and America.[6] It is doubtless referred to implicitly in some of the myths recorded in this volume, though the reporters of the myths have concealed it under such vague phrases as " the friction of wood," " rubbing two sticks together," and so forth, which would equally apply to the fire-drill, a different apparatus.

Deriving his fire thus commonly from the friction of wood or bamboo, primitive man naturally concluded that fire is something stored up in all trees, or at all events in those trees from the wood of which he usually extracted it ; hence many of the myths of the origin of fire attempt to explain how the igneous element came to be thus deposited in trees.[7] Sometimes it is said to have been so deposited by a thunderbolt striking a tree and setting it on fire.[8]

[1] Above, p. 103.   [2] Above, p. 95.
[3] Above, p. 221.
[4] E. B. Tylor, *Researches into the Early History of Mankind*,[2] pp. 239 *sq.*; W. Hough, *Fire as an Agent in Human Culture*, pp. 107-109 ; W. Marsden, *History of Sumatra* (London, 1811), pp. 60 *sq.* ; A. R. Wallace, *The Malay*

Archipelago (London, 1869), ii. 34.
[5] W. Hough, *op. cit.* p. 109.
[6] W. C. Farabee, *The Central Caribs* (Philadelphia, 1924), p. 38 (among the Caribs of British Guiana).
[7] See Index, *s.v.* " Trees."
[8] Above, pp. 151, 155 ; compare pp. 90, 92.

In many of the myths the fire is said to be deposited in trees of a particular species, or extracted from them by friction.   Among the trees mentioned in one or other of these connexions are the grass-tree,[1] the bamboo,[2] the hibiscus,[3] the *Eugenia*,[4] the coco-nut,[5] the bread-fruit tree,[6] the *Cordia*,[7] the *Urtica argentea*,[8] the banyan-tree (*Ficus Indicus*),[9] the cotton-wood tree,[10] and the cedar.[11]   Of these trees the oftenest mentioned is the hibiscus, and according to Darwin the very light wood of the *Hibiscus tiliaceus* was alone used for the kindling of fire by the stick-and-groove method in Tahiti.[12]   The Thonga of South-eastern Africa find that a species of hibiscus, which they call *bulolo*, is the best wood for fire-making.[13]

But the savage sometimes gets fire, not by the friction of wood, but by the percussion of stones, or even, at a more advanced stage, by the percussion of flint and iron.   This mode of fire-making appears to be much rarer and much less widely diffused in the world than the method by the friction of wood.   The stones used for the purpose are iron pyrites (" fire-stone "), or pyrites and flint.   This mode of procuring fire has been practised by the Eskimo and some Indian tribes of Canada, and again by the rude inhabitants of Tierra del Fuego, but in the vast intermediate regions of the American continent it is said to be unknown.[14]

In the myths of the origin of fire, which we have passed in review, there are allusions which suffice to prove that the myth-makers were acquainted with the process of eliciting fire, or at least sparks, from the percussion of stones.   Thus the Taulipang Indians of northern Brazil say that in the olden time fire was transferred from the body of a woman to the stones called *wato*, which, on being struck, give forth fire.[15]   Again, the Sia Indians of New Mexico say that the

---

[1] Above, pp. 12, 14.

[2] Above, pp. 26, 28, 94, 95.

[3] Above, pp. 26, 71, 77, 79, 85, 92.

[4] Above, p. 26.

[5] Above, p. 70.

[6] Above, p. 71.

[7] Above, p. 71.

[8] Above, pp. 77, 79.

[9] Above, pp. 77, 79.

[10] Above, pp. 85, 95, 135.

[11] Above, pp. 186 *sq.*

[12] Charles Darwin, *Journal of Researches* (London, 1870), p. 409.

[13] Henri A. Junod, *The Life of a South African Tribe*, Second Edition (London, 1927), ii. 33.

[14] E. B. Tylor, *Researches into the Early History of Mankind*,[2] pp. 249 *sq.*; W. Hough, *Fire as an Agent in Human Culture*, pp. 111-113.

[15] Above, p. 131.

spider, the creator of men and animals, used to make fire
in his underground house by rubbing a sharp-pointed stone
on a round flat stone.[1] These two myths seem to prove that
both the Taulipang and the Sia Indians were acquainted
with the mode of eliciting fire from stones, whether they
practised it or not. Again, the Kaska Indians of British
Columbia say that long ago, before men had got fire, the
bear was in possession of a fire-stone from which he could
elicit fire at any time. But a bird stole the precious stone,
which, after passing through several hands, or rather paws,
was finally carried off by the fox, who smashed it on the top
of a mountain and threw a fragment of it to each tribe of
Indians ; thus all men obtained fire, and there is fire in the
rocks everywhere down to the present time.[2] Again, the
Morioris of the Chatham Islands relate how the fire-god
Mauhika threw fire into flints, so that it can be extracted
from them.[3]

Among people at a more advanced stage of culture, or
in closer contact with civilization, the myths contain allusions
to the production of fire by flint and steel, or at all events
by stone and iron. Thus the Toradyas of central Celebes
relate how a cunning insect contrived to oversee the Creator
in heaven making fire by striking a flint with a chopping-
knife.[4] Again, a Tartar tribe of southern Siberia has a
tradition that, soon after the creation of man, three women,
acting on a hint dropped by the deity, contrived to strike
fire by the percussion of stone and iron.[5] The Sakalava and
Tsimihety of Madagascar tell how, worsted in a great battle
with Thunder, the flames hid in many things, such as wood,
iron, and hard stones ; and that, say these people, is why
you can make fire either by rubbing one dry stick against
another, or by knocking flint and steel together.[6] According
to the Tlingit Indians of Alaska, in the early days of the
world, when there was no fire on earth except on an island
of the sea, the raven flew thither and picked up a brand in
his beak ; but the fire burnt half his beak off, and on reaching
the shore he dropped the glowing embers on the ground,
and the scattered sparks fell on stones and wood. That,

[1] Above, p. 139.
[2] Above, pp. 183 *sq.*
[3] Above, p. 59.
[4] Above, p. 93.
[5] Above, p. 104.
[6] Above, pp. 108-110.

say the Tlíngit, is the reason why both stones and wood still contain fire ; for you can strike sparks from stones by knocking them with steel, and you can draw fire from wood by rubbing two sticks together.[1]

When we consider how often, in the long ages which preceded the discovery of the metals, men in palaeolithic and neolithic times knocked stones together for the purposes of fashioning those rude implements which still exist in countless thousands scattered over the face of the globe, we can hardly avoid concluding that the mode of kindling fire by the percussion of stones must have been discovered independently over and over again in many parts of the world ; and as little in this as in the case of the fire-drill need we resort to the hypothesis of a single discoverer, a solitary Prometheus, whose fortunate invention was spread from hand to hand to all the ends of the earth. The Yakuts of Siberia tell how fire was at first accidentally discovered by an old man who, having nothing better to do, amused himself by knocking two stones together, till sparks leaped from the stones and set fire to the dry grass.[2] We need not accept the tale as historical, but it is probably typical of what must almost certainly have happened over and over again in prehistoric times.

Thus, in spite of the fantastic features which distort many of them, the myths of the origin of fire probably contain a substantial element of truth, and supply a clue which helps us to grope our way through the darkness of the human past in the unnumbered ages which preceded the rise of history.

[1] Above, p. 187.   [2] Above, p. 104.

INDEX

THE END

Printed in U.S.A. by
NOBLE OFFSET PRINTERS, INC.
New York, N.Y. 10003